D0856077

1

We want freedom. We want power
to determine the destiny of our
Black community.

2

We want full employment for our people.

3

We want an end to the robbery by the
White man of our Black community.

4

We want decent housing, fit for shelter
[of] human beings.

5

We want education for our people that
exposes the true nature of this decadent
American society. We want education that
teaches us our true history and our role in
the present day society.

6

We want all Black men to be exempt
from military service.

7

We want an immediate end to *police
brutality* and *murder* of Black people.

8

We want freedom for all Black men held in
federal, state, county, and city prisons and jails.

9

We want all Black people when brought
to trial to be tried in court by a jury of
their peer group or people from their Black
communities. As defined by the constitution
of the United States.

10

We want land, bread, housing, education,
clothing, justice and peace.

Ten-Point Program by The Black Panther Party

FREEDOM!
THE STORY OF THE
BLACK PANTHER PARTY

Jetta Grace Martin
Joshua Bloom
Waldo E. Martin, Jr.

LEVINE QUERIDO

Montclair | Amsterdam | Hoboken

COPYRIGHT PAGE

This is an Arthur A. Levine book
Published by Levine Querido

www.levinequerido.com •
info@levinequerido.com
Levine Querido is distributed by
Chronicle Books LLC
Copyright © 2022 by Jetta Grace Martin,
Joshua Bloom, and
Waldo E. Martin, Jr.
All rights reserved
Library of Congress Control Number:
2021932072
ISBN 9781646140930
Printed in China

Published January 2022
Second printing

DEDICATION

For Josephine

There is an ancient saying: knowledge is power. The secret is this. Knowledge, applied at the right time and place, has the potential to change history. Knowledge is more than power. It's magic.

That's what the Black Panther Party did. They called up this magic and began a revolution.

In the beginning, it was a story like any other. It could have been yours and it could have been mine. But once it got going, it became more than anyone could have imagined.

It's the story of Huey and Bobby. Eldridge and Kathleen. Ericka, Elaine, Fred, and David.

It's the story of the women and the men of the Party. Their supporters and allies. The community survival programs and the Ten-Point Program. It's about Black revolution, Black radicalism, about Black people in America. It's about loyalty, community, and sacrifice. It's about what it takes to be free.

This is the story of the Black Panther Party.

PART ONE:
IN THE BEGINNING

The Black Panther Party's legacy is eternal. It will live on, always, in the hearts and minds of those who stand for the truth, of those who stand for justice and are willing to do whatever is needed to create the world we all deserve to live in: a world free of poverty, hunger, greed, fear, and hate—a world full of love and abundance.[1]

**Aaron Dixon, Chairman, Seattle
Black Panther Party**

CHAPTER 1

CRUISIN'
HUEY
BOBBY
A LONG FREEDOM STRUGGLE

CRUISIN'

In the dark, anything can happen. Blackness, darkness, has a power unto itself. Faces reside there: strong, determined, and proud. Unapologetic in their blackness. A large afro. A halo of power. Dark sunglasses, glinting in the half-light. Crisp leather jackets and cocked berets. A uniform with meaning. Figures cutting across the frame—Black and proud.

▲

It was late at night. Huey Newton, Bobby Seale, and Lil' Bobby Hutton were cruising around in Bobby's car. The year was 1967. The place, Oakland, California.

As Huey drove, they noticed a police car patrolling the area. Huey sped up to tail the car, keeping him in his sight.[2] They glided behind, silent and watchful.

What the officer couldn't see was Huey's shotgun. Or Seale's .45 caliber handgun. Or Lil' Bobby's M1 rifle.

When the officer turned right, Huey turned right. When the officer turned left, Huey turned left. After a while, they all pulled up at an intersection, side by side.

The three men turned, looking into the police car. Bobby held Huey's gun. Their weapons were clearly visible. Huey's law book lay waiting, across the backseat.

They paused, waiting for a breath. Then they accelerated, moving ahead of the officer. His high beams started flashing, but Huey refused to stop. A flashing light meant nothing to him. When the officer put on his siren, Huey finally pulled over, right across the street from Merritt Community College. Huey knew the area well. Merritt was a mostly Black school, where both Huey and Bobby were students.

The officer burst out of his car, yelling. Young Black men and women stood, having just come out of class, observing the scene. Quickly, a crowd began to gather.

The officer came closer, screaming. "Get out of that car!"

Huey turned, cool and collected. "You ain't putting anybody under arrest. Who the hell you think you are?"

The officer snapped. He pulled open the car door and stuck his head inside, reaching across Huey to grab the barrel of the shotgun that Bobby was holding. Bobby pulled back.

Huey sprang into action. He grabbed the officer by the collar, slamming his head against the roof of the car. Huey then turned in his seat, kicked the officer in the stomach, and threw him out of the car.

Huey jumped out, holding his shotgun. Standing tall, he jacked a round of ammunition into the chamber. He spoke loudly, for all to hear. "Now, who in the hell do you think you are, you rotten fascist swine, you bigoted racist? You come into my car, trying to brutalize me and take my property away from me?" Bobby and Lil' Bobby Hutton jumped out of the passenger side of the car. Bobby pulled back the hammer on his .45.

The officer lifted his hands from his own gun, backing away.

The crowd was in awe. People began to stream out of their houses, their excitement growing. Huey and Bobby encouraged the people to observe, to witness what was happening. The people listened. They were captivated by these Black men, standing up to the police.

Bobby told the crowd just what was on his mind. That the police were "occupying our community like a foreign troop that occupies territory. Black people are tired of it."[3]

Several more police cars arrived. An officer walked up to Huey, yelling, "Let me see that weapon!"

5

The men refused to surrender their weapons. They weren't under arrest and didn't have to comply with the officers' orders. They invoked the Second Amendment to the Constitution, which supported their right to bear arms. They cited the California law that allowed them to carry guns publicly, as long as they were visible and in the open. Huey, Bobby, and Lil' Bobby did not submit to the police.

The gathered crowd could feel the tension rising like a thick smoke, covering them all, ready to envelop them in violence. Someone would have to back down. Huey, Bobby, and Lil' Bobby refused to do so. The crowd held its breath while the police circled, looking for reasons, anything to take these men down.

Finally, the police lieutenant called his men off. He couldn't find sufficient grounds for arrest. One officer, frustrated, noticed Bobby's license plate attached by a coat hanger. The officer stopped and wrote Bobby a ticket for the license plate. This action was a last-ditch attempt at saving face. In that moment, the police were ineffective. Their power had been stripped.

The question on everyone's mind, police officers and civilians alike, was the same. Who were these people?

HUEY

In Huey Newton's young world, family came first. He was the youngest of seven children born in Monroe, Louisiana, in 1942. From early on, Huey understood the importance—and the power—of the group. His parents set an important example. When you put family first, when you put the needs of others before your own, you can achieve great things.

Huey's father, Walter, was a charismatic and powerful man, who worked several jobs to support his large family. Throughout his childhood, Huey saw his father stand up to White men. Once, when Walter got into an argument with a particular White man he worked for, the White man told him that if a "colored" person disputed his word, he whipped him. Walter replied that no man would do such a thing to

Huey Newton

him, unless he was a better man. Shocked by this uncharacteristic response, the White man backed down.[4] Walter's example encouraged Huey to stand up for himself, no matter the circumstances.

Huey's mother, Armelia Johnson, stayed home to take care of her home and children. At that time, many Black women were forced to work as servants in White households to make ends meet. Unlike Armelia, they were unable to spend that precious time with their own children. For Huey's family, Armelia's time at home was an act of rebellion. Both Armelia and Walter subverted the stereotypes that sought to confine them.

In 1945, when Huey was just three years old, his family moved to Oakland, California, looking for better opportunities. But just a few months later, World War II ended and most Black people lost their wartime jobs. Even though the Newtons fared better than many others, they still lived on the edge.

Huey's oldest brother, Walter Newton, Jr., became a hustler, working illegally to keep poverty at bay. Lee Edward joined the military, after gaining a reputation as a street fighter. Melvin took a different path, finding his purpose in books and learning, eventually teaching sociology at Merritt Community College in Oakland.

Huey became all of these things and more: a hustler, a fighter, and a scholar.

From a young age, Huey was small. He was light-skinned like his father, who was half-White. Huey had a reedy, high-pitched voice too. In many ways, he was the type of kid that bullies picked on. They looked at Huey and thought he would be an easy target. They were wrong.

Huey never backed down from a fight. He didn't believe that anyone was better than him and he refused to let anyone break him down.

When Huey reached high school, he still couldn't read. As a result, his teachers didn't consider him intelligent. They overlooked Huey, not bothering to get to know him. During all his time in the Oakland public schools, Huey didn't have a single teacher who taught him anything relevant to his own life experience. Instead, they tried to rob him of his self-worth.[5] As Huey said, "At the time, I did not understand the size or the seriousness of the school system's assault on Black people. I knew only that I constantly felt uncomfortable and ashamed of being Black."[6]

But Huey refused to let others define him. He knew that to find a healthy, powerful understanding of himself, he would have to rely on himself. He knew that he was the only one who could protect his basic humanity. Huey would nurture his own curiosity. He would question life as it was and he would work to change it, to make the world a better place for all Black people.

When his high school counselor told him he was "not college material," Huey set out to prove him wrong. Huey taught himself to read, graduated from high school, and in 1959, enrolled in Merritt College.[7] When he was unable to afford his tuition, Huey supported himself through theft and fraud. When he was caught, he defended himself in court, impressing the jury and defeating several misdemeanor charges.

Huey was an unusual combination: an intellectual and a man of action. In the years to come, he became the principal theoretician of the Black Panther Party, applying his knowledge and intelligence in ways his teachers never could have imagined. Huey always looked for real-world solutions to the injustice in his community. He fought for true freedom for Black people.

Whenever something got in the way of his goal, Huey removed the obstacle. Throughout his life, Huey refused to take no for an answer. He became a person that, in time, would go on to do what others thought impossible.

BOBBY

Bobby Seale was born in 1936 in Dallas, Texas. He was the oldest of three siblings and five years older than Huey.[8] Bobby was raised in Oakland by his mother, Thelma, and his father, George. Bobby's father was a carpenter by trade, who taught Bobby how to hunt and to fish. His father also taught Bobby about injustice.

From an early age, Bobby experienced random beatings from his father that filled him with a rage he didn't have an outlet for. But instead of becoming a bully, Bobby stood up for the underdog.

When Bobby's family first moved to Oakland, his sister Betty was pushed off the swing on the neighborhood playground. Even though

Bobby Seale

Bobby was the new kid, and outnumbered, he knocked the bully out of the swing, proclaiming that all the kids could use it. Bobby would go around the neighborhood taking on bullies twice his size, many times being beaten badly. But he never stopped standing up for himself, or for others.[9]

As Bobby grew, he learned how to channel his rage. And as he got older, he helped others channel their own anger, hurt, and frustrations, in a way that would change the world.

When he was fifteen, Bobby befriended another loner named Steve Brumfield. They would spend hours running through the nearby Berkeley Hills, dreaming and practice-fighting in the semiwilderness.

They communed with nature as a way to better understand themselves in the present and to dream of who they could be in the future. As a result, Bobby became faster and stronger and the bullies began to stay out of his way. It was the happiest time of Bobby's young life.[10]

But after high school, Steve joined the military and moved away. Bobby felt adrift without his best friend. He wandered from city to city, unable to hold down a job or have a meaningful relationship. Eventually he wound up back at home. But Bobby knew he couldn't stay there, where he would have to constantly defend himself against his father.

So, Bobby joined the U.S. Air Force. There he mastered the use of firearms, improved his metalworking skills, and worked on ways to channel his anger in a calculated fashion. When three soldiers refused to pay back a debt they owed Bobby and threatened to beat him if he mentioned it, Bobby bottled his anger and waited. Later that week, when the main soldier was least expecting it, Bobby attacked him.[11]

Bobby had multiple run-ins with officers. He broke the rules that he felt unjust. He returned after curfew and he spoke back to his superior officers. As Bobby said, "I cussed Colonel King out for what he was. I cussed him all the way down the streets. I had a whole big crowd of cats jiving and watching me cuss him out while they were taking me down in front of the barracks and all the way back across the lawn in front of the squadron headquarters."[12]

The Air Force put Bobby in jail and court-martialed him, letting him go with a bad conduct discharge. His colonel tried to threaten Bobby even as he was leaving, telling him that now, with this mark on his record, Bobby would never get a job.[13] Bobby didn't let that stop him. He worked as a sheet-metal mechanic, performer, and various other jobs.

Bobby had played jazz drums while he was in the military and now, at night, he performed in plays and comedy clubs. During the day, Bobby took college courses, an experience that helped him expand his mind. He began by studying engineering, but he soon shifted his focus toward what began to interest him most: African American history and politics.[14]

In time, Bobby would become the Chairman of the Black Panther Party. He would persevere amidst great pressure, unwavering. He would organize the Party and keep it running day to day, giving speeches that inspired countless people.

Once Bobby believed in something, he would never back down from his beliefs, regardless of the consequences.

A LONG FREEDOM STRUGGLE

Both Huey and Bobby grew up in Oakland in the 1960s. What they experienced was particular, but also part of a shared experience of being Black in America. Huey and Bobby had to deal with other people's prejudices and opinions of them, based sometimes purely on the color of their skin. They worked to prove people wrong, to stand up to stereotypes and embrace the best, most beautiful version of themselves. But, at every turn, they faced the reality of being a Black man in America.

Huey and Bobby were a part of a long Black freedom struggle in the United States, stretching back across the centuries to the first enslaved Africans that battled to free themselves.

After the American Revolution (1776–1783), the freedom struggle led by enslaved Africans increased. In ways large and small, the enslaved struggled to become free. They faked illnesses. They slowed the pace of work. They destroyed crops and tools. They torched buildings and crops and poisoned their masters and mistresses. Untold numbers ran away to freedom. In the Nat Turner Insurrection in Virginia in 1831, Turner led a band of slaves in an ill-fated yet extraordinary revolt to destroy slavery.

There were also Black people who were either born into freedom or successfully gained their freedom. These free Black people led the Abolitionist movement, which worked to end slavery. Together with a small but important group of White people, these free Black freedom fighters agitated for freedom for all Black people. Eventually, those who were enslaved led the movement that ultimately ended slavery during the Civil War (1861–1865).

Emancipation did not mean true freedom for those who had been enslaved. Even though they were technically free citizens, in practice Black people in the United States were far from free. From the 1890s down through Huey's and Bobby's childhoods, Jim Crow laws were common. These laws legalized the practice of racial segregation, keeping Black and White people apart. They were also created and used to oppress Black people—to keep them down and keep them from reaching equality.

These were just some of the conditions that shaped Huey and Bobby.

Now, the year was 1962. The Civil Rights Movement was gaining traction. During the twentieth century, the Civil Rights Movement became the largest and most powerful political movement in the United States. Those who agitated within this movement would successfully fight to abolish Jim Crow and to win voting rights for Black people. Important moments would include the 1941 March on Washington; the World War II Double Victory Campaign, which demanded victory over racism at home as well as over fascism and racism abroad; the *Brown v. Board of Education* decision (1954), which declared school segregation unconstitutional and, as a result, illegal; and the Montgomery Bus Boycott (1956–1957). The movement also used widespread economic boycotts, sit-in movements, voter registration campaigns, and desegregation campaigns throughout the nation, especially in the South.

The majority of people who fought during the Civil Rights Movement used a tactic called nonviolent civil disobedience. This kind of protest required people to literally put their bodies on the line to advance freedom. Instead of physically fighting back, protesters turned the other cheek, even when faced with violent retaliation. They were willing to suffer the penalties from their resistance to oppression—including being jailed, beaten, and killed—to advance the long Black freedom struggle.

13

Members of the Civil Rights
group SNCC, including John Lewis
on the left, protest a Whites-
only swimming pool in Cairo,
Illinois, 1962.

come let us build a
STUDENT NONVIOLEN

Lincoln Lithograph Company

ew world together

RDINATING COMMITTEE 8½ RAYMOND STREET, N.W. ATLANTA 14, GEORGIA

Danny Lyon

The raised fist became a prominent symbol of the Black Power movement.

In the early 1960s, the Black Power movement was also beginning to make strides. This movement worked to create pride in being Black and sought economic independence for Black people. It worked to create new social and cultural institutions for Black people. It did not seek necessarily to integrate with White society. Instead, the Black Power movement worked to advance the interests of the Black nation within the larger White American nation.

These movements overlapped in their struggles and their ideas. And of course, their ultimate goal—freedom for Black people—was the same. But at times these movements disagreed on the necessary methods. Some believed that freedom could be gained by operating within the system, by working within the current power structure to change it.

Others believed that, for true liberation, the system had to be overthrown and something new put in its place.

This was a time of great transformation. It was a time when people increasingly believed that change was possible. In campaign after campaign, Black activists and their allies put their bodies on the line, crossing the color line. They were brutally repressed by local White authorities. These Black activists drew the attention of the federal government, and, in many cases, the federal government intervened. Still, the movements continued, escalating and growing in numbers.

It was 1962. This was the year that Huey met Bobby.

Malcolm X speaks
at a gathering of
African American
Muslims, 1961.

CHAPTER 2

RALLY
MALCOLM X

RALLY

In 1962, Bobby Seale was walking through a rally near Merritt College. The purpose was to oppose the U.S. arms blockade against Cuba. During the rally, Bobby was drawn in by an unexpected sight. There were over two hundred people, gathered around just one man. Bobby moved in closer.

The speaker wasn't that tall. In fact, he was kind of small. But his energy, his presence, was commanding. The people around leaned toward him, like he was magnetic. He gestured wildly as he talked, fielding all kinds of questions and quickly providing answers.

When someone tried to best him by citing a passage from a book, the man took out a book of his own. It was *Black Bourgeoisie* by E. Franklin Frazier. The man immediately cited passages and page numbers right back to the other person, refuting his point. This was an impromptu speech that had little to do with the rally. The speaker was talking about race, about Black people in America.

Bobby was intrigued now. He decided to throw out some questions of his own.

Bobby asked the speaker about the National Association for the Advancement of Colored People. The NAACP was established in 1909, to address the ongoing violence against Black people in the United States. It committed itself to ending race-based discrimination and working toward not only equal rights for Black people, but also equality for all.[15] The organization didn't call for overthrowing the government, or for revolution. Instead it sought to work within the system, toward an integrated, more just society. Bobby argued that the NAACP was doing good work, helping Black people achieve a better future. An influential group in the Civil Rights movement, Bobby thought that, as a group, the NAACP was working hard and getting things done.

But the speaker had a different viewpoint. As Bobby put it, he got shot down, just like a whole lot of other people that day. The man argued that what the NAACP was doing wasn't the right way to go, politically. People didn't need to try to work with what was already in place. Instead, they needed to change it. He said, "It's all a waste of money, Black people don't have anything in this country that is for them."[16] He went on to argue that Black people didn't need more laws. The ones that were there already weren't working. Instead, Black people needed something new.

Bobby Seale had just been schooled by Huey Newton.

Bobby appreciated that Huey offered practical examples to theoretical problems. He took the lofty ideas and brought them back down to earth, where they mattered. As Bobby said, "He gets to a point where you can't get around, so you have to face things."[17]

Huey could debate theory with his peers at Merritt Community College while still understanding and relating to the "brothers on the block." He was a budding intellectual, but he never lost his connection to the street. Lots of people on campus were impressed by Huey. As Bobby said, "We would all wig out behind brother Huey, and I guess everybody respected Huey's mind and Huey's guts. He had something about him, that he didn't drive over people, but he would never let anyone drive over him."[18]

After meeting Huey, Bobby knew he had to do something. He wanted to be a part of this movement, of this larger revolutionary force that he could feel. A few days later, he went around campus searching for Huey. When Bobby went to the library, he saw Huey there, sitting amongst his books.

Bobby asked Huey where he could go to get involved and learn more. Huey gave him the address where the Afro-American Association met and the name of the book they were discussing. It was the same book Huey had taken out at the rally: *Black Bourgeoisie*.[19]

Bobby joined the Afro-American Association, where he saw more of Huey. The association was a space where Huey and Bobby discussed books and topics that shaped their growing minds. It encouraged them to think in ways they hadn't before, expanding their sense of possibility. They considered what it meant to be a Black

21

person in America and what it might mean to be Black in a just, more egalitarian society. It was there that Huey and Bobby read W.E.B. Du Bois and Booker T. Washington, James Baldwin and Ralph Ellison.

The Afro-American Association was itself inspired by Black nationalism, a movement that went back as far as the nineteenth century, when some Black people emigrated out of the United States to Black nations like Haiti and Liberia. In the twentieth century, the Universal Negro Improvement Association, led by Marcus Garvey, and the Nation of Islam, led by the Honorable Elijah Muhammad, both supported a vision of this Black nationalism. This vision required that Black people control their own economic, political, social, and cultural development.

Huey and Bobby were very influenced by this idea. They believed that Black people had to create what they wanted. They couldn't try to find it in the society that currently existed.

The two were also influenced by Donald Warden, the founder of the Afro-American Association. Warden embraced a kind of transcontinental Black pride that appealed to Huey and Bobby. This pride was not limited to Black people living in the United States. It also stretched back to its African roots, to what many Black nationalists would call the Motherland. Warden was also ready and willing to debate anyone, a quality that made a strong impression on Huey, Bobby, and many others.[20]

But, in the end, Huey and Bobby were men of action. What good was all this talking if it led nowhere? Even though they learned something while with the Afro-American Association, the group wasn't enough. Huey believed that Warden "offered the community solutions that solved nothing."[21] Huey left the group and Bobby soon followed.

For a while, Huey and Bobby were a part of the Soul Students Advisory Council (SSAC), which was an offshoot of the Revolutionary Action Movement (RAM). The Revolutionary Action Movement was a nationwide radical and internationalist Black organization, while SSAC was local to the Oakland area. In the SSAC, Huey and Bobby were exposed to important revolutionary texts, including works by Martinique's Frantz Fanon, China's Mao Zedong, and Cuba's Che Guevara. In the SSAC, Bobby and Huey were introduced to the idea that Black Americans were an oppressed colonial people, like other colonized groups across the world. This meant that Black people in America were a part of a global struggle against colonialism and capitalism.

In spite of what they learned, the SSAC wasn't a good fit for Huey and Bobby either. They eventually resigned from the group because they felt that, at its core, the SSAC was elitist. There would never be any room for the "brothers on the block." As Bobby said, "We're going to the black community and we intend to organize an organization to lead the black liberation struggle. We don't have time for you . . . You're hiding behind the ivory-walled towers in the college."[22]

In Huey and Bobby's eyes, these early groups that they joined and left weren't taking practical steps toward that revolution. Most of their time was spent reading and theorizing. It was intellectual work oriented mainly to college students, not to Black people as a whole.

Huey and Bobby still needed the right group: the appropriate philosophy, program, and leadership.

In 1964, the Civil Rights Movement was at its height. Protesters were working, through nonviolent civil disobedience, to eradicate violence and racism in America. But even with the passage of the Civil Rights Act that year and the Voting Rights Act in 1965—even as Jim Crow laws began to disappear—violence and racism persisted.

Officially, the federal government was making concessions to the demands of Black Americans. But these official moves were doing little to actually improve the lives of Black people in America.

In stepped Malcolm X.

MALCOLM X

Malcolm X was a "brother on the block" who would go on to become one of the primary architects of the Black Power movement. During his life, he would rise up to become an inspiration for people of all colors. Malcolm X was born Malcolm Little in Omaha, Nebraska, in 1925. He was one of eight children. When Malcolm was six, his father, Earl Little, was killed. Louise Little, Malcolm's mother, believed that her husband was murdered by White people who didn't want Earl to continue speaking out and preaching the ideas of Black nationalists like Marcus Garvey.

When Malcolm's father died, the year was 1931. The country was in the midst of the Great Depression. After his mother was hospitalized, Malcolm lived the rest of his childhood in and out of foster homes, was involved in crime as a teenager, dropped out of high school, and was incarcerated by age twenty.[23] Throughout his life, Malcolm experienced hardship and the violence of racism. But he refused to let it define or defeat him.

After Malcolm left prison in 1952, he became famous as a minister for Elijah Muhammad's Nation of Islam. From the years 1959 to 1965, Malcolm X was one of the most visible and important leaders of the Black freedom struggle. He had the courage of his convictions, but also a willingness to grow and change. When he spoke, people listened. And, above all, he never apologized for his blackness.

In direct contrast to the leaders of the Civil Rights Movement, Malcolm X declared a call to arms. While Civil Rights leaders promoted nonviolent civil disobedience as the best way forward for Black people, Malcolm X believed in liberation "by any means necessary." He asserted the necessity of armed self-defense.[24] If a person was being physically attacked, Malcolm X argued that that person could, and should, physically fight back. He asserted, "Concerning nonviolence, it is criminal to teach a man not to defend himself when he is the constant victim of brutal attacks."[25]

Malcolm X also believed that for Black people to get ahead, integration into White society was not the answer. His politics were separatist, like those of many in the Black Power and Black national-ist movements. Malcolm X argued that Black people had to take care of themselves by owning their own organizations and running their own businesses. They needed to create their own places to live, learn, and work. It wasn't about fighting for a seat at the table. Sit-ting down with the oppressor would not solve the fundamental problem. Black people needed to make their own spaces, their own systems, and their own structures.

Malcolm X's ideas resonated with many young Black people, like Huey and Bobby. They had not seen the Civil Rights Movement bring about any real change in the condition of their lives. As Malcolm X said, "And now you're facing a situation where the young Negro's coming up. They don't want to hear that 'turn-the-other-cheek' stuff, no . . . It'll be Molotov cocktails this month, hand grenades next month, and something else next month. It'll be ballots, or it'll be bul-lets. It'll be liberty, or it will be death."[26]

Malcolm X could foresee that his own days were numbered. As he wrote, "Each day I live as if I am already dead."[27] He predicted that he would die a violent death, but still, he took each hour as a gift. He used this borrowed time to further his mission of Black libera-tion. "I believe that it would be almost impossible to find any-where in America a Black man who has lived further down in the mud of human society than I have," he wrote. "But it is only after the deepest darkness that the greatest joy can come; it is only after slavery and prison that the sweetest appreciation of freedom can come. For the freedom of my 22 million black brothers and sisters here in America, I do believe that I have fought the best that I knew how."[28]

When Malcolm X was assassinated on February 21, 1965, gunned down in the Audubon Ballroom in Harlem, New York, the Black community was shaken. When Bobby heard the news he was filled with pain and rage. He went into his mother's garden, gath-ered up the bricks there, and began hurling them at passing cars driven by White people. He wanted to become his own version of Malcolm X. He felt that "if they want to kill me, they'll have to kill me."[29]

Like so many others, Bobby was deeply affected by the murder of Malcolm X. In Malcolm X they saw a leader, a role model, and a hero. His words hit home for many young Black people growing up in poor neighborhoods. Too many lived in substandard housing, without the promise of adequate employment or the hope for advancement. Who were they supposed to turn to? Where were they supposed to look? It was impossible to trust a racist system. And it was impossible to let things remain as they were.

Malcolm X's teachings encouraged people to seriously question that racist system and to question the status quo. Malcolm X didn't want people to blindly believe what they read in a history book, what they learned in school. He didn't encourage them to aspire to the "American Dream." He believed that, for Black people, that aspiration was no dream. It was a nightmare. Instead, Malcolm X demanded a new and different dream: a better life, made by Black people, for Black people.

Malcolm X provided an attractive, powerful, and necessary alternative. This vision of Black liberation struck a chord with Huey and Bobby. The Civil Rights Movement tried to operate within the system. Leaders like Malcolm X sought to overturn and dismantle business as usual.

What could be done, if peaceful coexistence was not an option? Who would carry on Malcolm X's legacy?

"THE RACIST DOG POLICEMEN MUST WITHDRAW IMMEDIATELY FROM OUR COMMUNITIES, CEASE THEIR WANTON MURDER AND BRUTALITY AND TORTURE OF BLACK PEOPLE, OR FACE THE WRATH OF THE ARMED PEOPLE."

HUEY P. NEWTON, Minister of Defense

Huey and Bobby outside their first office, February 1967.

BLACK PANTHER PARTY
P.O. Box 8641, Emeryville, Calif.

CHAPTER 3

BOILING POINT
WATTS
THE BLACK PANTHER

BOILING POINT

It was a bright, warm evening in March 1966. Huey and Bobby walked down Telegraph Avenue, headed toward the University of California, Berkeley campus. They were in the midst of a bohemian mecca, filled with color, with the sights and sounds of liberated, free thinkers. The streets were brimming with hippies and students, young people milling about and congregating in shops, bars, cafés, and restaurants. Even at nine at night, the street buzzed with energy.

Bobby and his friends were on their way to the record store. They were looking for some good blues music, by some "downhome brothers" like T-Bone Walker, Howlin' Wolf, Lightnin' Hopkins.[30] As they walked, Bobby's friends asked him to recite some poetry. Bobby had always been a natural performer, and this moment was no exception. He spoke loudly enough for everyone to hear, and, when they reached the outside of the Forum Restaurant, their friend "Weasel" pulled out a chair for him.

Bobby climbed up on the chair and continued with an antiwar poem called "Uncle Sammy Call Me Fulla Lucifer."[31] When he finished someone yelled out, "Do it again. Run it down again, man."[32] Bobby began to draw an excited and enthusiastic crowd. People stopped to listen. They leaned into his voice, into the cadence of his words and the passion behind his speech.

The Vietnam War was escalating. By 1965, North Vietnam was controlled by Ho Chi Minh, a Communist and nationalist leader. The U.S. became further involved because they didn't want all of Vietnam— and as a result, they feared, all of Southeast Asia—to fall under Communist rule. In 1965, President Lyndon Johnson increased the number of troops that were already in Vietnam. In that year, 25% of all the American soldiers killed in Vietnam were Black men. As the war continued to escalate, the U.S. accelerated a draft that required men ages 18–25 to fight in Vietnam when their number was called.[33]

The students were angry and scared. They felt conflicted about the draft and the role that the Vietnam war would play in their lives. How many of them would be called to serve? How many of them might lose their lives as a result? When Bobby finished speaking, the crowd began cheering, urging him to deliver the antiwar poem again.

To put a stop to it, an off-duty police officer pushed through and grabbed Bobby. A scuffle broke out, and Bobby and Huey were arrested for disturbing the peace.[34] Their friend and fellow Merritt College student Virtual Murrell came to their aid, bailing them out with money from the Soul Students Advisory Council treasury.[35]

A few weeks later, Huey and Bobby saw a police officer pushing around a Black man for no apparent reason. They followed the man to the station and bailed him out with the same method.[36] The stranger started to cry. Bobby was deeply touched. This was a tangible, immediate response to what they had done. It was an action, taken in the moment, that changed someone's life.

What would it be like if they could do this on a larger scale? Could they find a way to address police brutality, to make a positive change in their own communities and beyond?

The money Huey and Bobby used for this act was from the SSAC treasury. This led to a disagreement over where SSAC money could and should go. Huey and Bobby felt that what they had done was right, and it was then they decided to fully break away from the SSAC. They wanted to help people in the community. They wanted to stand up for the individual and for the group. To work against police brutality in their neighborhoods. This was the feeling they longed for, the experience they needed.

Huey and Bobby were not alone. Throughout the country, Black people wanted to rebel against racism and police brutality. Increasingly, many Black people felt that nonviolence wasn't the answer. In 1965, in response to police brutality, one of the largest urban rebellions in U.S. history had taken place. It occurred just 400 miles south in Los Angeles, in an area known as Watts.

WATTS

Watts was a mostly Black neighborhood, but very few officers in the Los Angeles Police Department were Black.[37] In 1957, Los Angeles Police Chief William Parker went so far as to write that "I don't think you can throw the genes out of the question when you discuss the behavior patterns of people." With this statement, he implied that Black people were inherently criminal.[38] The Black people of Watts were targeted to such an extent that one activist said, "You just had to be black and moving to be shot by the police."[39]

On August 11, 1965, twenty-one-year-old Marquette Frye was driving near his family's house in Watts. He was with his younger brother Ronald, who had just been discharged from the U.S. Air Force. They were pulled over by a California Highway Patrol officer and charged with drunk driving. Quickly, more police began to arrive. A crowd of more than two hundred people gathered to witness. Their mother, Rena Frye, came out to check on her sons. The police officers beat her with a blackjack, slapping her and twisting her arm behind her back.[40]

An aerial shot of the Watts rebellion.

The Frye family's violent experience was not unique. But it was galvanizing. The people had had enough.

The Watts rebellion spread over forty-six square miles. Some were calling themselves "followers of Malcolm X" yelling, "Let's burn . . . baby, burn!" There were more than 7,000 looters rampaging stores. Many armed themselves, stealing weapons like guns and machetes. When fire trucks and ambulances tried to enter the area, they were attacked. The rebels were firing shots at helicopters, airplanes, and the police. They hurled bottles full of gasoline and Molotov cocktails into cars and stores. The streets were ablaze.[41] The local CBS radio station reported, "This was not a riot. It was an insurrection against all authority . . . If it had gone much further it would have become civil war."[42]

A year later, in Hunters Point in San Francisco, a similar situation brewed. Hunters Point was a primarily Black neighborhood, just across the bay from Huey and Bobby. The tensions between police and citizens ran high in Hunters Point. Just like Watts.

On September 27, 1966, Matthew Johnson and his friends were riding in a stolen car. When the police stopped them, Matthew and his friends panicked. They jumped out of the car and began to run. The police gave chase, shooting Matthew in the back. They left him bleeding on the ground for over an hour. When the ambulances arrived, it was already too late. Matthew was dead.[43]

The people of Hunters Point took to the streets. Before it was all over, they destroyed thirty-one police cars and ten fire department vehicles. To put a stop to the uprising, the police arrested 146 people. Forty-two people were injured, ten of them by gunshots.[44] As quickly as it had started, the uprising ended.

The communities in Watts and Hunters Point did not have an organized, calculated response to this police brutality. Instead, they responded at an emotional, visceral level to an unacceptable situation. Bobby and Huey identified with this motivating rage. They knew what it meant to feel powerless. They understood the urge to fight back. Huey and Bobby had worked in their personal lives to

Heavyweight boxer Amos Lincoln guards the family drug store.

Two men talk in the aftermath of the Watts rebellion.

channel their own feelings of anger and hopelessness in an effective, targeted way.

Now, they wanted to channel this energy on a much larger scale. They knew that, if they could take this emotion, if they could harness this energy, they could create something powerful. They could direct the efforts of a whole group of people toward something that would rise and swell, a growing tide that could, with time, sweep across the entire American landscape.

Huey and Bobby knew that something had to change. Human life, Black life, had to be protected.

How could they organize and harness the power of the group? How could Huey and Bobby create something that would uplift not just the individual, but also the people as a whole?

THE BLACK PANTHER

Huey was determined to find the answer. He turned, as he so often did, to the written word. He pored through his books, his pamphlets and newsletters, searching for inspiration.

While reading the West Coast Student Nonviolent Coordinating Committee newspaper, the *Movement,* Huey learned about the Community Alert Patrol (CAP) in Watts. The members of CAP monitored police activity, driving around the Black neighborhoods of Watts and documenting police activities.[45]

But even with their careful patrolling, CAP members were routinely pulled over, beaten, and arrested. A new approach was necessary.

Huey was studying law at San Francisco State College and Merritt College when he made an important discovery. In California, it was legal to carry a loaded gun in public as long as the weapon was not concealed. Citizens also had the right to observe a police officer if they stood a reasonable distance away.[46]

This was what Huey had been looking for. He and Bobby could use this law to their advantage. They could directly address the issue of police brutality in Black and Brown communities. They would arm themselves in self-defense.

Huey had found a way to use the law in a revolutionary way. By arming themselves in self-defense, as Malcolm X and other Black nationalists called for, Huey and Bobby could begin to dismantle the system from the inside. With the law on their side, they would start to take apart the structures that had systematically oppressed them and so many other Black people in America.

Huey and Bobby would use the system against itself.

Instead of continuing to search for the right group, for the appropriate leadership, Bobby and Huey decided to create what they wanted. They would form the group. And they would lead it.

They called themselves the Black Panther Party for Self-Defense.

Now, Huey, Bobby, and the other "brothers on the block" could organize. They would have patrols like the CAP in Watts. But their group would be armed and ready.

That fateful night, cruisin' in Bobby's car, they all knew what was at stake. With Lil' Bobby Hutton beside them, Huey and Bobby made a decision that would change their lives.

When the police pulled them over, it could have ended in violence, or even death. Still, they refused to back down. These young Black men challenged law enforcement. They stood up and claimed their rights. And they lived to tell the tale.

The excited crowd gathered around, trying to figure out who these men were and what they stood for. Bobby and Huey described their organization, and, the very next day, the Black Panther Party for Self-Defense had new recruits.

Patrolling the police over the next few months, Huey and Bobby gained a small following. They began to collect more firearms to

Lil' Bobby Hutton

defend themselves against the police. The first weapons came from Bobby's own collection. Richard Aoki, a Japanese-American man, donated a shotgun and a pistol to their cause.[47]

37

To purchase more weapons, Huey and Bobby sold Mao Zedong's Little Red Book on the Berkeley campus.[48] Bobby also got Huey a job where he also worked, at the North Oakland War on Poverty Youth program. That's where they met Lil' Bobby.

Huey and Bobby liked Lil' Bobby right away. Lil' Bobby was only fifteen, but he was already mature and responsible. He was the youngest of seven children, just like Huey. Lil' Bobby's family moved from Arkansas to Oakland when Lil' Bobby was three years old, the same age as Huey when he moved.[49]

Lil' Bobby was serious about the cause, the revolution, and helping Black people. But he wasn't a serious person. In fact, he was quite the opposite. He had a contagious smile and an easygoing personality. As Huey said, "[Lil Bobby had] a disarming quality that made people love him."[50]

After work at the center, Lil' Bobby would go to Bobby Seale's house and they would spend time together, talking and reading. At this point, Lil' Bobby had already been kicked out of school. So, when he joined the Party as their very first recruit, Lil' Bobby devoted all of his free time to the organization.[51]

Once Huey, Bobby, and Lil' Bobby made enough money, they combined their paychecks. For their new organization, the Black Panther Party for Self-Defense, the trio rented an office on Grove Street and Fifty-sixth in North Oakland near Merritt College.[52]

As 1967 began, the Black Panther Party for Self-Defense had only a handful of members. They didn't have any coverage in the press. And only a few people had heard of them.

But that was all about to change.

PART TWO: TAKE A STAND

Let us go on outdoing ourselves; a revolutionary man always transcends himself or otherwise he is not a revolutionary man, so we always do what we ask of ourselves or more than what we know we can do. [53]

Huey Newton

Eldridge Cleaver

CHAPTER 4

ELDRIDGE AIRPORT

ELDRIDGE

It was early 1967. Huey and Bobby sat, listening intently to the radio. "Who is this cat?" Huey asked. He was intrigued by the voice he heard coming over the airwaves. The more Huey heard, the more intrigued he became. The voice was cool and compelling, self-assured and convincing. Huey made up his mind. He turned to Bobby and said, "I'm going to talk to this cat."[54] They headed over to the radio station to meet Eldridge Cleaver for the first time.

Leroy Eldridge Cleaver was born in Wabbaseka, Arkansas, in 1935. His mother, Thelma Hattie Robinson Cleaver, was an elementary school teacher, and his father, Leroy Cleaver, was a waiter and played piano in nightclubs.[55] Like Huey's family and many other Black families from the South, Eldridge's family moved out west for work during World War II. They ended up in Los Angeles, where Eldridge got caught up in petty crime. He went to jail a few times and then was sent to Soledad prison for two and a half years at age nineteen. "In Soledad state prison, I fell in with a group of young blacks," wrote Eldridge, "who, like myself, were in vociferous rebellion against what we perceived as a continuation of slavery on a higher plane. We cursed everything American . . . We knew that in the end what they were clashing over was us, what to do with blacks, and whether or not to start treating us as human beings."[56]

Eldridge's politics, his experiences, his eloquence and charisma all resonated with Huey. Once he heard Eldridge on the radio, Huey really wanted Eldridge to join the Party.[57] Bobby was indifferent to begin with. As he said, "Huey related to Eldridge more than I did, initially. I just had a tendency to follow Huey. I was never ashamed of the fact that I always followed Huey. I just followed him, and listened to him, and tried to understand what he was saying. If I disagreed with him, I tried to disagree properly."[58] At the time, Bobby saw nothing to disagree with. They both had heard of Eldridge, but they didn't know much about him. Still, Huey felt, in his gut, that the Party needed Eldridge.

When they arrived at the station, Eldridge was still on the air. Huey and Bobby waited. Right after the interview, Huey approached him.

They had a long discussion, with Huey doing most of the talking. He was trying to persuade Eldridge to join the Party, but he couldn't tell what Eldridge thought. Eldridge was barely talking. So Huey kept filling up the pauses. Every now and then Eldridge would nod his head and say, "I know," but that was about it.

Eventually, Huey was done. There was nothing more to say, so he stood still and waited. When Eldridge finally spoke, it wasn't what Huey wanted to hear. Eldridge didn't want to join up with Huey and Bobby. He made it clear that his commitment was to Malcolm X and his legacy. Eldridge's concern was protecting Betty Shabazz, Malcolm X's widow. Eldridge wanted to work with her to continue Malcolm X's work. That was all he had time for. With that, Eldridge turned and left.[59]

Very soon, Eldridge would gain acclaim from his book *Soul on Ice,* written while he was incarcerated. Beverly Axelrod, a White civil rights lawyer, had smuggled the manuscript out of prison—when she visited Eldridge, she hid his writing between the pages of her legal documents. Beverly showed Eldridge's work to Edward Keating, the publisher of *Ramparts* magazine, an independent Catholic publication and an influential voice in the mounting opposition to the Vietnam War.[60] Once Eldridge was out on parole, he became a writer for *Ramparts.*

But Eldridge didn't just want to write. He wanted to create a new organization that represented the true legacy of Malcolm X. He wanted to further Malcolm X's goals and his mission. That was the driving force behind the decisions Eldridge made, the places he went, and the people he worked with.

Eldridge helped to found Black House in San Francisco, a place he hoped would be a true cultural center for the Black Power movement in the Bay Area. A place he hoped would further the legacy of Malcolm X.

Eldridge also joined the Revolutionary Action Movement (RAM), the same RAM Huey and Bobby had been briefly associated with as a part of the Soul Students Advisory Council. Eldridge wanted to organize a memorial for the two-year anniversary of Malcolm X's death, so he proposed the idea at a RAM meeting. He thought they should bring in Betty Shabazz as the keynote speaker. The memorial was Eldridge's idea, but Roy Ballard, a longtime member of RAM, was appointed the event coordinator.[61] Even though Eldridge wanted the position, he was new to the group and the members of RAM overlooked him.

A few of the RAM members were worried. They knew that Betty would need protection. So, Roy called Bobby. He had heard about what Huey and Bobby were doing, and he knew them from their time with the Soul Students Advisory Council. He told Bobby about the event and that a few of the organizers were afraid for Betty's safety. Her husband had been murdered two years before. They didn't want to take any chances. Roy asked Bobby if the Panthers could provide protection for Betty.

After the call, Huey and Bobby sat down to talk it over.

Huey had heard about Betty's earlier visit to Los Angeles. The police managed to break up the people escorting her at the time, Ron Karenga's group US. In the end, Betty was left, standing alone, in the middle of the street.[62] Huey and Bobby refused to let that happen. If they were going to organize an escort, they were going to do it the Black Panther way.

AIRPORT

On February 21, 1967, eight members of the Black Panther Party walked into the lobby of the San Francisco Airport. They were all dressed in uniform. The men and the women wore sky blue shirts under dark, waist-length leather jackets. All of the Panthers were armed. They openly displayed their shotguns and pistols.

The Panthers met up with Kenny Freeman, Roy Ballard, and a few other members of RAM. When the airport security chief asked them to leave, confronting them with armed deputies, Huey refused. He had studied his books late into the night and he knew exactly what he and the other Panthers could legally do. As the security chief later admitted, the Panthers were "quite hip on the law."[63]

The Panthers proceeded to the gate where Betty was scheduled to arrive. They set themselves up at various stations, waiting, rifles in hand. Like sentinels, watchful and ready.

As soon as Betty left the plane, the Panthers formed a circle around her. They created a shield with their bodies. The other people in the airport stopped and stared. They had never seen anything quite like it.

The airport police were on edge. They weren't sure if they could intervene. What was the protocol in a situation like this?

While everyone hesitated, the Panthers swept through, unconcerned. Their mission was to protect Betty Shabazz, and that's exactly what they did. They walked with precision, protecting Betty all the way out of the airport. Once outside, the Panthers led her to the waiting cars.

From the airport, the Party members escorted Betty to the San Francisco office of *Ramparts*, where they had planned an interview with Eldridge.

But from there, things didn't go as planned.

The Panthers were confronted outside the *Ramparts* office by law enforcement. They could have predicted this. But not the sudden, aggressive attempt by a reporter who stepped in after, trying to push his way through the Panther bodyguard. Then the reporter made his biggest mistake. He tried to push Huey aside. In response, Huey grabbed him by the collar, pushing him back against the wall.

The surrounding officers reacted. Several flipped loose the straps that held their pistols, ready to grab them at any moment. One officer began shouting at Huey. Huey stopped, staring at the cop. Bobby tried to get Huey to leave. Instead, Huey walked right up to the officer, looking him in the eye. "What's the matter?" he said. "You got an itchy finger?"

47

The cop didn't reply. Both men continued to stare each other down. The other officers called out for the cop to cool it, but he kept his hand on his gun. Huey called out, "Okay, you big fat racist pig, draw your gun." But nothing happened. The officer made no move.

Huey stood there for a moment and then shouted, "Draw it, you cowardly dog!" And with that, he pumped a round into his shotgun chamber. The other officers spread out. They stood that way for a while: Huey ready to fire. The other officers standing out of the way. Everyone waiting for someone else to make the first move. While all this was going on, Betty was whisked away by the other Panthers.

Eventually, the officer gave up, sighing in defeat. He hung his head and Huey, triumphant, laughed in his face.

Eldridge had never seen a Black person behave this way. So bold, so seemingly unafraid. It was like watching "pure instinct."[64] At this time, not only was this strategy powerful—it was legal. Eldridge watched as this young Black man in America armed himself in self-defense. He stood up to the White police officers and won, all working within the law. For Eldridge, it was akin to a revelation.

Eldridge wanted to be a member of *that* Party. He wouldn't waste his time with RAM and Roy Ballard any longer. In RAM, there was too much theorizing and not enough action. Eldridge put his full support behind Huey. Huey had given Eldridge something new to believe in. In Eldridge's eyes, Huey was the legitimate heir to Malcolm X's legacy.[65]

In the months that followed, word began to spread about the bold new Black Power organization called the Black Panther Party for Self-Defense. Even though the first handful of members were men, women began to join the Party right away too. Still, most people would think of the Black Panthers as a male organization. But from the very beginning, women were right alongside men, doing the work of the Party.

The erasure of Black women's stories and their voices was not particular to the Black Panther Party. These omissions have happened far too often throughout history. A story untold. A name left unsaid.

These acts try to bury a person's experience, to rob it of its power. But the act of revolution, of seizing one's freedom, was also an act of reclamation.

The women of the Party worked to center their own experience, to step out of the shadows and away from the margins. They walked away from the places that they were expected to occupy because of their race and their gender. They proclaimed their agency, their own subjectivity, rejecting the idea that their bodies were merely objects, that the work they did could be taken for granted. The women of the Party fought and took their place as agents of revolutionary change.

Tarika Lewis was one of the first women to join the Black Panther Party. She had attended Oakland Technical High School, just like Huey and Lil' Bobby. Even before she joined the Party, Tarika was involved in her community. She would attend meetings on Black culture and history with her older cousins, who were activists. Tarika was a member of the Black Student Union and she worked to create a Black History Club at her school.

Tarika knew that to get what you wanted and needed, you couldn't wait. You had to fight for it. Not just that, she knew it wouldn't be enough to go after it alone. You had to work for change on both the individual and the group level.

One day in the spring of '67, Tarika strode into the Panther offices, bold and confident. She sported a large and beautiful afro. "Ya'll have a nice program and everything," she said. "It sounds like me. Can I join? 'Cause y'all don't have no sisters up in here." Bobby quickly agreed.[66]

Tarika would go on to create artwork for the Panthers' newspaper under the name Matilaba. Her angular line drawings were seen in the paper, alongside those of Emory Douglas, from 1967 to 1969.[67]

Elendar Barnes also joined the Party in the spring of '67. She learned about the Party through Laverne Williams, Huey's girlfriend and Elendar's best friend. For Elendar, being a part of the Panthers was an organic next step in her life. She knew about self-defense politics already. She grew up surrounded by it while her family lived in the

51

South. Elendar said, "I remember asking 'Papa why you always got a gun?' He'd reply, 'It's for the white folks, baby.' 'Papa, why you get up so early?' 'To keep up with the white folks, baby.' . . . That's why I joined the Panthers. I came from that idea of standing up . . . And it wasn't for the white man who wasn't bothering you. It was for the KKK and the others. And that's what moved me into the Panthers."[68]

By the spring of 1967, the Panthers were consistently adding more members. Huey and Bobby hoped that through standing up to the police, the Panthers could begin to organize even more Black people and build greater political power. They wanted to become a larger organization, with a membership outside the Oakland area.

But the Party's numbers remained low. They were known only through word of mouth. For now, their main tactic was their community patrols of the police. They operated in just a small area, not yet reaching beyond their own neighborhoods.

The Panthers needed a catalyst. A certain series of events that would vault them into the limelight.

HOOVER

FEB 19 1993

The BLACK PANTHER

BLACK
COMMUNITY
NEWS
SERVICE

VOLUME 1   APRIL 25, 1967   NUMBER 1

P.O. BOX 8641 OAK. CALIF. EMERYVILLE BRANCH

PUBLISHED BY THE BLACK PANTHER PARTY FOR SELF DEFENSE

WHY WAS DENZIL DOWELL KILLED

APRIL FIRST 3:50 a.m.

"I BELIEVE THE POLICE MURDERED MY SON" SAYS THE MOTHER OF DENZIL DOWELL.

Brothers and Sisters of the Richmond community, here is the view of the family's side of the death of Denzil Dowell as compiled by the Black Panther Party for Self Defense, concerned citizens, and the Dowell family. As you know, April 1st, 1967, Denzel Dowell (age 22), was shot and killed by an "officer of the Martinez Sheriff's Department", so read the newspaper.

But there are too many unanswered questions that have been raised by the Dowell family and other neighbors in the North Richmond community. Questions that don't meet the satisfaction of the killing of Denzil. The Richmond Police, the Martinez Sheriff's Department, and the Richmond Independent would have us black people believe something contrary to Mrs. Dowell's accusation. That is, her son was "unjustifiably" murdered by a racist cop.

There are too many questionable facts supporting the Dowell family's point of view.

These questionable facts are as follows:

1. Denzil Dowell was unarmed so how can six bullet holes and shot gun blasts be considered "justifiable homocide"? (Con't Page 2)

WE BLACK PEOPLE ARE MEETING SATURDAY 1:30 AT 1717 SECOND STREET LET US SUPPORT THE DOWELL FAIMLY EVERY BLACK BROTHER AND SISTER MUST UNITE FOR REAL POLITICAL ACTION

CHAPTER 5

NORTH RICHMOND
THE PANTHERS INVESTIGATE

NORTH RICHMOND

It was 3:50 a.m. on April 1, 1967. That late at night, most people were asleep. George Dowell, though, was awake. Suddenly, he heard ten gunshots. Something was wrong. He could feel it in his bones. He got up and went out into his neighborhood, North Richmond. Sometime after 5:00 a.m. he found his older brother Denzil, lying in the street. He was shot in the back and in the head. Twenty-two-year-old Denzil Dowell was dead.[69]

The official story appeared in the morning newspaper. Reportedly, an unidentified caller tipped off the police about a burglary in progress. When the sheriff's deputies arrived, Denzil and another man ran from the back of a liquor store. They didn't stop when ordered to. According to the newspaper story, the sheriff deputy, named Mel Brunkhorst, fired once, hitting Denzil and killing him. The other man escaped.[70]

The Dowell family didn't believe what they read in the paper. They knew something else was at work. Brunkhorst had issued Denzil citations in the past. At one point, Brunkhorst had even threatened to kill Denzil. Unfortunately, there were no eyewitnesses. No video or pictures taken. The Dowell family would have to try to piece together what happened to Denzil from evidence after the fact.

Right away, the official story began to fall apart. There was no sign of entry at the liquor store where the supposed robbery took place. The police reported that Denzil had run and hopped two fences while they pursued him. This was impossible. Denzil had a bad hip and he couldn't run. There was no way he could hop over multiple fences.

The coroner's report confirmed the Dowell family's suspicions—things weren't what they appeared. According to the report, Denzil bled to death. But where he was found, there had been no blood. Instead, twenty yards away from where the police claimed Denzil died, there was a pool of blood. There were also six bullet holes in his body. This confirmed the multiple gunshots that George and his neighbors heard, not the official story of Brunkhorst firing a single shot. In addition, a doctor working on the case informed the family that, judging from the way the bullets entered his body, Dowell had been shot with his hands raised.

When the county refused to let the family take pictures of the corpse, or to have the clothes Denzil was wearing, Denzil's mother publicly announced, "I believe the police murdered my son."[71]

Just a few months before, two unarmed Black men had also been shot and killed in North Richmond. They too had had their hands raised. There was a rumor that the police were responsible. Similarly, a Black woman who lived in North Richmond had recently had a run-in with the police, suffering a brutal beating at their hands. Denzil's killing was a part of this pattern of police brutality.[72] Tensions between the people and the police were reaching a boiling point. The North Richmond community demanded justice.

That was where the Panthers came in.

North Richmond was only a few miles from Oakland, the birthplace of the Panthers. At the time, North Richmond was predominantly Black. It had been the site of several major shipyards during World War II, which attracted many families, including Black families, to the area for jobs. After the war, the shipyards closed and the jobs went with them.

In the neighborhood where Denzil was shot, six thousand people lived between a garbage dump and the Chevron Oil refinery. The refinery pumped out toxic fumes, which the residents were forced to breathe. When a new playground opened, the children couldn't play—they were scared away by rats.[73] The community was physically isolated too. Most people lived in ghettos consisting of public housing units. There were only three streets to enter or exit the neighborhood. Sometimes the police blocked all of those streets, sealing off the area.[74] As Huey said, "North Richmond is no different from countless Black communities in California and the rest of the United States. Cut off, ignored, and forgotten, the people are kept in a state of subjugation, especially by the police."[75]

Mark Comfort, a local Black activist, brought Denzil's case to Huey and Bobby's attention. Mark knew the Dowell family personally and knew how high the stakes were. He drove to Huey and Bobby's office in Oakland. He wanted them to know what was going on, how upset the community members were, and that something needed to be done.

Central Headquarters in Oakland, CA.

Denzil's sister Ruby was calling a meeting at Neighborhood House, a community center in North Richmond. Huey and Bobby decided to attend.[76]

Emotions ran high at the meeting. Denzil's father and mother had mostly remained in the background during the heightening crisis, but in the meeting, Denzil's mother stepped forward. Mrs. Dowell was angry, but also scared. She was losing hope. She and her husband had worked so hard just to survive in North Richmond, to provide for their family and raise their children. Now, the very people who were sworn to protect them, had taken one of her children from her. When she tried to speak to authorities, to go through the appropriate channels, she wasn't taken seriously.[77] Where could she and her family turn? Would there ever be justice for Denzil? For the murders of so many Black people?

Huey and Bobby began to speak about their new organization. They explained the Panthers' belief—that only through armed self-defense could Black people find safety and security. But Huey and Bobby didn't just talk. They listened too. They asked questions about the case, trying to understand what really happened that night.

Denzil's brother George could see that Huey and Bobby actually cared. Not only did they want justice for Denzil, they were concerned about the people as a whole. For the first time, George had a hope for justice.

"I was really impressed," George said. "They made me feel like they were really interested in the people, and they knew what they were doing . . . When I listened to Huey and Bobby talk, I could tell that they were talking from their hearts. A person can tell when another person is telling the truth and that's what all our people been waiting to hear."[78]

THE PANTHERS INVESTIGATE

The very next day, the Party took matters into their own hands. They began to conduct an investigation. Huey, Bobby, and a few other Party members started to spend time in North Richmond. They spoke to George and other young people. They spent time in the Dowell family home. They spoke with the neighbors and other people in the community. They tried to find witnesses. They talked to forensics experts and the coroner's office.[79] They were determined to find the truth.

One Sunday later in April, while Huey was visiting with Mrs. Dowell, a policeman knocked on the door. "Policemen were constantly coming to Mrs. Dowell's house and treating her like dirt," said Huey. "They would knock on the door, walk in, and search the premises any time they wanted."[80] The officer thought Mrs. Dowell was alone, but this time Huey was there.

Mrs. Dowell answered her door and the officer pushed his way in. He began asking her all sorts of questions. Before she said anything, Huey grabbed his shotgun and placed himself in front of Mrs. Dowell. He told the officer to produce a warrant or leave. The officer stood for a minute, shocked. Then he turned and ran to his car.[81]

Word spread through the community about what Huey had done. Many people in the neighborhood felt especially vulnerable to police attacks. Now there was someone who met the police head-on, offering protection. Here was a group that would stand up for the community: the Black Panther Party for Self-Defense.

Mrs. Dowell continued to fight for her dead son. She went to have a meeting with the county district attorney. Then she went to Martinez to speak with the county sheriff, Panthers in tow. She tried to get the local authorities to listen. But the county sheriff refused to change anything. He said he cared about North Richmond, but he refused to suspend Brunkhorst or revise the department's policy on when to shoot potential suspects. An undersheriff said mockingly, "If you want the policy changed, you should go to the legislature."[82] The Dowell family had hoped that their local authorities might do something, but after the meeting in Martinez, it was clear that it was all a dead end. Still, they persisted.

On Saturday, April 22, the Panthers held a street-corner rally, telling the North Richmond community more about their group. The Panthers had already held rallies in Oakland and San Francisco; now, North Richmond. The Panthers maintained that if Denzil could be murdered with impunity, so could any member of the community.

That day the crowd began to grow. People were inspired by these young Black men and women: committed, disciplined, organized, and armed. Cars began to stop and traffic began to back up. Over 150 people gathered. Huey and Bobby had captured the community's energy and imagination.

To publicize their second rally, Eldridge started the Party's newspaper, with fellow Party member Emory Douglas. They called it *The Black Panther.* By creating their own paper, the Panthers created a place where they would control the words and images that represented the Party. This control was essential. Much would be said about the Panthers, but the paper provided a place for them to speak for themselves.

At its height, *The Black Panther* would have international distribution and a circulation in the hundreds of thousands. But this first issue consisted of just two mimeographed sheets stapled together. Even though the beginnings were humble, Eldridge and Emory, Huey and Bobby, believed in its future. The first headline read "Why Was Denzil Dowell Killed?" Three thousand copies were printed and the kids from the neighborhood distributed them door to door on their bikes.[83]

Emory Douglas

Distribution of *The Black Panther* soon became an essential Party endeavor.

The Panthers' second rally in North Richmond, a week after the first, was a huge success. Huey, Bobby, and Eldridge all spoke, encouraging Black people to take their safety into their own hands. They all had their weapons openly displayed.

Police began to line up around the area during the rally. A Contra Costa County helicopter buzzed ominously overhead. Unfazed, all three Panthers kept speaking. The crowd continued to grow.

At one point, Huey pointed to Panther John Sloan stationed on a rooftop. Sloan performed a weapons demonstration as the crowd cheered. Neighbors even showed up with their own guns. No one in the crowd had ever experienced anything like this.

During these rallies, there were confrontations with officers, but the police backed down. The Panthers had the people, and the law, behind them.

A couple listens at a Black Panther rally in Oakland.

Bystander Earl Anthony reported that he "had never seen Black men command the respect of the people the way that Huey Newton and Bobby Seale did that day."[84]

What Anthony witnessed was a powerful testament to what the Panthers had already accomplished—and the remarkable things they would go on to achieve. Anthony used the word "never." As in, completely new.

Huey and Bobby refused to step into the roles expected of them. They sought to create a new and different way of being, of walking through the world. They commanded respect by forging their own path. They took matters into their own hands. They made room for their unique personhood; for the kind of Black man, the kind of person, they wanted to be.

Unfortunately, Earl Anthony turned out to be more than just a bystander. He was an FBI informant. The government was already watching the Panthers.

CHAPTER 6

MULFORD'S BILL
SACRAMENTO

MULFORD'S BILL

As the Panthers' strategy attracted more attention in 1967, government officials took greater steps to undermine the Party. On the local level, the Oakland Police Department circulated internal memos. These memos identified members of the Party and described their vehicles.[85] On the national level, the FBI began to increase its monitoring of the group, to see if they posed a real threat.

Donald Mulford, a Republican assemblyman from Piedmont, found the Panthers particularly troubling. Piedmont was a tiny city, surrounded on all sides by Oakland. So, while Piedmont was predominately White and upper class, it was nestled inside the birthplace of the Panthers.

On April 5, 1967, Mulford introduced a bill into the California legislature called AB 1591, which would make it illegal to carry a loaded firearm in public.[86] If it passed, the Mulford bill would criminalize the Party's main strategy—armed patrols of the police. The open displays of guns at the Panthers' "self-defense" rallies would also be against the law.[87] Mulford hoped that his bill would take down the Panthers, and he was clear that this was his aim. He even called in to a radio show where Huey and Bobby were being interviewed. He declared on air that his bill would "get" the Panthers.[88]

Huey and Bobby were not surprised. "We knew how the system operated," said Huey. "If we used the laws in our own interest and against theirs, then the power structure would simply change the laws. Mulford was more than willing to be the agent of change."[89]

How would the Panthers respond? How would they stay one step ahead?

Huey and Bobby began to strategize. They further analyzed the Mulford bill as well as the murder of Denzil Dowell. The undersheriff had suggested that the Dowell family try to go to Sacramento, the state capital. He suggested that they could get their case heard in the legislature. But the undersheriff didn't really think the Dowell family could win. Instead, he knew they would be chewed up by the system.

"Institutions work this way," explained Huey. "A son is murdered by the police, and nothing is done. The institutions send the victim's family on a merry-go-round, going from one agency to another until they wear out and give up. This is a very effective way to beat down poor and oppressed people, who do not have the time to prosecute their cases. Time is money to poor people. To go to Sacramento [to protest] means loss of a day's pay—often a loss of job. If this is a democracy, obviously it is a bourgeois democracy limited to the middle and upper classes. Only they can afford to participate in it."[90]

The Panthers knew that one visit to Sacramento wouldn't necessarily change anyone's mind. By going to the state capital, the Panthers wouldn't be able to create a whole new set of just laws.

So instead, they decided to go as a form of protest. Against racism and against police brutality. They wanted visibility. Huey and Bobby wanted to get their message across. They didn't let Mulford's bill stop them—instead, they let it motivate them.

Before the group left, Huey worked on something he called Executive Mandate #1. Both Bobby and Eldridge contributed to it. The mandate was meant to be a message to Black people and to the greater world. Executive Mandate #1 was the Panthers' first public declaration of who they were and what they were fighting for. This wasn't just about Sacramento and the Mulford bill. The Panthers were part of a bigger, longer story. The Black Panther Party was a part of a long freedom struggle, fighting against imperial and colonial power.

SACRAMENTO

On Tuesday morning, May 2, 1967, thirty Panthers headed to Sacramento, headed by Bobby Seale. There were twenty-four men and six women, armed and in uniform. Emory Douglas was there, and so was Lil' Bobby Hutton. Some of Denzil's family, including Ruby Dowell and George Dowell, came to show their support.

Huey stayed away. Even though he wanted to be there, he was on probation. The Party couldn't afford to have him violate the terms of

69

his probation.[91] Everyone knew that the members who went might get arrested. So Huey reluctantly stayed at home. He made sure to caution the Panthers not to shoot unless someone fired at them.[92] No one wanted unnecessary violence.

Even though Eldridge was on parole, he went to Sacramento. He, like Huey and the others, knew that members of the Panthers might get arrested. So Eldridge officially traveled as a part of *Ramparts* magazine.

When the Panthers arrived at the capitol building, they got out of their cars, openly and heavily armed. Bobby asked bystanders where they could find the assembly chambers, as several TV cameramen began to gather around. They all hurried to the chambers and several reporters barged into the room first. They turned around to get a better picture of the Panthers' entrance. Now that the doors were open, twelve Panthers swept inside.[93]

The assembly sessions were open to the public. But the public was not allowed on the assembly floor. Now there were people all over the assembly floor, Panthers and reporters alike. "This is not where you're supposed to be," one of the guards said to the Panthers. "This is not where you're supposed to be," he repeated. It didn't matter. The group pushed forward.

In the ensuing chaos, an officer came up behind Lil' Bobby and grabbed his gun. Lil' Bobby began to shout, chasing after the officer. The Panthers streamed back into the hallway.

Seizing the opportunity, Assemblyman Mulford rose, lobbying for his bill. "A serious incident has just occurred," he said. "People with weapons forced their way into this chamber and were ejected."[94] Mulford was intent on undercutting the tactic of Black armed self-defense.

Outside, tensions were rising. The state police grabbed the Panthers, seizing more of their weapons. Bobby began to shout, "Am I under arrest? Take your hands off me if I am not under arrest! If I am under arrest, I will come. If I am not, don't put your hands on me."

Bobby demanded the Panthers' guns back, but instead the police officers pushed the Party members into an elevator. "Is this the way the racist government works, won't let a man exercise his constitutional rights?" Bobby asked. Once they were all downstairs, the police had to concede. The Panthers had broken no formal laws and their guns were returned.[95]

Outside, the reporters began to swarm around Bobby. He understood the importance of the moment. The energy around him was electric, like the charged air before a storm. With the world watching, Bobby Seale turned toward his captive audience. He stood tall and commanding, ready to make his statement. He began to read from the Black Panther Executive Mandate #1:

"The enslavement of Black people from the very beginning of this country, the genocide practiced on the American Indians and the confining of the survivors on reservations, the savage lynchings of thousands of Black men and women, the dropping of atomic bombs on Hiroshima and Nagasaki, and now the cowardly massacre in Vietnam, all testify to the fact that toward people of color the racist power structure of America has but one policy: repression, genocide, terror and the big stick . . . The Black Panther Party for Self-Defense believes that the time has come for Black people to arm themselves against this terror before it is too late. The pending Mulford Act brings the hour of doom one step nearer. A people who have suffered so much for so long at the hands of a racist society, must draw the line somewhere. We believe that the Black communities of America must rise up as one man to halt the progression of a trend that leads inevitably to their total destruction."[96]

Bobby read the entire mandate several times to the press. He wanted to make sure that the Party's message was clear. That what the Panthers wanted and what they stood for would be broadcast to the nation and the world. This mandate was not just meant for Black America. It also called out to their potential allies and comrades, linking them all together in a global struggle against a common enemy. Bobby kept reading, driving his point home.

Panthers enter the state capitol building in Sacramento.

Once Bobby was done, the Panthers returned to their cars. Shortly afterward, several police officers with riot guns and pistols began to follow them, accompanied by reporters.[97] When the Panthers pulled into a service station, the police surrounded them. A couple of officers grabbed one Panther, Sherman Forte, forcing his hands behind his back. When Sherman asked if he was under arrest, the police said yes. Sherman turned to Bobby and Bobby told him to accept it.

As national TV crews covered the scene, the police searched the rest of the Panthers. They arrested Bobby for carrying a concealed weapon, even though he was openly displaying his pistol on his hip. Other Panthers were arrested on an obscure Fish and Game code violation that prohibited loaded guns in a vehicle.[98] In total, twenty-four people were arrested.

Eldridge, covering the story for *Ramparts,* was not a part of the action. He only had a camera in his hands. But he too was arrested. A Black woman who lived in Sacramento who happened to be buying gas at the time was also arrested.

When Beverly Axelrod later represented Eldridge in court, she asserted that he was arrested because he was Black. Beverly drew the court's attention to the woman who was just trying to buy gas. The Panthers didn't even know her. She had no ties to them, but the officers saw the color of her skin and decided, based on that fact alone, that she should be arrested.

It was a dangerous time, a dangerous moment, to be Black.

Bobby and Mark Comfort were bailed out of jail that evening. When Bobby got home, Huey was waiting for him. Huey reached out and shook Bobby's hand, but then quickly moved in and put his arm around him. They were becoming brothers now, connected by the struggle. Their loyalty would only grow stronger from here. Bobby had been the first to believe in Huey, to look at him and see what he could do. Bobby knew the things they could accomplish working together.

"Brother, you were good," Huey said. "You were beautiful. You were a true revolutionary. You did the job you were supposed to do."[99] Bobby could tell that Huey was emotional. Bobby let him have this moment. There was a promise in the air. They could feel that the world was ready for something different. Something more.

▲

Huey and Bobby both believed that Sacramento would be a turning point. And they were right. They had seized the opportunity and declared their vision to the world. Now that they had issued the call, it was only a matter of time before the people answered. The Panther vision would spread and the Party would grow.[100]

The *San Francisco Chronicle* printed at least twelve stories on the Panther "invasion" of the state capitol. The confrontation appeared repeatedly on television. It was all over the local newspapers and even major newspapers throughout the country—*The New York Times*, *Chicago Tribune*, and *Washington Post* all covered the event. Now people throughout the country were watching and waiting for the Party's next move.

Students at San Francisco State and UC Berkeley began flocking to Panther rallies, numbering in the thousands. Young Black people now had a new political organization they could call their own. As Emory said, "It was like being a part of a movement you had seen on TV and now being able to share and participate in that movement . . . it brought a sense of pride."[101]

Those involved knew that the Panthers were on to something. Denzil's brother George explained it this way, "We are tired of police brutality. We want something done about it . . . The Panthers took the first [step] in my brother's investigation and [were] the first to show the world that black people need protection and that we never had it. That's why we are arming ourselves. We are just tired of living like this. We want freedom now."[102]

After Sacramento the Panthers gained even more visibility. They decided to use this moment to talk to the oppressed people across the world. The Panthers would say who they were, what they believed in, and what they wanted. They would take control of their destinies and lead the people to freedom.

CHAPTER 7

TEN-POINT PROGRAM NEWARK

TEN-POINT PROGRAM

Three days after Sacramento, the Panthers got to work on the second issue of their newspaper. They were all huddled together in Beverly Axelrod's house: Huey and Bobby, Eldridge and Beverly, and a new Party member named Barbara Arthur. Bob Dylan's song "Ballad of a Thin Man" played on repeat. Eldridge and Barbara were busy writing.

Huey turned to Bobby, the notes of Dylan's song drifting in the background. "Listen, listen—man, do you hear what he is saying?" Huey asked.[103] Huey could tell that Bobby wasn't really listening to the words. He was focused on the melody and the beat: Dylan's haunting piano chords, the growling guitar, the organ that sounded like it came out of a horror movie. It was a surreal song, poetic, and at times, disturbing. That's what Huey liked about it.

The song called attention to the underclass, the dispossessed, those who were different, or in the minority. In the song, a circus "geek" ran into hard times. He was forced to do the worst kind of work—caged and eating live chickens for the entertainment of the audience. At one point, he handed a chicken bone through the bars of his cage toward the audience members, forcing them to confront themselves. There was a dichotomy there. The person who was forced to debase himself to make a living—and the person who watched it and called it entertainment. For Huey, this circus "geek," the person seen as a "freak," was like the Black person in America.

And Huey saw it on a broader social level too. The idea that people in the upper classes sometimes liked to go down into poor, working-class Black neighborhoods. To see the people hanging out on the street corners, to witness the reality of their daily struggles. Those in the upper classes watched it like they watched a sideshow. They could go to the nightclubs and the bars, drinking and dancing and having a good time. Experiencing and reveling in a world so different than theirs. But when you confronted them with the actual complex reality of Black life, when you handed them that chicken bone, it was just too much for them to face.

"This song is hell," Huey said to Bobby. "You've got to understand that this song is saying a hell of a lot about society."[104] That was Huey. His mind was always working. Even while there was other work to do.

When the photographer arrived to shoot pictures for the second issue, the group switched into high gear. Eldridge began moving things around, dragging in a large wicker chair reminiscent of a throne. He put it over a layer of zebra-skin rugs. A shield and a spear were brought out too, along with a gun. "Take the gun and put the spear here," Eldridge said gesturing, arranging. But while Eldridge was the one composing the shot, everyone agreed that Huey should be the one in the picture.[105]

The photographer set up his tripods and brought out his camera. When Huey sat down, they took some pictures. Huey's face was half in the light, half in the shadow. His feet lay on the zebra-skin rug, with a pile of live ammunition in the corner. In one hand he held the long rifle. In the other, a pointed spear. His leather jacket lay crisply across his torso; his black beret was cocked to the side. Huey's feet were positioned one in front of the other, ready to stand. Ready to protect.

The shields in the back, the rug beneath his feet, the spear in his hand—all were a nod to the motherland. To Africa. The picture positioned Huey as the protector of Black people, displaced in White America. He was Huey P. Newton. The Black Panther Party's Minister of Defense.

It took them days to finish that first full issue of the newspaper, but all of the hard work was more than worth it. *The Black Panther* newspaper would become a key tool in their revolution.

In the early days, Eldridge's circle of progressive friends, many of whom were White, provided important help with technical aspects, editing, and publishing. Without him, the paper would not have had the reach that it did.

For many people, the words and images of *The Black Panther* became their first introduction to the world of the Black Panther Party. Through the newspaper, the Panthers were able to spread the word

and reach new members beyond their local area. They were able to gain support and raise funds. *The Black Panther* was a place where the Panthers could explain their ideas and give voice to their cause. Most importantly, they could do so guided by their own vision, in their own words.

The Panthers wanted freedom of the mind, body, and spirit for Black people as individuals and for Black people as a whole. The Panthers wanted better housing, full access to a first-rate education, high-quality jobs, and increased opportunities for Black people. The shackles of racism, institutionalized and otherwise, had to be destroyed. With physical force if necessary. The Panthers had always believed this, from the moment they armed themselves in self-defense.

The Panthers had no doubt that the Mulford bill would pass, and they were right. In just a couple of months, the state of California would outlaw carrying a loaded firearm in public.

The Panthers had to shift their focus. Huey, Bobby, and Eldridge began to craft a platform and a program that would define the Black Panther Party. The Ten-Point Program was meant to directly address the immediate needs and interests of the Black community. Their platform drew inspiration from the Nation of Islam's ten-point program, which Malcolm X had helped to create. The Panthers' own program was both a declaration to the world and an important act of self-definition. Directly above this Ten-Point Program was the photograph of Huey, armed and ready in his wicker throne.

Now every issue of the newspaper, from the second to the last, would include this program, starting with the words "We want freedom."[106]

WHAT WE WANT
1. We want freedom. We want power to determine the destiny of our Black community.
2. We want full employment for our people.
3. We want an end to the robbery by the White man of our Black community.
4. We want decent housing, fit for shelter [of] human beings.

5. We want education for our people that exposes the true nature of this decadent American society. We want education that teaches us our true history and our role in the present day society.
6. We want all Black men to be exempt from military service.
7. We want an immediate end to *police brutality* and *murder* of Black people.
8. We want freedom for all Black men held in federal, state, county, and city prisons and jails.
9. We want all Black people when brought to trial to be tried in court by a jury of their peer group or people from their Black communities. As defined by the constitution of the United States.
10. We want land, bread, housing, education, clothing, justice and peace.[107]

What the Panthers articulated was specific, but also universal. It was the basic human desire for self-determination. These were goals worth striving for, and, for many, worth dying for.

The images in the *Black Panther,* created by Emory Douglas, Tarika Lewis, and others, were unique and evocative. Many people read the paper for the inspiration that these visuals provided. In every issue, there were powerful pictures of Panther members working and fighting, armed and ready. These illustrations and photographs positioned Black people as the subjects, placing their experiences front and center. For many, seeing Black people as the stars of their own stories was an empowering and uplifting experience.

The paper also used another important image: the Black Panther. This symbol would become strongly associated with the Party. Even though the image started with the Lowndes County Freedom Organization in Alabama and was being used by others, it would become most associated with the Black Panther Party.[108]

After Sacramento, the Panthers found themselves in the public eye. The speaking engagements began to come in, and the Panthers seized the opportunity. While out on bail from the Sacramento incident, Bobby spoke at the Young Socialist Alliance held at UC Berkeley. Activist Peter Camejo, who would go on to help found the Green Party, organized the event. "Why don't cops who patrol our community live in our

IS THIS THE PARTY YOU WANT?

DEMOCRATIC PARTY

OF ALABAMA

or

IS THIS ?

LOWNDES COUNTY FREEDOM ORGANIZATION

ONE MAN -- ONE VOTE

The original Black Panther logo.

"All Power to the People" became a powerful Panther refrain.

community?" Bobby asked the crowd. "I don't think there would be so much police brutality if they had to go and sleep there." The audience of several thousand people, the majority of them White, clapped loudly.

Bobby also emphasized that the Black Panther Party was not racist. "You've been told that the Black Panthers . . . make no bones about hating whites. That's a bare-faced lie. We don't hate nobody because of color. We hate oppression."[109]

Bobby wanted to clarify this point, especially in front of the crowd of mostly White listeners. The Party's mission was not to attack a particular group of people. It was to dismantle the system that supported and reinforced oppression and racism.

Panther Barbara Arthur, a fellow student of many in the crowd, stepped forward. "I represent the women's department of the Party," she said. "We believe that an education system which still teaches and preaches that white is right, black is wrong, is itself wrong."[110] This remained a fundamental struggle. To get at the root of the problem, the Panthers had to attack a central American ideal—that whiteness equaled purity and goodness, while blackness was undesirable and evil. In order to claim one's own blackness in a whole, healthy, and powerful way, the systems, the structures, even the very language itself had to be changed.

Around this time, Huey, Bobby, and Eldridge decided to take on more formal positions within the Party. Huey became the Minister of Defense, while Bobby became the Chairman of the Party. Bobby was a masterful organizer and public speaker. He was also a great comedian and an actor. He liked to be in front of a crowd. He enjoyed leading and wanted to be an administrator.

Huey didn't want to worry about things like formalities and the demands of running an organization. He wanted to theorize, debate, and take action. Eldridge would become the Minister of Information. He was a great writer, well networked, and an expert at public relations.[111]

Together, these three young people had a powerful synergy that could take the Party to incredible heights. They had a revolutionary program and support from individuals in the local Black community. But for now the Party itself was made up of just a handful of committed organized people.

Soon the tactic that Huey and Bobby used to build their organization would be outlawed. Mulford's bill would pass. Up until this point, in all of the armed confrontations with police, no shots had been fired. But this couldn't last. And now carrying these weapons would be against the law.

The Panthers wouldn't let that stop them. They refused to settle for the world as it was. Instead, they began to shape it into something new. They worked and organized. They took what they knew of the Black experience and used it to make a Party that offered people a source of dignity, agency, and pride.

NEWARK

In June 1967, Bobby published an article in the *Black Panther* entitled, "The Coming Long Hot Summer." He predicted that the number of rebellions, like the ones in Watts and Hunters Point, would only expand and multiply, creating the conditions for a Black revolution. He wrote this with the belief and the understanding that the Black Panther Party would lead this revolution.

Bobby knew that, since July 1964, there had been fifty rebellions in Black communities across the nation. Almost every one began in the same way. As he wrote, "[In] every rebellion a racist cop was involved in the starting of that rebellion."[112]

Black people across the nation were all too familiar with this painful reality. They knew that they would be judged based on the color of their skin. And all too often, the assumptions made would be of criminality and guilt.

When Black people interacted with police officers, their lives hung in the balance. Combined with all the other pressures of being Black in America, it was too much to take. It was too much to live under. So, people took to the streets.

Huey and Bobby aspired to turn the raw energy of these rebellions into something organized, powerful, and unstoppable: a revolutionary force. "The Party wanted no more spontaneous riots," wrote Huey, "because the outcome was always the same: the people might liberate their territories for a few short days or hours, but eventually the military force of the oppressor would wipe out their gains. Having neither the strength nor the organization, the people were powerless."[113] The Panthers' goal was to take the impetus for these rebellions and use it in a direction that would have a lasting impact.

Before he was murdered, Malcolm X had also pointed to the power and potential of these uprisings. As he said in his autobiography, "The 'long hot summer' of 1964 in Harlem, in Rochester and in other cities, has given an idea of what could happen—and that's all, only an idea. For all those riots were kept contained within where the Negroes lived. You let any of these bitter, seething ghettoes all over America receive the right igniting incident, and become really inflamed, and explode, and burst out of their boundaries into where whites live!"[114] Then, the country would really see what might happen. As Malcolm X, Bobby Seale, and others predicted, it was only a matter of time before these rebellions would spread across the country.

In North Richmond, instead of a rebellion, the Panthers organized an investigation into Denzil Dowell's death. They took the energy and rode it, all the way to the state capitol, where everyone could see and feel it.

But as the summer of '67 wore on, more and more rebellions began to take place. The first, like the one in Hunters Point protesting the killing of Matthew Johnson, were sporadic incidents, squashed quickly. Nothing reached the level of Watts.

Not until Newark, New Jersey.

In 1967, there were 400,000 people living in Newark. Over half of those people were Black. The police force was almost entirely Italian American, while nearly everyone the police arrested was Black. Things had escalated to the point that the mayor enlisted the FBI to address investigations of police brutality. Most of the people

Residents of Newark and National Guardsmen confront each other during the Newark rebellion.

convicted of crimes were Black. Most of the victims of these crimes were also Black.[115]

On Wednesday, July 12, just three weeks after Bobby's article appeared, a Black cabdriver was pulled over by two Newark police officers. Neighbors watched from their windows as the police dragged John Smith across the pavement and into the police station. The police beat him so badly that he couldn't walk. Still, Smith was arrested on assault charges. By 10:00 p.m., a crowd began to gather, mostly made up of residents from the housing projects across the street and other cabdrivers, who had been notified by radio.

The police began to assemble, ordering the crowd to disperse. In response, a glow started. Just a few tiny flames. Suddenly, two bottles sailed over everyone's heads, full of liquid and topped with burning rags. The Molotov cocktails hit the wall of the police station, which burst into fire. The flying glass glittered with light, the faces of the people suddenly illuminated. The police officers inside scrambled out and others moved to clear away the crowd. Already people were hurling stones and breaking windows. A nearby car exploded into flames.

The next day Black Power groups in Newark met to discuss further action. They assembled to have a "police brutality rally" early that evening, right in front of the Fourth Precinct Station. At 7:00 p.m., the Black director of the Human Rights Commission announced that the mayor was forming a citizens' committee to investigate what had happened to John Smith. In a political move, to try to quiet the rising unrest in the Black community, one Black police officer was promoted to the rank of captain.

The gathered crowd was not appeased. Someone shouted, "Black Power!" In response, the people began to throw rocks. The police tried to disperse this crowd, but they were outnumbered. The rebellion grew and spread throughout the city. The local police could not control it alone. The state police were called in. Eventually, so was the National Guard.

Law enforcement officers shot looters and fired randomly into crowds. They also targeted businesses labeled "Black Owned." The police ended up injuring uninvolved bystanders and people in their homes. Twenty-three people were killed. All but two of them were Black. These included six women, two children, and a seventy-three-year-old man.

The well-known Black writer LeRoi Jones, later known as Amiri Baraka, was arrested and beaten by police during the rebellion. He declared that, after years of appealing to a racist government, "[now] we will govern ourselves or no one will govern Newark, New Jersey."[116] This was a sentiment that many Black people shared.

The Panthers devoted an entire issue of their paper to the Newark rebellion. On July 20, the front-page headlines read "The Significance of the Black Liberation Struggle in Newark" and "Police Slaughter Black People." The cover showed a photograph of three police officers holding down a Black man, his face pressed into the sidewalk. The paper also featured a centerfold with photos from Newark. Many of the pictures showed Black men and women bloodied and brutalized. One of the large pictures showed several people lying facedown on the concrete with armed officers standing over them, while other officers held back the crowd. Another showed a military jeep driving past a burned-out building, with officers holding machine guns aloft. The caption read, "Racists call it 'rioting,' but actually it's a political consequence on the part of black people who have been denied freedom, justice and equality."[117]

The Panthers argued that it was just a matter of time before there was another, larger rebellion. The people had begun to demand what was theirs.

Then came Detroit.

Three year old Thomas Allen in the aftermath of the Detroit rebellion.

CHAPTER 8

DETROIT

DETROIT

Just three days after the *Black Panther* issue on Newark, Detroit, Michigan, erupted. In Detroit, as in so many other U.S. cities, racism fueled violence and prevented justice. Even while White supremacists burned crosses outside Black people's homes, even when a mob of eighty White people smoke-bombed the home of an interracial couple in a suburban White neighborhood, even when a Black couple went to visit a White neighborhood and the husband was shot to death and his wife miscarried, the racist status quo was upheld. In 1967 no White person had ever been found guilty of murdering a Black person in Detroit. The value of Black life had been diminished to a point that justice could not be served.[118]

The message was clear: Black people were not free. If they stepped outside of the bounds set up for them, by going into White neighborhoods or engaging in interracial relationships, there would be real and often deadly consequences.

Early in the morning on July 23, 1967, the Detroit police raided an "underground" bar. This particular bar served mostly Black patrons after 2:00 a.m., when alcohol sales were against the law in the city. A party was going on for two veterans returning from the Vietnam War and another man who was leaving to go to war. The police routinely took bribes from the operators of these bars. Those that refused to pay were raided.

That morning, more than eighty people, almost all Black, were taken from the bar and loaded into the backs of police vehicles. The gathering crowd grew more and more upset by the officers' actions and the amount of force being used.

"Black Power," someone in the crowd yelled. "Don't let them take our people away; look what they are doing to our people. Why do they come down here and do this to our neighborhood? If this happened in Grosse Pointe [a rich White neighborhood], they wouldn't be acting this way."[119] In response, someone flung a beer bottle into the air. Those assembled began to rise, their energy increasing and their defiance mounting. The rebellion had begun.

In the Detroit rebellion, there was widespread arson. Snipers fired from the rooftops. These fires and these bullets, this anger and this rage, were aimed at the Establishment. These people meant to attack the idea of a society that lied, mistreated, and disregarded them—that took their lives wantonly and with impunity. The rebellion was a challenge to the social order.

The National Guard was called in later that day. The guardsmen were told "to shoot any person seen looting." That evening the state police, the National Guard, and the local police were all firing at fleeing looters. The state sought to reassert its "dominance and control." One guardsman went so far as to say, "I'm gonna shoot anything that moves and that is black."[120]

Eventually the army was called in. The people on the ground were met with bayonets and armor. Behind these officers, tanks pounded through the streets and machine guns sliced through the air. Overhead, army choppers circled.

Dispersed bands of looters roamed the streets, some using shortwave radio to coordinate their movements in the dark. The rebels stole hundreds of guns, and, when fired upon, shot back. The rebels knew that they would be repressed. Still, they fought for what they believed in. During the day, one of those fighting turned toward an officer and yelled, "You can't do anything to me White man. Black Power!"[121]

The Detroit News called parts of the city a "bloody battlefield," comparing the streets to those in war-torn Vietnam. The mayor said that it looked like Berlin during World War II. The executive secretary of the establishment Committee for Equal Opportunity, Hubert Locke, called it a "total state of war."[122]

In the end, 552 buildings were damaged or destroyed. 7,231 people were arrested, more than twice as many as in Watts and four times more than in Newark. Forty-three people were killed, thirty-three of them Black. Of the ten White people who were killed, a number of them were government officials.[123]

In the first nine months of 1967, 164 rebellions erupted across the United States. These were not flukes. They were not isolated incidents. They were a trend and an assertion of power. The Panthers had seen this power in advance and acted to harness it.

The Kerner Commission, appointed by President Johnson, was supposed to investigate these incidents. What the commission reported proved to be tainted by their own biases. They described the rebellions as apolitical and spontaneous. By removing their political motivation, the commission delinked the rebellions from the larger struggle. By robbing the rebellions of their context, the commission sought to rob the rebellions of their power and historical significance.

A few social scientists, working under Research Director Robert Shellow, argued that racism pervaded all US institutions. They wrote that, "A truly revolutionary spirit has begun to take hold . . . an unwillingness to compromise or wait any longer, to risk death rather than have their people continue in a subordinate status." These scientists were fired and their words removed from the report.[124] For many in power, the truth was too much to accept.

Huey and Bobby and the members of the Party understood and were a part of this "revolutionary spirit."[125] They also understood the impetus for these uprisings. It was the very real and constant threat of state violence hanging over the heads of Black people. The Panthers knew that Black people in the United States were reaching a limit. They had begun tapping into that feeling with an armed strategy that appealed to many young Black people. They continued to arm themselves in self-defense, for many of the same reasons that Black people were rebelling throughout the country.

The Panthers saw that Oakland could be another Watts. The potential was there for another uprising that would be squashed just as quickly. What the Party did was harness this energy that existed in all these cities, like Oakland, Hunters Point, and North Richmond; Watts and Newark and Detroit. They took this wave of rage and rode it in a different direction. They turned Oakland into the birthplace of a movement. A Party that would persist and thrive.

The Panthers recognized the power of Black voices, of Black people's minds and bodies. They looked at their comrades and saw a way to organize. The Panthers reared up, ready to fight and take their place as true revolutionaries.

PART THREE: THE PANTHERS RISE

If we must die, let it not be like hogs
Hunted and penned in an inglorious spot,
While round us bark the mad and hungry dogs,
Making their mock at our accursèd lot.
If we must die, O let us nobly die,
So that our precious blood may not be shed
In vain; then even the monsters we defy
Shall be constrained to honor us though dead![126]

Claude McKay

Kathleen Cleaver

CHAPTER 9

BLASTED OFF THE STREETS
KATHLEEN
ALLIANCES

BLASTED OFF THE STREETS

"You can do six months for the Party, can't you?" Huey asked Bobby. It was the fall of 1967 and Bobby was headed to jail because of the incident in Sacramento. Bobby had no prior charges against him; he and a few other Panthers had agreed to accept misdemeanor charges. That way, the Panthers with prior convictions wouldn't go away for longer.

"Sure I can," Bobby replied. "I can do it easily."[127] Huey knew Bobby was ready. In a revolution, sacrifices had to made. This would be just one of many along the way.

What Huey didn't know was that it would be almost four years before he saw Bobby again.

Huey had a good feeling on Friday, October 27. The weekend was just getting started. Huey's parole, a condition of an assault conviction, was finally over. He began to dream of what he could do now that he could go where he wanted and wouldn't have to keep reporting to his parole officer.

Being able to move without limitations was a freedom that some people took for granted. But Huey didn't. He knew what it meant to be watched, to have his movements tightly controlled. He had done what he had to and now his parole was lifted.

Huey was ready to celebrate. He set up a date with his girlfriend LaVerne for that evening. But first, as usual, he had work to do.

In the afternoon, Huey spoke at San Francisco State University as part of an event sponsored by the Black Student Union. The forum was entitled "The Future of the Black Liberation Movement." If Bobby hadn't been in jail, he would have given the speech. Huey wanted to be on the ground, debating one on one, or working with people instead of standing behind a podium. But the Party couldn't afford to turn down public speaking engagements—so Huey did as many as he could.

Back at home in the evening, he had a "happy, righteous dinner of mustard greens and cornbread" with his loved ones.[128] Feeling jubilant, he headed to his girlfriend LaVerne's house on foot, planning and dreaming. He wasn't just thinking of what they would do that night. He was also thinking of all the nights of freedom stretched out before him.

But when Huey arrived, LaVerne wasn't feeling well enough to go out. Huey was disappointed, but LaVerne encouraged him to still make the most of his freedom. She would see him soon enough. LaVerne lent Huey her car and he left, driving out into the night.

First, Huey went to Bosn's Locker, a bar where he had already started recruiting people for the Party. He ordered a rum and Coke, also known as a Cuba libre or "free Cuba." He wanted to celebrate that night with a drink of liberation.[129] After talking with his friends for a while, he left for the nearby church, where the Friday night social was already in full swing. At the social, he met up with his friend Gene McKinney, whom he had known since elementary school. Around 2:00 a.m., Huey and Gene headed for a party on San Pablo Avenue in Oakland.

Huey was feeling great. He was officially a free man, no longer on probation. It seemed that everywhere he went there was happiness and a good time to be had. Huey and Gene stayed at the party until around 4:00 a.m., when they decided to go to West Oakland, where an all-night restaurant was serving soul food. They drove through the misty darkness, not realizing that everything was about to change.

Alone in his police car sat twenty-three-year-old officer John Frey. He had been on the force for only a year and a half, but he already had a reputation. Earlier that evening, Frey had intervened in a dispute between a White man and a Black grocery clerk named Daniel King. The White man had no pants on and claimed that the Black clerk had stolen them. According to King, Frey responded by holding the Black clerk's arms behind his back so that the White man could beat him, all the while calling King the "N-word."[130]

When giving a speech at Clayton Valley High School, Frey had told the class that the Black people in the neighborhood he patrolled were "a lot of bad types." He also called them the "N-word"—a word created to dehumanize and demean. Later, a ten-year veteran of the force told *Ramparts* magazine, "Frey is not what I would categorize as a good cop." Once, when he was accused of behaving like the Gestapo, Frey put his hand on his gun and said, "I *am* the Gestapo."[131]

This was the man Huey and Gene encountered that night. On Officer Frey's dashboard was a list of twenty cars identified as Black Panther vehicles. Frey knew exactly who had just driven by. He pulled out after Huey, calling for backup.

When Huey saw what was happening, he parked his girlfriend's car. Officer Frey came up beside them and looked inside. "Well, well, well, what do we have here? The great, great Huey P. Newton." He was trying to antagonize Huey, but Huey didn't take the bait. He said nothing, just handed over his license and registration.

A second officer, Herbert Heanes, pulled up. The two men asked Huey to get out of the car. Huey knew this was when things could get most dangerous. He reached for his criminal evidence book, so he could refer to the lines and passages he needed if the officers attempted to arrest him. In his haste, he accidentally grabbed his law book, which would be of no use.

Huey asked if he was under arrest. Officer Frey said, "No, you're not under arrest; just lean on the car." Huey put his hands on the car, on top of his law book.

The officer ran his hands along Huey, searching him in a way Huey described as both "disgusting and thorough." The officer untucked Huey's shirt and moved his hands across Huey's entire body. It was more than just a routine search. It felt like a violation. Huey stood there, hands up, until the officer was finally finished.

"You have no reasonable cause to arrest me," Huey said afterward, opening his book. Quickly, words were exchanged. The officers refused to give up. Huey was never going to back down. It's unclear what happened next, but shots were fired, seeming to come from all directions. By the end of it, both officers were wounded, and so was Huey. Huey fell to his knees, the world spinning before his eyes.[132]

"Long after I was shot I hovered between consciousness and unconsciousness," Huey said. "I remember some things and have no memory of others. It was a terrifying time: the blood pounding in my head, waves of pain engulfed me, and everything around me receded into a vast blur."[133]

Huey admitted that "I did not think I would live for more than one year after we began; I thought we would be blasted off the streets."[134] Still, even in the face of death, he had remained committed to the goal of Black liberation, through the Party he helped to found.

Now Officer Frey was dead. Officer Heanes was seriously wounded. Law enforcement began to search for clues. What they found, on the ground at the crime scene, was a book on its side. A law book belonging to Huey P. Newton.

In the next issue of the *Black Panther,* Huey sat in his wicker throne, just like in all the other issues. But it was only an image. The actual man was now locked away, severed from his beloved Party. Huey, the Minister of Defense for the Black Panther Party, was the prime suspect in Officer John Frey's murder.

Eldridge wrote the lead article in the paper, entitled "Huey Must Be Set Free!" Eldridge discussed the immediate circumstances leading up to Huey's arrest. Then he explained what Huey's arrest meant politically, placing the event in its historical context as part of a long freedom struggle.

"The shooting occurred in the heart of Oakland's black ghetto," wrote Eldridge. "Huey is a black man, a resident of Oakland's black ghetto, and the two cops were white and lived in the white suburbs. On the night that the shooting occurred, there were 400 years of oppression of black people by white people manifested in the incident. We are at that crossroads in history where black people are determined to bring down the final curtain on the drama of their struggle to free themselves from the boot of the white man that is on their collective neck . . . Through murder, brutality, and the terror of their image, the police of America have kept black people intimidated, locked in a mortal fear, and paralyzed in their bid for freedom."[135]

The Panthers decided to flip the script. In their eyes, Huey was not the one on trial. It was America. For all of its crimes, for all of its transgressions against Black people. Huey was a Black man who stood up and fought back against this system, fighting not just for his own freedom, but also for freedom for all Black people. To have control over their own minds and their own bodies. To be able to have a night out, to celebrate, without ending up violated, traumatized, and imprisoned.

The Panthers began to use Huey's case to mobilize support and bring more awareness to their cause. They wanted to emphasize that, in their eyes, he was a political prisoner. Huey was standing up to a long history of police brutality and oppression against Black people. He was being held without bail for murder. Not because he had committed a crime, but because of his radical political beliefs. The Panthers began to rally around the cause to "Free Huey!" It was a cause embraced by a new member named Kathleen Neal.

KATHLEEN

Kathleen Neal grew up in Tuskegee, Alabama, and other college towns. Both of her parents were academics. Her father, Ernest, mostly worked as a sociologist and her mother, Juette, had a master's degree in mathematics. Kathleen herself was an honor student. She attended boarding school, Oberlin College, and then worked a government internship in Washington, D.C.[136]

Kathleen grew up as a Black woman in the South. This experience lit a fire inside her. Kathleen wanted to challenge injustice. She wanted to work for Black liberation, for Black women and men alike. She, like so many women of the Party, worked toward both group liberation and, specifically, the liberation of Black women. Kathleen's fight was not a new one. "I think it is important to place the women who fought oppression as Black Panthers within the longer tradition of freedom fighters like Sojourner Truth, Harriet Tubman, Ida Wells Barnett," she wrote, "who took on an entirely oppressive world and insisted that their race, their gender, and their humanity be respected all at the same time."[137]

Kathleen began working at the Student Nonviolent Coordinating Committee (SNCC) offices in New York in 1966, then moved to Atlanta to work as the secretary of SNCC's Campus Program. She helped to organize a Black student conference in Tennessee, where she first met Eldridge Cleaver. She was deeply affected by their meeting. As she said, "What startled me most about him—a brilliant writer, and eloquently lucid speaker, as well as a tremendously handsome and magnetic person—was that he referred to himself as a "convict" . . . He exuded strength, power, force in his very physical being."[138]

On Kathleen's flight back from the conference, she couldn't stop thinking about Eldridge. She wanted to put her feelings into words. She decided to write a love poem to him. She entitled it "My King, I Greet You," a direct response to Eldridge's open love poem, "My Queen, I Greet You."[139] Eldridge's poem was meant as a love poem to all Black women from all Black men. In contrast, Kathleen's words were personal and passionate, meant only for the charismatic man she had just met.

Soon after, Kathleen moved to San Francisco. She arrived just three weeks after Huey's arrest, ready to become a part of the Black Panther Party. Kathleen later reflected that "of all the things I had wanted to be when I was a little girl, a revolutionary certainly wasn't one of them. And now it was the only thing I wanted to do."[140]

Kathleen threw herself headlong into the work of the Party, devoting most of her time to the new campaign to free Huey. The Panthers argued that Huey could not get a fair trial in America. The trial would be about more than just Huey—it was about the racism and violence that Black people faced in their daily lives. The Free Huey! campaign gave the members of the Party a cause to rally around and a place to pour their energy. And Kathleen did just that.

She contributed in all areas, writing leaflets and organizing demonstrations, designing posters and attending court hearings, holding press conferences, speaking at rallies, and appearing on television. She created the position of Communications Secretary, modeled after what she had seen Julian Bond do with SNCC.[141] Just a few weeks after she arrived in San Francisco, Kathleen and Eldridge were married. Theirs was a swift, passionate, and intense love affair.

On January 16, 1968, at 3:30 in the morning, police knocked down the door of Kathleen and Eldridge's apartment. They didn't have a warrant, but they swept through the rooms, cursing and yelling at the Cleavers, throwing their furniture, and scattering their papers. The officers had shotguns and pistols, while the Cleavers were unarmed. As a condition of his parole, Eldridge didn't own any guns. Finally, when they couldn't find anything of interest, the officers left.[142]

Huey responded by issuing Executive Mandate #3 from prison. He ordered all Party members to keep guns in their homes. These weapons were meant as protection against police officers who might try to enter illegally. The Panthers had begun by publicly arming themselves in self-defense, and this mandate was an extension of that strategy, in private.[143]

Beside the mandate was a picture of Kathleen. She was dressed in a long black leather jacket. Her face was framed by a full afro, her cat-like eyes hidden behind dark glasses. In her arms was a large shotgun, perched and aimed at the camera. The heading read "Shoot Your Shot!"[144]

Kathleen was ready to defend herself if necessary, as were so many other young Black men and women. That's why they were attracted to the Panthers.

As Kathleen observed, "My generation became conscious during a period of profound world turmoil, when the Vietnam War and countless insurgencies in Africa, Asia, and in Latin America challenged the control of resources of the world by the capitalist powers . . . When we looked at our situation, when we saw violence, bad housing, unemployment, rotten education, unfair treatment in the courts, as well as

Kathleen, on left, with other Party members.

direct attacks from the police, our response was to defend ourselves. We became part of that assault against the capitalist powers."[145]

ALLIANCES

From the very beginning, the Black Panther Party made it clear that they were committed to Black liberation. Still, they did not believe in working only with other Black people. The members of the Party were all Black, but they saw creating diverse coalitions as an important step to creating a powerful Party. With the Free Huey! movement, the Party gained more visibility. As their popularity grew, other groups began to seek alliances with them.

One of their first coalitions was announced on December 22, 1967 with the Peace and Freedom Party, which had started just a few

A Free Huey protest outside the Alameda County
Court House, California 1968.

months before on June 23. A strong voice in the antiwar movement, the Peace and Freedom Party was founded in part by Robert Scheer, an editor of *Ramparts* magazine, where Eldridge worked. The Peace and Freedom Party was primarily made up of White people. "We made our slogan 'Peace and Freedom' just to make it clear that we stood not only for ending the war in Vietnam and other wars but also for ending oppression," wrote committee member Mike Parker. "We were looking for groups in the Black community to work with and we found that the only group in the Black community that was even willing to talk with us about these kinds of questions in a serious way . . . was the Black Panther Party for Self-Defense."[146]

Working with a group like the Peace and Freedom Party put the Panthers at odds with many Black nationalist groups. Some of these other groups had a separatist political stance. This meant that they believed the work of Black liberation should be done only by Black people. But as one Panther wrote, "The increasing isolation of the black radical movement from the white radical movement was a dangerous thing, playing into the power structure's game of divide and conquer. We feel that in taking the step of making a coalition with the Peace and Freedom Party, we have altered the course of history on a minor, but important level."[147] While it was an unpopular stance among some, it proved to be extremely advantageous for the Party.

Then, in February 1968, the Black Panther Party announced another bold merger that would change how they were viewed on a national and international scale.

At this point, the Student Non-Violent Coordinating Committee was starting to collapse. The SNCC was a student-led organization which had grown out of the southern Black protests against lunch counter discrimination. Its main initial concern was the fight to end Jim Crow. By the early 1960s, the organization had become an important force in the Civil Rights Movement, representing the voices of young Black people. Under strong leaders like John Lewis, Ruby Doris Smith, Julian Bond, and Stokely Carmichael, SNCC flourished.

From the very beginning of the Black Panther Party, Huey and Bobby drew inspiration from SNCC. As Huey wrote, "I had to respect the

Bobby Seale speaks at a Free Huey rally in Oakland; the bus
and sound speakers were on loan from the Peace and Freedom
Party.

Student Nonviolent Coordinating Committee for having some of the most disciplined organizers in the country. When we had first talked of forming a party, Bobby and I read about their work in the South—registering people to vote and organizing co-operatives."[148] Even though SNCC's main tactic of nonviolent civil disobedience was at odds with the Panthers' strategy of armed self-defense, the Panthers wanted to create some kind of merger.

The Panthers even tried to draft one of SNCC's leaders, Stokely Carmichael (later known as Kwame Ture), before the merger. Huey issued "Executive Mandate #2," for this purpose. Bobby read it on the steps of the San Francisco Hall of Justice on June 29, 1967, with television cameras rolling. The mandate gave Stokely the position of Field Marshal, which Bobby called upon him to accept, "to establish revolutionary law, order and justice." And he went even further, challenging Stokely. Bobby asked, "Whose Authority and Program is Stokely Carmichael going to acknowledge, that of the warmonger Lyndon Baines Johnson or Minister of Self-Defense, Huey P. Newton?"[149] Would Stokely side with the American government and the president? Or would he answer the call of the revolution and the Black Panther Party for Self-Defense? Stokely wouldn't join in that moment, but he would eventually become a member of the Panthers.

The merger was announced in the Oakland auditorium on February 17, 1968. It was Huey's twenty-sixth birthday. Center stage in the auditorium was his wicker chair from the now infamous picture. But the chair sat empty. Huey was still in jail.

That night, Bobby spoke, as did three SNCC leaders: H. Rap Brown, Stokely Carmichael, and James Forman. Eldridge was the master of ceremonies.

During his speech, Bobby emphasized the need to Free Huey! and also, more broadly, to stand up to police brutality. When Stokely spoke, he implied that the Black Panther Party's primary concern was their self-defense activities. A distinction was being made, between what he saw as the power of other groups, like SNCC, and the limitations of the Panther Party.

Stokely Carmichael and Bobby Seale.

In the very next issue of their newspaper, the Panthers changed their name. They dropped "for Self-Defense" and became the Black Panther Party. They refused to be put in a box.

Stokely would not stay with the Panthers for long. In fact, the merger wouldn't last long. Even though the idea of Black Power and the larger goal of Black liberation was shared, the two groups were not well matched. As SNCC continued to decline, the Black Panther Party stepped in to fill the void on their own.

The Panthers understood and spoke to the struggle of oppressed people across the world on a deep and powerful level. They knew that Black people, like many people of color across the world, were part of this global war against oppression.

At this time, many groups and individuals rallied around the desire to end the war and to end oppression. One of the most inspirational figures of this era wanted an end not just to the Vietnam War, but to all wars. He worked to put an end to racism, violence, and oppression on a large scale. He was one of the most important leaders of the Civil Rights Movement and one of the greatest proponents of nonviolent civil disobedience. He was a man who would be remembered long after he was gone.

That man was Dr. Martin Luther King, Jr.

CHAPTER 10

DR. MARTIN LUTHER KING, JR.
LIL' BOBBY

DR. MARTIN LUTHER KING, JR.

Born in Atlanta, Georgia, Dr. Martin Luther King, Jr. was a deeply religious person. His father was a Baptist minister, and King received his doctorate in theology, becoming a reverend himself. In 1955 and 1956, he was one of the main organizers of the Montgomery Bus Boycott, one of the major protests of the Civil Rights Movement.

King was influenced by the nonviolent civil disobedience practices of Mahatma Gandhi (1869–1948). Ghandi was the most prominent leader of the Indian independence movement. He fought to free India from British imperial rule. King travelled to India to learn more about Gandhi, his philosophy, and his teachings through the land and the people who knew him. When King left India he was "more convinced than ever before that non-violent resistance [was] the most potent weapon available to oppressed people in their struggle for freedom."[150] In 1964, King would receive the Nobel Peace Prize for his efforts to protect and fight for Black people and for human rights, using the practice of nonviolence.

King stood out for his incredible ability to mobilize and inspire. He was accepting of all kinds of people—and deeply committed to working across racial and class lines. King hoped and fought for the time when true racial integration would be a reality. To this day, he remains one of America's most influential and revered spokespeople for both nonviolence and racial integration.

King's oratorical style, rooted in the Black church, was unique and singularly inspiring. His speeches were not one-way events. They were communal experiences. As King paused, people reacted, providing affirmation, appreciation, and encouragement. Those who listened also responded with their own truths, allowing themselves to feel all kinds of emotions, not the least of which was hope. King made the people feel seen.

On the evening of April 3, 1968, King spoke at the Mason Temple in Memphis, Tennessee. His impassioned speech reached its height at the very end, when he acknowledged his own mortality. Many people feared for King's safety and his life. Still, he always pressed on. As he said, "Like anybody, I would like to live a long life. Longevity has its place. But I'm not concerned about that now. I just want to do God's will. And He's allowed me to go up to the mountain. And I've looked over. And I've seen the Promised Land. I may not get there with you. But I want you to know tonight, that we, as a people, will get to the promised land! So I'm happy tonight. I'm not worried about anything. I'm not fearing any man. Mine eyes have seen the glory of the coming of the Lord."

King finished then, turning from the microphone at the height of emotion. He was determined and his path was clear.[151]

The next day King helped lead a strike by thirteen hundred Black sanitation workers in Memphis. His support for the strike was a part of his efforts to alleviate poverty and express his opposition to the Vietnam War. King had shifted his focus in the last few years, once the Civil Rights Movement defeated legalized Jim Crow. It wasn't enough to end Jim Crow—the movement had to keep going.

Now King was working to end poverty in America. He was trying to change the capitalist foundation of the country in a way that would serve the vast majority of people, rather than a chosen few. The Panthers saw capitalism in the same light, as a structure that had to change for Black people to truly be free. While King had always been radical in his own views, those in power saw this turn as even more of a threat to the Establishment. But King knew that for people to be truly free, they had to have their basic needs taken care of. With a huge wealth gap and intense poverty, that would never happen for many Americans.

King was heading out to dinner. Later he was going to lead a rally in advance of the next day's strike. Below his hotel balcony, he saw Jesse Jackson and musician Ben Branch. "Do you know Ben?" Jackson asked.

King smiled, calling out, "Yes, that's my man!" He asked Branch to play the gospel song "Precious Lord, Take My Hand" at the rally. King loved that song. Little did he know that, only a few days later, Mahalia Jackson would sing it at his funeral.

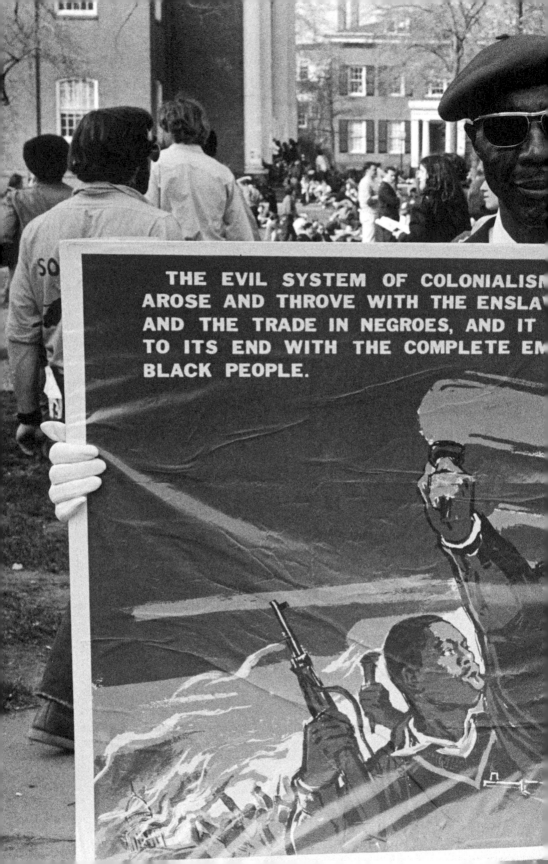

Before the men could finish their conversation, a shot rang out. Someone had been watching him, and on that balcony, he was exposed. King fell to the ground as those with him crowded around, trying to help. They rushed him to the hospital, but only an hour later, Dr. Martin Luther King, Jr. was pronounced dead.

That night, Memphis caught fire. For the next few weeks after King's assassination, rebellions swept across the country in over one hundred cities.[152] Twenty-one thousand people were arrested and forty-six people were killed.[153]

After that day, many Black people stopped seeing nonviolent civil disobedience as an effective means of protest. That idea died with Dr. King. As Stokely said, "When White America killed Dr. King last night, she declared war on us."[154]

The reverberations of Dr. King's murder would be felt for years and generations to come. If a Black man who stood for nonviolent resistance could be murdered in cold blood, what then? What was the message to America, to Black people as a whole?

LIL' BOBBY

Two days after Dr. King's death, a group of armed Panthers was riding along at night. This close to the murder of Dr. King, the police were out in full force. There was disagreement among the Panthers about whether they should be out at all. Everyone was deeply upset about Dr. King's murder, but Eldridge was more than upset. He wanted revenge. And if Eldridge said so, the comrades would ride.

David Hilliard, an important member of the Party and one of Huey's friends since childhood, was especially concerned. In fact, he feared for his life. But, as David said, "without Huey's presence or Bobby's objections no one can resist the power of Eldridge's logic."[155]

The front car, driven by Eldridge, was an old white Ford that the Peace and Freedom Party had donated to the Panthers. David Hilliard was there, as well as Lil' Bobby and six other Panthers. At a little after 9:00 p.m., Eldridge pulled over and stepped out of the car. Just a few seconds later several police officers pulled up. They shone a light on Eldridge, and all too soon there was gunfire both ways.

The Panthers split up, running for cover. Eldridge and Lil' Bobby ended up in the basement of a nearby building. David Hilliard tried to hide in the house of a friend of a friend, crouched under the bed. Outside it was raining fire and gunshots. Neighbors began to gather, trying to make sense of the situation as the police cordoned off the area. Everyone was separated, except Eldridge and Lil' Bobby, hiding together. But they couldn't stay where they were. The building had caught fire.

An hour and a half later, Eldridge emerged from the basement of the burning building. His lungs were full of smoke. He came out with his arms over his head, completely naked. He wanted to make it clear that he was unarmed. He surrendered and the officers grabbed him, taking him into custody.

Lil' Bobby stumbled out from the basement behind Eldridge. The fire burned behind him, the smoke curled around his naked chest. He'd taken off his shirt, but he was embarrassed by the idea of taking off his pants, so he left those on.[156] He too was unarmed, with his hands over his head. But when he came out, the police shot Lil' Bobby in the head, killing him on the spot.[157]

Lil' Bobby, the Black Panther Party's first recruit, was dead at age seventeen.

Lil' Bobby's funeral had a deep effect on all who attended. Two thousand people came out, packing themselves into the Ephesian Church of God in Christ in Berkeley. Circled around Lil' Bobby's open casket were one hundred Black Panthers in uniform. They created a ceremonial guard for their fallen comrade.

The Panthers held a rally outdoors directly after the funeral. They told anyone that would listen that Lil' Bobby was killed precisely because of his politics. That this was a racially and politically motivated murder of a seventeen-year-old.

Bobby Seale was furious. He believed that the police meant to shoot him instead. Now out of prison, he had been driving in that white Ford all day long. Instead, they shot Lil' Bobby, with his hands up.[158]

Bobby looked around, seeing the police presence even there, at a funeral. He yelled into the crowd, "There are pigs on top of the library behind you. They are up there on other buildings . . . They must know that every time these racist pigs attack us we are going to defend ourselves." Bobby took a deep breath, steadying himself. Then he said, with all the strength in his body, "Free Huey!" The crowd responded back with force. "FREE HUEY!"[159]

But Huey was not free. He was still in jail. When the Panthers came to visit after Lil' Bobby's death, they found Huey uncharacteristically quiet and despondent. David begged his old friend to speak, to lead the Panthers in some sort of service to honor Lil' Bobby. David remembered his speech this way:

"We're afraid of death because we imagine it as the end of life. But death is a part of life. So the question of how you die is really a question of how you live."[160]

When Huey began to speak again, reworking a quotation from Mao Zedong, the words came down to David like rain: calming, renewing, invigorating

"To die for the reactionaries is lighter than a feather—because you are already dead, spiritually dead, stripped of the pride and will that are our human traits. But to die for the people is heavier than a mountain—because then humanity has lost someone who has helped change the intolerable conditions in the world."[161]

One thing was clear: Lil' Bobby died for the cause. As Huey wrote, "[Bobby] died courageously, the first Black Panther to make the supreme sacrifice for the people. We all attempt to carry on the work he began."[162]

David's daughter Patrice called Lil' Bobby "wonderful." "He related to us as if he were one of us," she remembered. "He was the one who,

BOBBY HUTTON

Social Protest Project
Bancroft Library

murdered

Malcolm X was *murdered.*

Martin Luther King was *murdered.*

Both were 39; both were ministers, one Baptist, one Muslim. *Both were unarmed.*

Minister of Defense Huey P. Newton was shot by Oakland pigs attempting to murder him. He is charged with murder and attempted murder, facing a death sentence.

Minister of Information Eldridge Cleaver was shot by Oakland pigs attempting to murder him. He is charge with 3 counts of attempted murder, and now that his parole has been revoked, faces life imprisonment.

Brother Malcolm, Dr. King, Huey P. Newton, and Eldridge Cleaver all laid their lives on the line for BOBBY HUTTON. Brother Bobby is dead, murdered by an Oakland pig. *He died fighting for our freedom.*

FUNERAL AT STAR BETHEL CHURCH Stanford and San Pablo, Oakland 11:15 Friday, April 12

MEMORIAL AT MERRITT PARK 1:30 pm (across the street from Alameda County Courthouse)

PROCESSION TO JAIL for

Eldridge Cleaver

following memorial

BODY IN STATE at Fouchette-Hudson Funeral Home, 37th and Telegraph Oakland

BLACK PANTHER PARTY

A notice for Lil' Bobby Hutton's funeral.

before a meeting, would come in there and talk and hug and kiss us." She remembered the change in his pocket, the way she and her little brothers liked to go in the room after Lil' Bobby left because his change would be all over the floor. With the money from Lil' Bobby's pockets the kids would go and buy candy and bubble gum.[163] But now they would never see his smile again, or feel his hugs and kisses. Lil' Bobby was gone.

Those who attended Lil' Bobby's funeral were still reeling from the murder of Dr. King. The deaths of King and Lil' Bobby, so close to one another, emphasized just how dangerous it was to fight for the cause of Black liberation. In this moment, many young people felt that they had to make a choice. They were witnessing the limitations of nonviolent resistance. As Bobby Seale put it, "Our brother Martin Luther King exhausted all means of nonviolence."[164]

In the Black Panther Party, many now saw a powerful and important alternative. Panther Billy John Carr explained it to *The New York Times*: "As far as I'm concerned it's beautiful that we finally got an organization that don't walk around singing," he said. "I'm not for all this talking stuff. When things start happening I'll be ready to die if that's necessary and it's important that we have somebody around to organize us."[165]

The Panthers were seen as an alternative to the groups that focused on nonviolent civil disobedience. But while the individuals of these separate movements were portrayed as opponents, in reality, they were all fighting for the same thing, just with different methods.

For example, Dr. King was a radical, revolutionary leader. Black people and their allies fought hard to secure this legacy. But, as time passed, the Establishment deradicalized Dr. King, putting him in opposition to other leaders like Malcolm X. Before he was killed, Malcolm X predicted that the Establishment would use him in this way: "[The white man] will make use of me dead, as he has made use of me alive," he wrote , "as a convenient symbol of 'hatred,'—and that will help him to escape facing the truth that all I have been doing is holding up a mirror to reflect, to show, the history of unspeakable crimes that his race has committed against my race."[166]

Rather than show how Dr. King and Malcolm X were part of the same tradition, the strategy was to reduce and oversimplify what both men stood for. The idea that one person stood for love and the other hatred wasn't the whole picture. The truth was much more complex and there was space within the long Black freedom struggle for everyone. Fundamentally, they were two sides of the same coin: courageous Black freedom fighters.

Lil' Bobby was not famous like Dr. King and Malcolm X. The Establishment could not co-opt his image, because Lil' Bobby wasn't even on their radar. Like so many of the Panthers, he was just another "brother on the block." But his death was not in vain. He would live on in the collective memory of the Party. And because he wasn't famous, because he was a hero in the Panthers' world, Lil' Bobby would become a martyr for the revolution.

Lil' Bobby died for what he believed in, standing up to the police and to oppression in America. He died for Black self-determination. He died so that one day Black people might be free to determine their own destinies, unfettered by the chains of racism. Lil' Bobby's death existed in a long line of resistance, one which was far from over.

Ericka Huggins

CHAPTER 11

ERICKA, ELAINE, AND L.A.
SEATTLE
NEW YORK
PIGS
BLACK STUDIES

ERICKA, ELAINE, AND L.A.

Lil' Bobby's death was a turning point for Ericka Huggins. She had already committed herself to working in her community, but when Ericka attended Lil' Bobby's funeral, she said, "What awakened in me, what changed my life and my mind . . . was Bobby Hutton's face at his funeral . . . My entire life and mind was changed from that point on . . . I had read about the Party and I had read about all the things in history that had been done to black people—lynching, murder, tortures, etc.—but I was convinced when I had direct confrontation with the brutality, the cruelty, and the doggishness of the police. His face had been entirely shot out. The entire portion of his face was gone and had been puttied into place and made up. He was no longer the seventeen year old person he had been, not physically or anything else. He wasn't. And the police were in the balconies of that church. They were everywhere. I had never seen anything like that in my life."[167]

Ericka was born Ericka Jenkins in Washington, D.C. She was thoughtful and quiet, hoping to one day become a teacher and work with children. Unfortunately, the college she went to didn't challenge or inspire her. Once she transferred to Lincoln University, another historically Black college, her outlook began to change. She was introduced to the ideas of Malcolm X. She joined the Black student organization and immersed herself in the Black political life on campus. Still, she felt that something was missing. She was removed from the real action, from the real work of the revolution. Ericka knew that she wanted to be involved in the community, to devote her life to the people—but the pathway wasn't clear. After Ericka moved to Los Angeles with her husband, John Huggins, they both joined the Black Panther Party. Once Ericka attended the funeral of Lil' Bobby, she was even more certain of the direction her life would take.[168]

Elaine Brown was one of Ericka's first recruits. Elaine grew up in Philadelphia, as an only child. She attended Temple University but left early and moved to Los Angeles. In L.A., she was soon immersed in a world of glamour and privilege. But even her rich White lover could not protect her from racism. After booking a hair appointment

Elaine Brown, in white coat.

over the phone, she was denied service when she appeared in person. She tried to speak up for herself, but her voice came out weak. Elaine hurried away, her head held high, before they could see her cry.[169]

At that time, Elaine's boyfriend was the owner of the Sands Hotel in Las Vegas. When she told him what had happened, he was irate. As he held her to calm her down, she could feel his whole body shaking with anger. He called and berated the management of the hair salon. They tried to apologize, but Elaine didn't want to hear it. The damage had already been done. She knew that no matter where she went, no matter who she associated with or chose to love, her blackness

135

would always follow her. But rather than run away from that reality, she turned toward it and toward the Black Panther Party.[170]

Elaine Brown, John Huggins, and Ericka Huggins were all members of the Los Angeles branch of the Party, run by Alprentice "Bunchy" Carter.

Elaine was there when Bunchy first announced the Los Angeles branch, in February 1968. She was attending a community poetry reading sponsored by the Black Student Alliance, which had been founded by Harry Truly at California State University, Los Angeles.

A few hours into the festivities, the double doors flew open. Everyone turned. In the doorway stood Bunchy, flanked by twenty of his men. He was dressed perfectly, as always. He swept into the room with his entourage. "No one invited us, but we thought we'd come anyway," he said.

The people around Elaine murmured. It was a public event. Bunchy didn't need an invitation. "I've got a few poems of my own," he declared, ascending to the podium. "Right on!" someone yelled in response.

After reading two of his poems, Bunchy got down to business. "I came here to make an announcement," he said, scanning the crowd. "We have just officially formed the Southern California chapter of the Black Panther Party for Self-Defense."

"Right on!" came the response. Bunchy snapped his fingers, and one of his men handed him a banner. Bunchy unfurled the now famous picture of Huey in his wicker throne.

"This is Huey P. Newton," declared Bunchy. "From this point forward, Brothers and Sisters, if the pig moves on the community, the Black Panther Party will deal with him . . . We will destroy him absolutely and completely or, in the process, destroy the gravitational pull between the earth and the moon!"[171]

It was no wonder that Bunchy became a leader of the Black Panther Party. He had a reputation throughout his community. As Elaine said, "Everybody had heard of Bunchy."[172] Not only did Bunchy have wide-reaching influence in Los Angeles, he also had a strong personal connection to Eldridge Cleaver.

Bunchy had met Eldridge in Soledad prison, in an African history class. They became friends right away.[173] In fact, they became so close that Bunchy was a witness to Eldridge and Kathleen's marriage. Kathleen even called Bunchy Eldridge's best friend. At Soledad, Bunchy also became a Muslim minister and a follower of Malcolm X.

Once Bunchy got out of prison, he wanted to continue his work toward Black liberation. He visited the Black Student Alliance to find out more. The head of the Alliance, Harry Truly, was working to form a coalition of all the Black student unions across the nation. The Black Student Alliance was already a part of the Black Congress, an umbrella organization created after the Watts rebellion to help rebuild the Black community. Both Harry and Bunchy wanted to create a Black revolution. Both were involved in a struggle for freedom. But they didn't agree on how to get there.

"We're struggling over a solution. Trying to initiate black revolution," Harry said when he first met Bunchy.

"Right on. That's right on," said Bunchy. "Even though I never heard of revolution without the gun . . ."

"We're not in a position to wage armed struggle right now, Brother," Harry said. "We have a ragtag army and a sorry arsenal . . . We'd only lose. Is that what you'd have us do, fight to lose?"

"In revolution, one wins or dies," Bunchy responded.[174] And Bunchy was in it to win. After Bunchy met and befriended Eldridge in prison, after he saw Huey stand up to the police at the airport, Bunchy was sold. The Panther way was the way to go. So, he decided to help form and run the Los Angeles chapter of the Black Panther Party.

SEATTLE

Aaron Dixon, who was a member of the Student Nonviolent Coordinating Committee, created the first Black Panther Party branch

Seattle office.

outside of California. After attending Lil' Bobby's funeral, Aaron was inspired to alter the course of his life, just as Ericka was. For Aaron, "looking into the casket of Little Bobby Hutton had been almost like looking into the future and glimpsing what the movement might hold. It was not the glory and the victory we romanticized."[175]

After Lil' Bobby's funeral, Aaron Dixon went to San Francisco State University, where he heard Bobby Seale speak. Bobby's words changed Aaron forever. "I had seen Martin Luther King speak in person," wrote Aaron. "I had listened to records of Adam Clayton Powell often, and to the taped speeches of Malcolm X. All these things had inspired me, but the speech I had just witnessed totally blew me away, pushing me off my safety perch, casting me out into the wind, my eyes wide open. I could not sleep that night. I only wanted time to move ahead; I wanted to speed up time, propelling me faster toward my fate."[176]

Aaron realized, then and there, what he was meant to do. The stakes were too high, the consequences too great—he had to act. Aaron went home, and, with his brother, worked to open a chapter of the Party in Seattle.

Bobby Seale flew to Seattle to help them get started. He went to Aaron's home, telling those gathered that people in the Party had to read "at least two hours a day," giving them a list of books to study. They talked about Frantz Fanon's *Wretched of the Earth* and *Black Skin, White Masks.* One of the women took out her notebook and started taking notes. "They got some righteous bookstores around here?" Bobby asked.

"Yeah, Mrs. Boyetta's bookstore!" someone shouted.

"And the books you can't find, we will send you some," Bobby insisted.[177] There was an air of excitement in the room. After all, Bobby Seale had actually flown up and was now in Aaron's living room. For the people sitting there, listening to Bobby, the idea of the Party quickly became more and more real. Aaron began to have

Members of the Seattle branch protest on the steps of the Legislative Building, Olympia, WA.

conflicting emotions. He felt pride and happiness at having Bobby and the rest of the group in his house. But he was also nervous and afraid. What would it really mean to commit his life to the people, to this revolution? He had just come from the funeral of one of the Panthers. He knew it would not be the last.

Bobby turned to the group and asked who the defense captain would be. Aaron looked at the fingers that were now pointing at him. Before he could respond, Bobby said, "Okay, Dixon. You're the captain. I want you to come with me back to New York on an organizing tour through the East Coast."[178]

Within two months, the Seattle Black Panther Party had over 300 members. Aaron attributed this not only to his experience at Lil' Bobby's funeral but also to the general mind-set of Black people at the time. "Since the death of Martin Luther King," he said, "my life and the life of many other Black youth throughout America had taken on an overwhelming sense of urgency. The movement was accelerating and transforming. We were now consumed with the fight for justice and the right to determine our own destiny."[179]

NEW YORK

In the weeks after King's murder, a branch of the party also opened in Harlem, New York. Harlem already had a rich history of rebellion and resistance, as well as Black nationalism. Marcus Garvey's Universal Negro Improvement Association had found its home in Harlem. In the 1950s and '60s Malcolm X made his greatest impact in Harlem. Harlem, in particular, was ready for the Panthers.[180]

Initially, Joudon Ford became the captain of the New York Black Panther Party. He had served in the Civil Air Patrol and worked as a part of the Student Nonviolent Coordinating Committee before joining the Party. He created a temporary office in the SNCC headquarters in downtown Manhattan and was overwhelmed by the response.[181]

Two of the first people to join the New York Party were Lumumba Shakur and Sekou Odinga. Lumumba became the section leader for Harlem, Sekou for the Bronx. They had gone to high school together

Harlem, New York office.

in Queens, and both became involved in politics while they were in prison. They had joined Malcolm X's Organization of Afro-American Unity in 1964, but in only a few short months, Malcolm X was killed. Both men searched for other organizations and all of them came up short. Until the Panthers. After King's death, Lumumba and Sekou were onboard with the Party.[182]

Lumumba and Sekou attended a meeting where members of the Black Panther Party spoke. Afeni Shakur, who would marry Lumumba, was there as well. Afeni remembered the excitement when Bobby Seale began to speak. "And then Bobby Seale says the Ten-Point Program of the Black Panther Party. Nothing sounds like Bobby Seale when he says the Ten-Point Program of the party . . . The way he said those ten points made me want that more than anything. So there I was wrapped in my Africanness. For the first time, loving myself and loving, now that there was something I could do with my life. There was now something I could do with all this aggression, and all this fear."[183]

Afeni was already impressed with the way the Panthers had stood up to the police in Sacramento. Watching the confrontation, she remembered a Panther asking, "Am I under arrest?" when a police officer tried to take his gun. The police officer responded that he was not. In response the Black Panther Party member demanded that the officer take his hands off the Party member's gun, that he had a constitutional right to have it. "In 1967 that in itself was enough to blow anybody's mind," Afeni remembered.[184] Afeni believed that the Panthers offered a very real and effective alternative to the politics of nonviolence. They talked the talk and they walked the walk.

In fact, many of the most politically active young Black people in New York sought out the Panthers. "We're revolutionaries and we're fighting a war," New York Panther Bill Hampton said to *The New York Times.* "People have to realize that 'the man' is not just moving on us Panthers, but he is moving on all black people . . . They see us as a threat and realizing this the man has to put it down. That's why the police run around here now trying to get something started."[185]

The Panthers were well aware that they would be met with oppression and, when it happened, they would rise up to meet it.

Abayama Katara went to a Panther meeting in New York because he heard that the Black Panther Party was tackling police brutality. He kept hearing the Panthers use the word "pigs." He couldn't figure out what they were talking about. When Abayama asked, the Panther member looked at him like he was crazy. "Man he looked at me as if I asked him what the earth was," Abayama said. "After he finished running it down . . . I left the house saying 'pig' over and over again. I got on a bus and everybody must have thought I was bugged out, because all the way home I just kept saying 'pig,' because the way the brother ran it down, it fit perfectly."[186]

When Abayama heard the word, it resonated with him powerfully. It made so much sense. "Pig" was more than an insult. It was a way of challenging the authority of the police force, of saying that their treatment of Black people was wrong and inhumane. It was a way of siding with and elevating the oppressed.

PIGS

From his reading of Friedrich Nietzsche's *The Will to Power,* Huey was convinced of the importance of harnessing and using words for a

The Sky's The Limit

25 cents

THE BLACK PANTHER

Black Community News Service

VOLUME II, NO. 7   SATURDAY, SEPTEMBER 28, 1968

PUBLISHED WEEKLY   **THE BLACK PANTHER PARTY**   P.O. BOX 8641 EMERYVILLE BRANCH OAKLAND, CALIF. 94608

PIGS WANT WAR

PANTHERS COOL

REAGAN ATTACKS ELDRIDGE

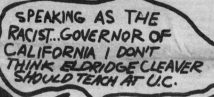

Sacramento, Calif.

The racist governor of the state of California, slobbering pitifully at the mouth, stated a few days ago that Eldridge Cleaver, Black Panther Party's Minister of Information, should not be allowed to express his views or relate any platforms of the Panthers' ten-point program on state property.

This is the same racist-Reagan that called Black people "Mad Dogs" for expressing their dissatisfaction with this decadent American society. It's the same pig that was considered too reactionary for the renowned swine, Ricky-boy Nixon.

Pig Ronald Reagan, no more than a by-product of Knotts Berry farm. A tool of the perverted publisher of the Oakland Tribune. The staunch supporter of the political line first expressed by George Wallace and Mayor Daley.

This greasy pig—the die-hard racist Reagan—oinked out publicly that the Honorable Eldridge Cleaver was "a racist!" The words should burn the hog's tongue!

Racist Ronald Reagan has once again shown that the dogs maneuvering this imperialist power structure keep on pushing their "big lies." They say to Black brothers and sisters that "war is peace;" that their brutalization of Black people is "law and order;" and, that for the Honorable Eldridge Cleaver to be lecturing "the black truth" on the University of California's Berkeley campus "is racism!"

The funky pig talks about Eldridge's jail record, but fails to mention that the brave warrior's jail record is the result of white "in-justice" related to all Black people.

Pig "in-justice" is charging Blacks with murder and attempted murder while their entire hog forces, national guards, and armed oink-oink army kill Black people with impunity!

Ronald "pigpen" Reagan is the perfect symbol of the white-racist power structure that Black people are up against.

The state's number one pig, Ronald Reagan, ain't nothing but a fugitive from the world of make-believe — a world that specializes in "lying."

But we, the members of the BLACK PANTHER PARTY, are willing to submit our case to the PEOPLE: "WHO'S THE RACIST—THE HONORABLE ELDRIDGE CLEAVER—or the pig, Ronald Reagan?"

specific purpose. "Words could be used not only to make Blacks more proud but to make Whites question and even reject concepts they had always unthinkingly accepted,"[187] Huey wrote. So, words could be used not just to empower Black people, but also to have other people question ideas and norms they might have taken for granted.

Huey and the Panthers were fighting to change stereotyping, prejudice, and implicit bias. The Panthers agitated for a world where police brutality wouldn't take place disproportionately against Black and Brown individuals. Where their criminality and guilt would not automatically be assumed based on the color of their skin.

The Panthers began with the word "policeman." Huey knew how important it was to recast the police force, to draw attention to the fact that, in many communities, they were not helping the very people they were sworn to "protect and serve." "One of our prime needs was a new definition for 'policeman,'" he wrote. "A good descriptive word, one the community would accept and use, would not only advance Black consciousness, but in effect control the police by making them see themselves in a new light."[188]

Huey tried "dog," the reverse of "god," but it didn't work. "Beast," "brute," and "animal" were also in the running, but none of them quite captured the quality the Panthers wanted to convey.[189] But the word "pig" caught on. This was not a new use of the word, but the Party helped to popularize it.

Famously, Emory Douglas drew a picture with a pig standing in three separate frames. The image in each was the same. Only the label was different. One said "local police," the next "national guard," and the last "the Marines." The point was that state violence was state violence, no matter who perpetrated it—the police against Black people, the national guard against protesters, or the Marines against the Vietnamese. This powerful image of the pig gained circulation outside the Party and the word kept spreading like wildfire. Just as it had in young Abayama's imagination.

After he rode home on the bus, repeating the word "pig" to himself, Abayama realized how powerful definition could be. He decided then and there to redefine himself. Still in high school, Abayama joined the Panthers.

Abayama became president of his Afro-American history club. He tried to educate his classmates, posting photos of the Black liberation struggle that depicted the beating of protesters, the Student Nonviolent Coordinating Committee taking nonviolent action, and the Black Panthers. One was the photo of Kathleen with a shotgun, first printed next to Huey's Executive Mandate #3, ordering all members of the Party to keep weapons in their homes as protection from unlawful entry by police officers.

The principal tried to get the students to take the posters down. He claimed that they were too violent. The students argued that what they had posted wasn't any more violent than what was already in their history books. The students knew that their teacher wasn't just reacting to the posters. He was upset by the idea of a Black revolution and the prospect of real liberation for Black people.[190]

BLACK STUDIES

Abayama and his classmates were a part of a larger movement, gaining momentum at this time, for Black studies to be a part of school curricula across the country.[191] As chapters of the Black Panther Party spread throughout the country, so did their influence on college campuses. By April 1968, George Murray, a prime advocate for Black Studies, was the Minister of Education for the Panther Party. He was also the director of the undergraduate tutorial program at San Francisco State University. George recruited young Black students, encouraging them to take advantage of the university's resources. He was one of the many people calling for the creation of a Black studies department at the university. The concept behind Black studies was to spark self-awareness among Black people. It was also to create an intellectual tradition based in blackness, even within the primarily White university system.

George believed that for Black people to be liberated, not only must imperialism come to an end, but there also had to be a cultural revolution for Black people. "We are changing," he said, "we are deciding

George Murray teaches at San Francisco State.

that freedom means change, changing from the slaves, the cowards, the boys, the toms, the clowns . . . of the 50's, 40's, 30's, into the wild, courageous, freedom fighting revolutionary black nationalists."[192]

George went to Cuba in August 1968 to promote the Free Huey! campaign. While he was away, the Panthers continued to influence the student movement at San Francisco State. When George came back, the Panthers were working hard to organize Black student unions throughout the state and the country.

On October 26, 1968, the Black Panther Party would organize a state-wide conference for Black student unions. The promotional materials for the gathering restated the fifth point of the Party's platform: "We want education for our people that exposes the true nature of this decadent American society. We want education that teaches our true history and role in the present day society." The speakers included George Murray, David Hilliard, Bobby Seale, and Eldridge Cleaver.[193] Out of the conference, Black student unions joined forces across the state. They put together a ten-point program and a platform that drew its inspiration from the Black Panther Party. Together they started to organize on a national level.[194]

Two days later, on October 28, the one-year anniversary of Huey's imprisonment, the Party's Field Marshal, Donald Cox (DC), and five other Panthers went to SF State. George organized a rally for the Black Student Union. "I think we should have a demonstration for Huey today," he said, making circles in the air, encouraging the students to gather around. "He'd lay down his life for the people, and we should honor him."[195] Students began to gather, chanting "Free Huey!" More and more people joined in the call and response. "Free Huey!" "Black Is Beautiful!" "Set Our Warrior Free!" "Free Huey!" The Black students marched around the campus. Now a group of two hundred people, they headed into the cafeteria, grabbing four tables and pushing them together. They wiped off the food and the plates and the forks, creating a platform for people to speak.[196]

George stood up and called for a student strike in November, citing the need for Black studies in the school system. In 1968, more than half of the young people in San Francisco were non-White or people of color. They were Black and Latinx, Asian American and Pacific Islander and Native American, but this was not reflected in the university's enrollment. Instead, the student body at San Francisco State was 75 percent White.[197] The people of the city weren't represented and neither were their interests. "There are four and one-half million black and brown people in California," George said, "so there should be five thousand black and brown people at this school."[198]

George Murray was arguing not just for freedom for Black people, but freedom for all peoples. As he wrote in a piece for *Rolling Stone* magazine, "Freedom is a state not limited to a particular culture, race or people, and therefore, the principles upon which a struggle for human rights is based must be all inclusive, must apply equally for all people. For example, the struggle at San Francisco State is based upon three principles: (1) a fight to the death against racism; (2) the right of all people to determine their economic, political, social and educational destinies; (3) the right for the people to seize power, to carry out all their goals, and to answer all their needs. In short—*All Power to the People*."[199]

147

The protest at SF State was the longest student strike in the U.S. Their protests led to the rise of ethnic studies departments around the country.

Ron Dellums, a Black city council member from Berkeley, predicted that the Black studies movement would spread. "The spin-off from San Francisco State will have implications for high schools, junior colleges, junior high schools, elementary schools as well as other colleges throughout the state and outside the state," he said.[200]

Across the country there were more Abayamas, more Georges, more Black people agitating for not only learning the history and culture of Black people, but also having more control over the production of that knowledge. The UC Berkeley chapter of the Third World Liberation Front put it best. "The people must be given an effective voice in the educational apparatus which either prepares or fails to prepare their children for life as it actually is. WE MUST HAVE SELF DETERMINATION!!"[201]

Through hardworking individuals who agitated and organized, Black Studies departments would spread across the nation. San Francisco

State and the Black Panther Party were at ground zero of this movement, informing its inception and forming its rise.

▲

After the deaths of Martin Luther King, Jr. and Lil' Bobby, branches of the Black Panther Party began to sprout up all over the country. "The murder of King changed the whole dynamic of the country," said Kathleen. That is probably the single most significant event in terms of how the Panthers were perceived by the black community."[202] Young activists across the country wanted to know how they could be a part of the movement. The Panthers were doing very little recruiting. The people came to them.

The Black Panther offices in Los Angeles, Seattle, and New York appeared first. By the end of the year there would be offices throughout California, in San Diego, Sacramento, Richmond, Long Beach, Bakersfield, and Fresno. Across the country offices would open in Albany, Boston, Chicago, Denver, Des Moines, Detroit, Indianapolis, Newark, Omaha, Peekskill, and Philadelphia.

"The offices were buzzing beehives of Black resistance," recounted Mumia Abu-Jamal. "It was always busy, as people piled in starting at 7:30 am opening time and continuing 'till nightfall. People came with every problem imaginable, and because our sworn duty was to serve the people, we took our commitment seriously . . . In short, whatever our people's problems were, they became our problems. We didn't preach to the people; we worked with them."[203]

Mumia was an example of how popular the Party was becoming, especially with young people. He picked up an issue of the paper, and, at just fourteen years old, was taken with the Party. He wouldn't formally join for a few months, but as soon as he touched the pages of the paper, he joined in his heart. For Mumia, it was like a "holy book."[204] The incisive and searing words of Eldridge, combined with Emory's striking, humanistic artwork, left an imprint.[205] Mumia couldn't get enough of the fierce visuals of powerful and beautiful young Black men and women, clad in leather, armed for revolution.[206]

149

Panthers drill outside the Philadelphia office.

But, on September 8, 1968, the Party suffered what at the time seemed to be a huge setback. Huey P. Newton, the Black Panther Party's Minister of Defense, was sentenced to two to fifteen years in prison. Even though he was acquitted of wounding Officer Herbert Heanes, he was convicted of manslaughter in the death of Officer John Frey. It was a blow to the Free Huey! movement and to all those who were expectantly awaiting Huey's release.

Eldridge had already coined the statement "Free Huey or the Sky's the Limit," implying that anything could (and would) happen if Huey was not freed. Huey's White lawyer, Charles Garry, who was recommended by Beverly Axelrod, would still seek an appeal. But the fact remained: Huey would not be returning to the Party anytime soon.

Nevertheless, the Party didn't slow down. Branches continued to form and Black people continued to join. On college campuses across the nation, the Panthers' message continued to spread. The Black Panther Party was fast becoming one of the most influential and visible groups fighting for Black liberation in the United States.

Panthers ready the newspaper for national distribution at headquarters in CA.

Panthers drill before a Free Huey rally.

PART FOUR:
THE GLORY

First you have free breakfasts, then you have free medical care, then you have free bus rides, and soon you have FREEDOM![207]

**Fred Hampton, Deputy Chairman,
Black Panther Party, Illinois**

Fred Hampton, speaking.

CHAPTER 12

FRED AND ILLINOIS
A WIDESPREAD INSPIRATION

FRED AND ILLINOIS

What was it like to be a leader of the Black Panther Party? How did a person hold all of that hope and all of that promise? What did it feel like, what did it look like, to be an inspiration for an entire movement?

In Fred Hampton's case, it didn't look extraordinary at all. He wore unassuming clothes. He drove a beat-up car and spent his time amongst the people. It wasn't about the appearance. It was about the commitment, the actions, and the internal drive. His deep belief, the force of his commitment to the struggle, changed those around him. He left them with hope and inspiration. When Fred spoke, people could hear the possibility of liberation. They could hear the sound of freedom.

Fred Hampton was born in Louisiana on August 30, 1948. He grew up in Maywood, Illinois. He was the youngest of three children, raised in a loving family, and attended church throughout his childhood. Fred was a straight A student, an athlete, and an activist from an early age. He became an excellent speaker through necessity. His father, Francis, said that when Fred was a child, he fell and injured his teeth. The accident made Fred speak with a kind of whistle. Fred worked hard to overcome this, spending many hours on the art of public speaking from a very early age.[208]

When Fred was in high school, he studied the speeches of Dr. Martin Luther King, Jr. and Malcolm X. He recorded them on his tape player and memorized them. He read political texts by Black authors like W.E.B. DuBois, Marcus Garvey, and Malcolm X. At his school, Fred spoke out about the lack of Black teachers and administrators, agitating for more diversity in the staff.[209] He also helped to set up a Black cultural center in his town, with a section on Black history. According to his mother Iberia, Fred always loved to read, especially history books.[210] In 1966, Fred turned eighteen. The Vietnam War was in full swing. Fred refused to register for the draft based on his political beliefs. That was the same year that Muhammad Ali refused to register.[211]

In 1967, Fred became the president of the NAACP's Youth Council in Maywood. He organized a boycott at his high school when the Black girls at the school were excluded from running for homecoming queen. When the Black students protested, the White students attacked them with bats and blackjacks.

Fred then organized the Black students to fight back with force. The Maywood police responded to the conflict by setting up checkpoints in Black neighborhoods. They also instituted martial law, usually used in times of war, rebellion, or civil unrest. Fred brought in members from the national NAACP and led a boycott at his high school to bring an end to the martial law declaration. He succeeded and the martial law ended.[212]

In 1968, Bobby Rush, who had worked as a member of the Student Nonviolent Coordinating Committee, cofounded the Illinois Chapter of the Black Panthers with Fred. Bobby Rush was an administrator and a scholar, but not a particularly gifted public speaker. Through his work with SNCC, Bobby met Stokely Carmichael, who introduced him to the Panthers. Bobby Rush soon went out to California to meet

Bobby Rush

Bobby Seale and David Hilliard. After speaking with them, Bobby decided to form a chapter in Chicago. But he couldn't do it alone. When he heard Fred speak at a Black leadership conference, Bobby knew that the Party needed Fred Hampton. Bobby would serve as the Illinois chapter's Minister of Defense, while Fred would be the Deputy Chairman.[213]

When Aaron Dixon first heard Fred speak, he too was blown away. It was a chilly Wednesday evening at the University of Chicago. Fred took the stage surrounded by other Panther members, including Bobby Rush. The Panthers secured the doors, and Fred proclaimed that no one would leave until they were finished. He stood up in an army fatigue jacket and proceeded to speak for the next thirty minutes. Aaron admitted that "my speech paled in comparison to the powerful words of this young Black man, my same age. I had no idea—nor did any of us at the time—that we were witnessing the next Malcolm X, the next Martin Luther King. In essence, Fred Hampton was poised to become the next great leader of Black America."[214]

Fred organized the original Rainbow Coalition in June 1969. The importance of this coalition was in its promising union of diverse groups of people. It was an effort to unite different racial liberation struggles in the fight to end poverty, and, in turn, upend the class hierarchy. As Carlton Yearwood, a leader of the New York Black Panther Party, said, "We believe that racism comes out of a class struggle, it's just part of the divide-and-conquer tactics of the Establishment and a product of capitalism."[215]

The Rainbow Coalition worked across these movements and across racial identities, including the Young Lords, the Black Panthers, and the Young Patriots. The Young Lords were a Puerto Rican organization, and the Young Patriots were an organization of young Whites originally from Appalachia. Fred Hampton proudly stated that "we got blacks, browns and whites . . . we've got a Rainbow Coalition!"[216]

Fred's charisma and energy, his commitment and his presence, were undeniable. His politics, personal and public, were an example to those around him. He was committed to unity. Not only through groups like the Rainbow Coalition, but also in the way he interacted with the members of his branch. He agitated for fair treatment for

people outside the Party as well as within it. He made sure that the women in his branch were treated with the same respect and dignity that was afforded the male members.[217] He believed in a future where all people would be treated equally, and he was willing to risk everything to make that future a possibility.

The Black Panther Party had begun not only to serve people outside of their own community, but also to inspire them, to give hope for a better future. And Fred Hampton was one of its rising stars.

But Fred remained down to earth. As Rory Guerra, a member of the Young Lords, said, "Hampton was a very humble person and didn't walk around like he was God's gift to the movement . . . He was a person who came in an old car, got out, shook people's hands, wanted

to really talk to people. I remember him saying, 'I'm glad to have met you. I'm glad to have met you.'"[218]

The Illinois chapter, headed by Fred Hampton and Bobby Rush, would become the most important hub in the Midwest for the Black Panther Party. They decorated the second-story windows of their office building with a sign that said, "ILL. CHAPTER BLACK PANTHER PARTY," in big block letters. On either side was the image of the black panther, leaping forward, claws bared. Underneath hung images of the Party and Black Power: the picture of Huey seated on his wicker throne; a portrait of Lil' Bobby Hutton, painted by Emory Douglas; an image of Malcolm X; a photograph of Eldridge Cleaver in action; and, finally, the now-famous image of Huey Newton and Bobby Seale, armed to defend the very first Black Panther office.[219]

The Illinois chapter grew in presence and power, even as the state tried to repress them. Their membership blossomed. People in the local Black community began to recognize them. Allies came forward from far and wide, offering support. The national headquarters took notice.

Bobby Seale went to Chicago, where he participated in a mobilization event held in a local church with Bobby Rush and Fred Hampton. Inspired, Bobby Seale spoke in front of a diverse audience. "I'm so thirsty for revolution," he declared. "I'm so crazy about the people. We're going to stand together. We're going to have a Black Army, a Mexican American Army, an alliance in solidarity with progressive Whites. All of us. And we're going to march on this pig power structure. And we're going to say: 'Stick 'em up . . . We come for what's ours.'"[220]

On April 9th, 1969, Fred Hampton and Bobby Seale spoke together at a rally in downtown Chicago organized by the Panthers and a predominantly White radical group called Students for a Democratic Society.[221] At the rally, Fred and Bobby both spoke about the Panthers and the coming revolution. Fred especially stirred the crowd with his words and his passion. Most importantly, the Panthers positioned themselves, stating in front of the crowd of more than 500 people that the Panthers were the "vanguard of the revolutionary struggle today."[222]

Fred had influence even before he became a part of the Black Panther Party. Afterward, his influence only grew. He was deeply rooted and committed to not only the local Black freedom struggle, but also the long Black freedom struggle and the broader human rights struggle. Fred was a revolutionary and a unifier.

As he said, "We're gonna fight racism not with racism, but we're going to fight with solidarity."[223]

A WIDESPREAD INSPIRATION

This solidarity that Fred Hampton spoke of, that Dr. King preached, that so many people working throughout the long Black freedom struggle tapped into, had great power. All of these activists knew that, by working together, oppressed people could change the world. And so the Panthers encouraged other groups to find ways to work toward their own freedom. Throughout the country, activists began to create radical organizations modeled after the example of the Black Panther Party. In turn, the Party helped to support these new movements.

Members of the Young Lords party.

A Young Lords march in Chicago, IL, 1969.

One of these groups was the Young Lords Party, who were also a part of the Rainbow Coalition. The Young Lords began as a Puerto Rican street gang, with José "Cha Cha" Jiménez as their leader. José was a young man with light skin, green eyes, and curly hair that he combed out to look straight. Because José was lighter skinned, he heard and experienced the racist views of others firsthand. A turning point for José came when he attended an all-White Catholic school. He heard the priests, "talking freely, using the N word, and I'm turning red [and thinking], 'Whoa, man, did this guy just say that?' And I'm wondering if he's gonna say something about Puerto Ricans . . . This is a man of God talking like this; that really affected me."[224]

When José was in jail in 1968, he met Fred Hampton. They had a serious discussion about the very real tensions that existed between the Black community and the Puerto Rican community. José was impressed with Fred and the Black Panther Party. He decided that theirs was the program to follow. "We see and we recognize the Black Panther Party as a vanguard party, a vanguard revolutionary party," stated José. "And we feel that as revolutionaries, we should follow the vanguard."[225]

Even in the early days, the Young Lords organized community picnics and events. The Young Lords gave away free clothing and food, but they knew that this wasn't enough. The group increasingly wanted to create real, meaningful change. "The Young Lords Organization turned political because they found out that just giving gifts wasn't going to help their people," said José, "they had to deal with the system."[226] As soon as he got out of jail, José led the transformation of the Young Lords from a gang into a radical, political organization.

The Young Lords weren't the only group who took inspiration from the Panthers. On May 1st, 1969, two officers approached a group of Latino men who were moving a TV into their apartment in San Francisco's Mission District. Insults were exchanged and a fight broke out. During the conflict, officer Joe Brodnik was killed with the other officer, Paul McGoran's, gun.

In response, the San Francisco Police raided over 150 residences in the Mission District. The police said they were searching for the person who shot Brodnik. In an article entitled "S.F. Pigs Attempt to Arrest Entire Brown Community," the Panthers questioned the motivations of the police. Was it necessary to search over 150 homes for seven people? Or were the police just using it as an excuse to harass and intimidate the residents of the Mission?[227]

A few hours later, three young people, Ralph Ruiz, Donna Amador, and Yolanda Lopez were all attending a Free Huey! rally. Suddenly, from behind them, they heard the crackle of a police radio. "An all-points bulletin went out for a number of Latin men, and coincidentally, one of the suspects [Ralph Ruiz] was standing beside me!" recalled Donna. "My priorities changed instantly. Education was important for the brothers and sisters, but the fight for freedom from the oppression and injustice of the real world suddenly took me away from SFSU [San Francisco State University]."[228]

Of the seven young Latino men charged, there was evidence that half of them weren't even at the scene of the crime. Without clear evidence and with no clear argument about who actually shot the officer, these men were charged with first-degree murder. The prosecution called for their execution.[229]

While all these men weren't necessarily at the scene of the crime, they were all activists. They had been working to create a Third World studies program and to diversify enrollment at the College of San Mateo. They wanted to see their own history, their own interests represented in the school system.

Now these seven men were imprisoned and up for execution. A group of young Latinx people living in the Mission District formed a group called Los Siete de la Raza, which roughly meant "the seven of the Latinx community." The group stood with the seven men charged and worked to free them.

In San Francisco there was also the radical Red Guard, which came out of Leway, a nonprofit organization serving low-income children in Chinatown. After taking part in Stop the Draft Week and the strike at SF State, the members of Leway concluded that the US government wasn't interested in the serious problems confronting poor

Chicanx activist Reies Tijerina, with Brown Beret security, at a Free Huey rally.

and working class Asian-American communities. To meet these challenges head-on, the Red Guard led a series of community-based programs and actions. They modeled themselves after the Panthers in many ways, calling for self-determination and community service programs and organizing against police brutality. They also had their own Ten-Point Program.[230]

In L.A, there were the Brown Berets. As cofounder of the Brown Berets, Carlos Montes described, "We were a group of young Chicano revolutionaries from the barrios of the Southwest fighting for the self-determination of our people. We organized in our barrios, published the newspaper *La Causa*, ran a free clinic and fought against police brutality as well as against the U.S. war in Vietnam."[231] They began as a youth group called the Young Citizens for Community Action and evolved into the radical political group, the Brown Berets. They were active leaders in the Chicano Civil Rights Movement in the 1960s and '70s.

The Panthers continued to inspire, to grow and to fly. Their power and their purpose lit a fire in others, like the Brown Berets, Los Siete de la Raza, the Red Guard and the Young Lords. As the Panthers' programs and beliefs spread, so did their influence. Chapters of the Black Panther Party continued to proliferate throughout the country. Even with attempts to repress the Party and their influence, at this point, there was no containing them.

As Kathleen Cleaver said, "What's going on here is spontaneous and somewhat organized, but most times quite chaotic, revolutionary change. It's one of those periods of time when people just throw off the bonds and say, 'Ready or not, here we come.' And young people loved it."[232]

As a group, the Panthers offered a blueprint toward freedom, not just for Black people, but for oppressed groups across the country.

CHAPTER 13

FREE BREAKFAST LIBERATION SCHOOLS

FREE BREAKFAST

The Panthers' community survival programs were another way that the Party created pathways for change. While these programs were not seen as the end goal of the Party's efforts, they were an essential step toward freedom. And in the end, the survival programs would become one of the Party's most important, long-lasting, and influential legacies.

In late 1968, under Bobby Seale's leadership, the Panthers announced the Free Breakfast for Children Program.[233] The initial program began in early 1969 at St. Augustine's Episcopal Church in West Oakland. Ruth Beckford-Smith, a dancer and choreographer who also attended the church, helped to coordinate the program. Ruth had first interacted with the Panthers when she taught Afro-Haitian dance to Huey's girlfriend LaVerne.

Ruth recruited mothers from the local Parent-Teacher Association and rallied other community support. Even though the work was difficult, "those women were happy to do it," Ruth said. "They felt that this was a very positive program for the Panthers. Where others might have been afraid of any association with the Panthers 'cause they thought they were violent . . . this program was their strongest point and was able to rally people from all sections of the community."[234]

The first day they served 11 children. By the end of the week there were as many as 135 children. Not only would the program become very successful, but, as the *San Francisco Chronicle* reported, the children in the program would learn a very important lesson: "Power in a community begins with people who care."[235]

As Panther JoNina Abron said, the Free Breakfast for Children Program became one of the "most respected and popular" of the Party's programs in the Black community.[236] It required Panther members to wake up early to make the food and sometimes transport children to and from the breakfast site and their schools. While at the program, children learned Black history and lessons about the Black Panther Party. Sometimes the Panthers fed not only the children but their parents too. They also organized food donations.[237]

The Panthers' community programs soon extended beyond free breakfast for school children.

During the 1968–69 school year, the Panthers estimated that they fed 20,000 children across the country. The next school year—1969–70—they hoped to feed 100,000.[238]

The Panthers worked to shed light on the very real issues of childhood hunger and poverty. Studies showed that hunger undermined a child's ability to learn. "Hunger among schoolchildren illustrates one of the basic contradictions in American society," said Yvonne King, the deputy of labor in the Chicago Black Panther Party. "America is one of the richest nations in the world, able to send countless numbers of rockets into space at the drop of a dollar, yet people are starving."[239]

Children going to school hungry, especially in impoverished Black communities, was a real and immediate issue that the Panthers could address. In the Los Angeles Party, Flores Forbes put it this way: "While we might not need their direct assistance waging armed revolution, we were hedging our bets that if we did, they would respond more favorably to a group of people looking out for their children's welfare."[240] And this was true.

Throughout the country, the Panthers offered many programs and services, depending on the specific needs in their communities. "The Survival Programs—Free Breakfast for School Children, the free medical clinics, Busing to Prisons, Free Food, Free Shoes and Clothing, and others to come—were simple, basic concepts that came mostly from rank-and-file members deeply embedded in the communities they had grown up in and now organized," wrote Aaron Dixon. "These programs were the perfect vehicle for the party to address the concrete, immediate needs of the people . . . That's what the Survival Programs were about, as was just about everything we did—transforming a problem into a solution that we created and controlled."[241]

The Panthers gave away clothes and shoes to people who couldn't afford them. They had a free busing program, so people could visit their family members in jail. There was a Free Ambulance Program, especially popular in Winston-Salem, North Carolina. There, fifteen-year old Alan "Snake" Dendy had died after he was shot and the

emergency medical technicians (EMTs) who came to the scene didn't touch his body, saying they lacked the authorization to do so. Dendy died before he could get to the hospital. To make sure this didn't happen again, the Winston-Salem branch of the Party created a free ambulance program that ran for two years and had twenty EMTs who belonged to the Party.[242]

The Panthers also opened free health care clinics. The services included "first aid care, physical examinations, prenatal care, and testing for lead poisoning, high blood pressure, and sickle cell anemia."[243] They contributed significantly to awareness of and treatment for sickle cell anemia, which affects 1 in every 500 African Americans.[244] The free health care clinics touched the lives of many Black people. For example, in the free clinic in Chicago, over 2,000 people were seen in the first two months.

The idea was simple. Good health was essential to liberation. The people as a whole could not be healthy—mentally, physically, spiritually, and otherwise—if individual members were sick. Physical health was just as important as social and economic welfare, as opportunities to have adequate schooling and housing. It was all part of a goal of advancing the individual and collective health of Black people. And the view was holistic. It wasn't just about the Black body but about the mind and the spirit too.

Largely because of the positive community impact of these survival programs, especially the Free Breakfast for Children Program, many individuals in Black communities throughout the country now rallied around the Panthers. In a particularly revealing moment, the community banded together after the Philadelphia police raided the Panther headquarters in that city.

"It was the most beautiful experience I've ever had in my whole life," Panther Clarence Peterson recalled. "I really cried because the people opened up our offices again . . . We did not think our office would open again. The people in the community put everything back in the office. They put furniture back . . . they fed us for about a week . . . they kept our kids. It was something . . . it was out of sight . . . they told the cops that these are our Panthers, so leave them alone."[245]

LIBERATION SCHOOLS

The liberation schools were another essential part of the survival programs. These schools existed throughout the country, beginning with those in the San Francisco Bay Area. The schools' motto was "Learning *how* to think, not *what* to think."[246] They were inspired by the fifth point of the Ten-Point Program: "We want education for our people that exposes the true nature of this decadent American society. We want education that teaches us our true history and our role in the present day society."[247]

Ericka Huggins ran the Oakland Community School from 1973 until 1981.[248] She wanted the children in East Oakland to have access to a quality education. In addition, she believed it was very important

175

A free health care clinic run by the Panthers.

that the process of education be democratic. She wanted to avoid what happened to Huey and so many other young Black children in schools where they were made to feel inferior, where they were disciplined in a way that made them distrust formal education.

"The feeling that we could not learn [the] material was a general attitude among Black children in every public school I ever attended," wrote Huey. "Predictably, this sense of despair and futility led us into rebellious attitudes. Rebellion was the only way we knew to cope with the suffocating, repressive atmosphere that undermined our confidence."[249]

The liberation schools sought to change this. Ericka, working alongside the other teachers and community members, fought tirelessly to change the relationship that so many Black youth had to school and to the education system. For many young Black people, school highlighted the ways they would never fit into an ideal of whiteness and, as a result, could not succeed. "Our image of ourselves was defined for us by textbooks and teachers," wrote Huey. "We not only accepted ourselves as inferior; we accepted the inferiority as inevitable and inescapable."[250]

The problem wasn't simply that the children were made to feel inferior: it was also the feeling that this inferiority was somehow fixed and could not be changed. This sense of stagnation, of hopelessness, took away the choice of freedom and possibility. It created a climate in which a child felt trapped and could not see opportunities for success, growth, and change.

But as Ericka said, "Real change occurs, because if you give people decent education and some nice clothing to wear and maybe a roof over their heads, that's a beginning. But the real change occurs within."[251] Only once a person's basic material and physical needs were met could the real revolutionary work take place. With adequate housing and food, with clothes and access to quality education, people could begin to lead more fulfilled lives.

The Panthers wanted Black people in America to do more than just hold on and eke out an existence. The Black Panther Party wanted

High school students listen to a Black Panther speech in Chicago.

Black people to thrive. Once thriving, a person could begin to craft a healthy self-concept. An individual could start to develop a political consciousness, to agitate to make the world a better and more understanding place. Communities could overthrow the vicious cycles of the oppressor and oppressed, of the haves and the have-nots. And it was much more difficult for that work to occur if a person could not operate from a place of safety—a place where their basic human needs were met.

The Panthers preached "All Power to the People," and "Black Power!" encouraging people to reclaim their political rights and freedoms. They also encouraged Black people to find beauty and solace in their

179

The Black Panther Party Children's Institute, a precursor to the Oakland Community School.

blackness. The Panthers were engaged in not just a political revolution, but a cultural one as well. Not only were they fighting for basic rights and freedoms like adequate food, shelter, clothing, and access to education, they were fighting for the right to self-determination and the freedom that comes with a whole and actualized sense of self.

The Black Panther Party incorporated these ideas into the way they presented themselves to the world. They were Black and proud of it, proclaiming it in their dress and their hair and their political consciousness. These young Black people stepped out and took up room, demanding their own space, demanding to be seen.

The Black Panther Party was a youth organization. Many of the people in the Party were under the age of twenty-one. Sixty percent of the Party members were women.[252] These were energetic and driven young Black activists who knew that, together, they had the power to change the world. As a teacher in the liberation schools put it, "We, the teachers, know that power belongs to the people and that youth makes revolution."[253]

Residents of Algiers with a Huey Newton poster.

CHAPTER 14

ELDRIDGE IN ALGIERS MONTREAL AND SCANDINAVIA

ELDRIDGE IN ALGIERS

In November 1968 Eldridge decided to run for president of the United States on the Peace and Freedom Party ticket. "We have been driven out of the political arena," he wrote. "We will not dissent from the American Government. We will overthrow it."[254]

For many, change could not come fast enough. Eldridge was speaking to thousands upon thousands who couldn't wait to hear what he had to say. Crowds who gathered to hear him speak packed so close together that they could hardly move. He was agitating for the Black Panther Party and he was getting things done. Eldridge's vision was clear: armed revolution as soon as possible. The people would not wait.

Then, on November 28th Eldridge disappeared. At this time, he was out on bail. Previously, he had been arrested for his involvement in the events that lead to the death of Lil' Bobby. If Eldridge had stayed in the United States, he would have been rearrested. Instead, he went into exile.

Eldridge was first seen again in Cuba on Christmas Day. Then he moved on to North Africa and Algiers, the capital city of Algeria. At that time, the United States and Algiers didn't have diplomatic relations. Eldridge could stay there without fear of getting arrested and the Panthers could work freely and openly.

Eldridge's first public appearance would come at the inaugural Pan-African Cultural Festival in Algiers. Algeria had just gained independence from France in 1962. They were a new socialist government, having fought for a decade to free themselves. The new president, Houari Boumedienne, was one of their military leaders. He was adamantly opposed to colonialism and wanted to help freedom fighters around the world. The Algerian government also worked to promote African unity and to support liberation struggles in other countries. That was one of the reasons they accepted the Panthers with open arms. As Eldridge explained, the Algerians thought of the Black Panther Party "as the nucleus of the future, American government."[255]

In May 1969, Kathleen, who was eight months pregnant, went to Algiers to join Eldridge. Emory Douglas accompanied her. David Hilliard and Masai Hewitt also flew to Algiers a few weeks later for the festival.[256] Masai would become the Minister of Education.

Julia Wright, daughter of the renowned author and activist Richard Wright, met the Panthers. She helped them by translating from French to English and with her knowledge of African cultures and politics.[257]

The festival began with Algerians on horseback galloping through the capital, firing rifles. Four thousand Africans from twenty-four countries came to meet and celebrate for over twelve days. The art and culture flowed freely, including visual art shipped in from museums and dance troupes from Mali, Tanzania, Guinea, and the Congo. There was a two-hour-long parade featuring jugglers, pipers, drummers, and dancers. Swordsmen from Guinea performed indigenous dances. There were plays and acting troupes and musicians, poets, and writers. This was all a celebration of the authentic culture of each nation. President Boumedienne made a point of highlighting this. He emphatically rejected the western idea of a colonial White "civilizing mission," which was what the colonizing French had tried to do in his country. Instead, he asserted that "culture is a weapon in our struggle for liberation."[258]

In the office assigned to the Panthers for the festival, Emory hung revolutionary artwork. Now the Algerians walking down the main street could see posters of Huey and Eldridge and enlarged graphics from the Party newspaper. One such picture was of a Black woman who carried both her baby and a rifle strapped to her back. Crowds gathered, standing, discussing, soaking in Emory's work.[259]

On July 22, 1969, Julia Wright introduced the Black Panther Party during the opening of their Afro-American Center. In French, she explained that Malcolm X came to Africa as one man, alone. Now the Panthers had come as a group, a revolutionary organization that was fully developed. They were the vanguard of the revolution, representing the Black liberation struggle in America.[260]

187

Eldridge Cleaver, David Hilliard, Emory Douglas, and the Palestinian delegation in Algiers.

The Afro-American Center in Algiers.

The Algerian government gave the Black Panthers official diplomatic status.[261] In fact, the Black Panthers were the only Americans that the Algerian government recognized. They also received a beautiful embassy building made of marble and white stucco from the North Vietnamese, who were moving into a different space.

The contrast between the Panthers' treatment in Algiers and in the United States was stark. As a reporter for *The New York Times* wrote, "In the United States, the Black Panthers are viewed in official quarters as a menace to society. They are harassed by police, and shot in battles with them. Many of their leaders are in jail or out on bail."[262]

On the other hand, in Algiers, "the Panthers are respected as one of approximately a dozen liberation movements accredited by the

Algerian Government and provided with assistance and support in their task of overthrowing the governments in power in their respective countries."[263]

The Black Panther Party had achieved something that many Black liberation groups and leaders—including Malcolm X—had wanted. The Party had an official headquarters for its new international wing, which they called the Intercommunal Section.

In Algiers, Eldridge could continue his work on the Free Huey! campaign. He could continue to agitate for freedom for Black people, all from a new home base. At the opening of the headquarters, Eldridge proudly announced that "this is the first time in the struggle of the black people in America that they have established representation abroad."[264]

MONTREAL AND SCANDINAVIA

The day after Eldridge disappeared in November 1968, Bobby Seale was also outside the United States. He was in Montreal attending the Hemispheric Conference to End the War in Vietnam. He had traveled there with a delegation of Black Panthers including David Hilliard.[265]

Bobby stepped up in front of 1,500 delegates from around the world, calling for an end to imperialism. His voice rang out in St. James Church in downtown Montreal, the light flooding through the stained-glass windows. Surrounded by the high Corinthian columns and the carved ceiling overhead, he maintained that peace could not be achieved without justice. Bobby thought of Huey, and of all the Black men and women trapped in the prison system in the United States.

Bobby was surrounded by beauty and spaciousness. This sense of openness, of true possibility, was rooted in the condition of ultimate freedom. That's what the Panthers were after.

But he was still aware of all the restrictions placed on him and so many others. Even as he and some of his fellow Panthers had the opportunity to travel abroad, to spread the word of the Panthers, other people were still at home working, struggling, and dying. Bobby finished his speech and watched as the delegates began to stand, applauding him, applauding the Party.

The Black Panther Party continued to influence the conference. A Panther member from Baltimore, Elijah Zeke Boyd, known as Brother Zeke, was elected as chairman. The programs were changed to highlight the Panthers' emphasis on anti-imperialism.[266] The Panthers captured the hearts and minds of those in attendance.

During the conference, the Black Panther Party compared the police brutality that Black people experienced in the United States to the occupation in Vietnam by the U.S. military. "We say that the oppressor has no laws and no rights that the oppressed are bound to respect. We cannot respect it," asserted the Party members. What the Panthers wanted, for themselves and other oppressed peoples, including the people of Vietnam, was the universal "right to self-determination."[267]

At the conference's end, the Americans handed their draft cards to the North Vietnamese. These cards were slips of paper with random numbers that corresponded to each man's birthday. When his number was called, that person was drafted and had to enlist in the army to fight in the Vietnam War. As a form of protest against the war, American men had begun burning their draft cards.

Now, at the Hemispheric Conference to End the War in Vietnam, these American men made a gesture that had real meaning and symbolism. Together, they were standing against the war in Vietnam.

The North Vietnamese delegates built a small fire on the stage and fed the draft cards to the flames. The audience cheered. They raised their hands in the air, making fists. Bobby looked out over the audience, full of people of all kinds lifting up the Black Panther salute. As he watched, they began to chant "Panther Power to the Vanguard!" It was one thing hearing his own voice ringing out in the halls of the church. It was another to hear all of these people chanting this phrase in unison, their voices swelling and arcing toward the rafters.

In a show of solidarity, the North Vietnamese minister of culture, M. Hoang Minh Giam, turned to David Hilliard and declared, "You are Black Panthers, We are Yellow Panthers!"[268]

The Panthers continued to travel internationally. Early in 1969, Bobby and Masai Hewitt toured Scandinavia, seeking support for the "Free Huey!" campaign. Connie Matthews helped to organize their trip. Connie was a Jamaican woman who worked with the the United Nations' Educational, Scientific, and Cultural Organization in Copenhagen. She was young, full of energy, a great speaker, and down with the cause. "I am only too willing time and time again to repeat to European audiences," Connie said to a reporter from *Land and Folk,* a Communist newspaper in Copenhagen, "that the BPP is speaking about a world proletarian revolution and recognize themselves as part of this. It is a question of the oppressor against the oppressed regardless of race."[269]

Across the world, the late '60s was a time of great change and possibility, where revolution seemed with reach. Bobby and Masai traveled to Finland; Norway; Stockholm, Sweden; and Copenhagen, also stopping in Germany for a brief visit. The trip brought prestige and funding and an expanded reach for the "Free Huey!" campaign.

The movement that Huey and Bobby had started just a few years ago was now inspiring people thousands of miles away. The Panthers created space where it had not existed before. They seized this opportunity of their own creation and claimed their place in the revolution.

But the Party didn't only have supporters. The more well known they became, the more opposition they would face.

Eldridge Cleaver and Bunchy Carter.

CHAPTER 15

JOHN AND BUNCHY

JOHN AND BUNCHY

Back home in L.A., the Black Panther Party branch was small, but still powerful and influential. A lot of that had to do with Bunchy. "Bunchy has become a key Party member," David Hilliard explained. "Bunchy exudes charisma. He's a lover, revolutionary, and warrior, a genuine tough guy who never fronts. A gang leader from Slauson—the area around South Central L.A.—he carries all the fascination, glamour, and repute of Los Angeles. His style is macho and lyrical."[270]

But the Panthers weren't the only ones with influence in the area. Another main player in L.A. was Ron Karenga, and his group US.

The members of US believed in changing society through a cultural revolution. It wasn't that they didn't believe in political action, but they believed that the heart of the revolution would come through a cultural shift. They dressed in dashikis—colorful garments originally from West Africa. Karenga spoke many languages, including Swahili, which he taught to the members. He was known as Maulana, which means "master teacher," and was the founder of the Kwanzaa holiday.[271] In L.A., US was well known and powerful. As the Panthers became a more important presence in the area, the conflict between the two groups increased.

And there had been tensions from the start. When US and Ron Karenga were assigned to protect Betty Shabazz in 1967, she ended up alone in the street. Huey and Bobby decided to take a different course of action, giving her an armed escort from the airport. This event helped define the Black Panther Party early on as a force to be reckoned with.

The tensions between US and the Black Panther Party only grew after that, especially once the L.A. branch of the Panthers opened. As the Deputy Minister of Defense in the L.A. chapter, Bunchy had a lot of power and influence. He was also a target. But Bunchy wasn't afraid of anything, or anyone.

Ron Karenga

Members of US began threatening and intimidating members of the Black Student Union at UCLA and other small groups, some of whom were Party members. US was using their influence in the area to try to assert their will. Bunchy wasn't having it.

He called up Bobby Seale and said he wanted to put a stop to what US was doing. "What you should do is get out in the community," Bobby said, "and forget Ron Karenga and the Black Congress too, and go and set up those community offices. You should have five, six, or seven offices set up throughout Los Angeles. Work from there at serving the people and move to implement the Party's ten-point platform and program, and politically educate the masses of the people. That's what has to be done. Forget Ron Karenga."[272]

US had come out of the efforts of the Black Congress.[273] These groups were all vying for power and influence. But Bobby believed that, through direct community action, the Panthers would stand out.

Still, the conflict persisted within UCLA's Black Student Union. The position of program chair opened in the university's Black Studies Program, and there was a disagreement over who should be appointed. The university had made Karenga a community adviser, so he had an official position. He supported one candidate, but the Panthers opposed this person. The Party agitated for a role in the decision-making process.

This was not the only time that the Panthers and US would disagree publicly. Bunchy continued to want to address their conflict head-on. But Bobby and others in power still thought this wasn't a good idea. As Bobby remembered, "One of the cleanest things about Bunchy was his deep seriousness and honesty about the need for revolutionary change. When Eldridge, I, or someone from Central Headquarters would give him an order to stop doing something, he would stop."[274]

This didn't mean that Bunchy never disagreed with them. But when he was given a direct order, he followed it. So, Bunchy and John Huggins, who was now the Deputy Minister of Information for the Los Angeles chapter, attended community meetings instead and didn't confront US.

Bunchy and John did go to a couple of meetings on the Black Studies Program chair in 1969, on January 15, and again on the seventeenth. Both John and Elaine Brown had been elected to a committee to represent the concerns of the Black Student Union. John, Bunchy, and Elaine were all attending UCLA at the time. So was fellow Party member Geronimo Pratt.

It looked like either Bunchy or John might win the election to become the president of the union. Things were going the Panthers' way. They had avoided direct violent conflict with the members of US and would instead gain more official influence through the Black Student

Union. The university was set to announce the new director of the Black Studies Program on January 21.

Still, the final meeting was long and contentious, with heated arguments on both sides. Everyone was ready for the meeting to adjourn. When one of the final motions was being discussed, John leaned over to Elaine and whispered dramatically, "I hope they go for this, I'm starv-ing." Elaine stifled a laugh. Luckily, the meeting was soon adjourned.

As Elaine was walking out, one of the members of US came up to her. "You need to watch what you say Sister," he said, but Elaine just brushed it off as she headed down the stairs.[275]

Moments later, Elaine heard gunshots. She started running back up the stairs. She could hear the thudding of feet above her. Around her, glass was breaking.

Elaine didn't know it yet, but John and Bunchy had been murdered. When they died, the men lay so close together their hands touched. Their bodies were trampled as the survivors ran to escape the gunfire.[276]

At the time Ericka was at home with their child. She and John had just had a baby girl, named Mai, three weeks ago. When Ericka heard what happened to her husband, she went into a state of shock. She stood up and began boiling water, to make everyone coffee. Before they could even drink it, police officers arrived outside.[277] All four women and the three week old baby were taken to jail.

After they were finally released, Ericka went to New Haven, Connecticut with Mai to attend John's funeral and be with his family there. In New Haven, Ericka would work to build a chapter of the Party.[278]

The incident shook the Party as a whole. The murders made it even clearer that there was danger in being a Panther. That, while it might be an important and even righteous decision, it truly was a dangerous

199

one. How many members would be ready not only to live for the people, but also to die for the people?

For days after John and Bunchy died, it poured rain. Sheets of water sliced through the air, drowning the earth below. Many couldn't believe that Bunchy, the "Mayor of the Ghetto," once the notorious leader of 5,000 men in the Slauson Gang, was now gone.[279] As Aaron Dixon wrote, "It rained for the next seven days, and some speculated that this was the gods' way of expressing their anger over the death of one of the most respected Black men on the streets of Southern California."[280]

John and Bunchy's murder would prove to be not just about Ron Karenga and US, though. There was yet another player still on the scene: the FBI.

FBI surveillance photo of Elaine Brown,
Ericka Huggins, and others.

CHAPTER 16

COINTELPRO

COINTELPRO

From the beginning, the federal government had trained its eyes on the Party. When the Panthers started to grow in power and influence in 1968—and especially following Richard Nixon's election that year on his "Law and Order" platform—the U.S. government began a targeted assault on the Party. Now there were chapters of the Party throughout the U.S. There was the International Section in Algiers and international alliances throughout the world. The armed self-defense programs had gained the Panthers an initial following, and with expanded efforts like the survival programs, the Party's influence became an undeniable force. Not just in the U.S., but throughout the world. By July 15, 1969, the director of the FBI, J. Edgar Hoover, declared that "the Black Panther Party, without question, represents the greatest threat to the internal security of this country."[281]

The Party had become too powerful. Hoover's message was urgent and obvious: the FBI had to take the Party down.

Earlier in the year, at the time of John and Bunchy's murders, it wasn't clear how involved the FBI was. Later, it was learned that government agents had intentionally escalated the conflict between US and the Black Panthers, knowing that it could end in violence, even death.

Back in November 1968, Hoover had sent a memo concerning US and the Black Panthers. "A serious struggle is taking place between the Black Panther Party and the US organization," he wrote. "The struggle has reached such proportion that it is taking on the aura of gang warfare with attendant threats of murder and reprisals. In order to fully capitalize upon [Black Panther Party] and US differences as well as to exploit all avenues of creating further dissension in the ranks of the [Party], recipient offices are instructed to submit imaginative and hard hitting counterintelligence measures aimed at crippling the [Black Panther Party]."[282] Hoover directed his agents in L.A. to exploit this rift.

During Bunchy's funeral, Bobby Seale boldly stated that Ron Karenga was a "tool of the power structure."[283] The Panthers were not naïve. They were fully aware that the Establishment saw them as a serious threat and that, as a result, they were already enduring government-directed repression. Even in the early days of the Party, the FBI had decided that the Panthers were a threat: "The extremist [Black Panther Party] of Oakland, California, is rapidly expanding," wrote Hoover on September 27, 1968. "[It] is essential that we not only accelerate our investigations of this organization, and increase our informants in the organization but that we take action under the counterintelligence program [COINTELPRO] to disrupt the group."[284] Still, in the beginning, the Panthers weren't aware of the full extent of the government's efforts to destroy the Party.

Decades ago, the FBI had targeted groups like the National Association for the Advancement of Colored People, Marcus Garvey's Universal Negro Improvement Association, the Communist Party, and the Wobblies (Industrial Workers of the World).[285] In the beginning of the Civil Rights Movement, the FBI closely monitored the activities of key individuals, including both Martin Luther King, Jr. and Malcolm X.

In 1963, as the Civil Rights Movement gained increasing international influence, the FBI stepped up its efforts to discredit King. The intensity increased further in 1967, when King publicly opposed the Vietnam War.[286] And now both the Black Power movement and the long Black freedom struggle—of which the Black Power movement was an essential part—were entering a new period.

The Black urban rebellions spreading across the country struck fear in many. These rebellions signaled a powerful upswell of resistance from below, from those who were oppressed. The government's response made it clear that those in power felt threatened.

In 1967, Hoover and the FBI targeted what they called six "black nationalist hate-type" organizations. One of these was Dr. King's Southern Christian Leadership Conference (SCLC). This group was nonviolent; they worked within the system to get what Black people needed, rather than disrupt and dismantle the government. They wanted reforms, and they didn't advocate a violent overthrow of the government. They were integrationist and didn't call for armed defense, as the Panthers did.

But once the Civil Rights Movement defeated Jim Crow, King and the SCLC shifted their attention to class. They sought to help poor Black people and to end poverty for all people in America. King and the SCLC also wanted an end to the Vietnam War, stemming from their belief in nonviolence. Even though they weren't a Black nationalist group, and even though they advocated unity and non-violence, because of their political positions Hoover labeled the SCLC a "black nationalist hate-type" group and a threat to national security.[287]

On March 4, 1968, Hoover expanded COINTELPRO. In a memo, he named Martin Luther King, Jr., Stokely Carmichael, and Elijah Muhammad as serious threats to the Establishment. He wrote that COINTELPRO's job was to "prevent the rise of a 'messiah' who could unify, and electrify, the militant black nationalist movement. Malcolm X might have been such a 'messiah;' he is the martyr of the movement today."[288]

As of that memo, Malcolm X had already been murdered. One month after the memo, Dr. Martin Luther King, Jr. would also be assassinated. A few months after this, in January 1969, Bunchy and John would be murdered.

The Panthers knew that the government was watching them, but only later did they realize that it wasn't just people working on the outside to destroy them. There were people posing as members of the Party, trying to take the Party down.

"What we didn't understand was how infiltrated we were," Party member Brenda Presley later admitted. "We suspected some folks but we didn't know the extent."[289]

In fact, the FBI paid visits to Brenda's mother in Alaska and her father in San Francisco. Brenda's mother "actually freaked out . . . because the FBI went to her job a couple of times and asked her if she knew what her daughter was getting involved with." The agents encouraged Brenda's mother to talk to her. They said she was "too nice a girl to get mixed up with the Panthers."[290]

They tried to appeal to Brenda's mother through a sense of respectability. The theory was that "nice girls" could take part only in certain activities in certain ways.

But that just wasn't the case. "Nice girls" could be revolutionaries. A revolutionary was just that—someone engaged in the making of a revolution. What held these particular revolutionaries together was their bold commitment to a common goal: the liberation of Black people. The Panthers worked to destroy the idea that to be a certain thing (i.e., a "nice girl" or Black in America), a person must behave in a certain way and have their options limited as a result. In contrast, the FBI deployed the idea of "niceness" as a weapon to undermine the Party. To be seen as "nice," not as a revolutionary, was what mattered.

But the Panthers were not aiming for "nice." And clearly, from the FBI's perspective and the perspective of many, the Black Panther Party was not made up of "nice" people. Fortunately, those who joined the Panthers didn't do so out of concern for how they were perceived. They did so out of a commitment to freedom, for themselves and for others.

Still, it wasn't easy for members of the Party to live that way, with their mortality hanging over their heads. Panther Janice Garrett-Forte said that she "kinda expect[ed] to get killed," she "expected to die." How might a person face each day with that kind of mentality? She began to experience a kind of numbness. "The only question was, how was it going to feel when it happened? What kind of situation am I going to be in? It felt inevitable. You didn't think that you were going to get out alive."[291]

The FBI came down hard. In their eyes, there was no more dangerous organization in the United States than the Black Panther Party. They worked to create suspicion amongst the leaders and rank-and-file members concerning money and its uses. They suggested that spouses and others might be cooperating with law enforcement. They also hoped to turn the public against the Panthers and create opposition to them even in their own neighborhoods.[292] The FBI

sent forged letters to create confusion and cast suspicion. They tapped phone calls to gain information. They sent people working for the FBI in to pose as members of the Panthers.

On the local level, the raids of Panther offices had already begun. Members of the Party were consistently targeted and attacked. Eventually, members were instructed to take off their berets and leather jackets—which had swiftly become the recognizable uniform of the

WANTED BY THE FBI

INTERSTATE FLIGHT - ASSAULT WITH INTENT TO COMMIT MURDER

LEROY ELDRIDGE CLEAVER

FBI No. 214,830 B

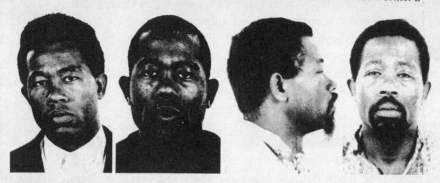

Photograph taken 1966   Photographs taken 1968

Aliases: Eldridge Cleaver, Leroy Eldridge Cleaver, Jr.

DESCRIPTION

Age:	33, born August 31, 1935, Little Rock, Arkansas		
Height:	6'2"	**Eyes:**	Brown
Weight:	185 to 195 pounds	**Complexion:**	Medium
Build:	Medium	**Race:**	Negro
Hair:	Black	**Nationality:**	American
Occupations:	Author, clerk, laborer, magazine editor, reporter, writer		
Scars and Marks:	Numerous pock scars on back		
Remarks:	Sometimes wears small gold earring in pierced left ear lobe		

Fingerprint Classification:

CRIMINAL RECORD

Cleaver has been convicted of assault with intent to commit murder, assault with a deadly weapon and possession of narcotics.

CAUTION

CLEAVER ALLEGEDLY HAS ENGAGED POLICE OFFICERS IN GUN BATTLE IN THE PAST. CONSIDER ARMED AND EXTREMELY DANGEROUS.

A Federal warrant was issued on December 10, 1968, at San Francisco, California, charging Cleaver with unlawful interstate flight to avoid confinement after conviction for assault with intent to commit murder (Title 18, U. S. Code, Section 1073).

IF YOU HAVE ANY INFORMATION CONCERNING THIS PERSON, PLEASE NOTIFY ME OR CONTACT YOUR LOCAL FBI OFFICE. TELEPHONE NUMBERS AND ADDRESSES OF ALL FBI OFFICES LISTED ON BACK.

DIRECTOR
FEDERAL BUREAU OF INVESTIGATION
UNITED STATES DEPARTMENT OF JUSTICE
WASHINGTON, D. C. 20535
TELEPHONE, NATIONAL 8-7117

Wanted Flyer 447
December 13, 1968

Party—to make them less recognizable. As Aaron Dixon wrote, "The party also ordered all members to take off the leather jackets and berets in the interest of our dressing more like the people. By wearing a uniform, we had isolated ourselves from the very people we had pledged to uplift and also made it easier for the police to identify, arrest and kill us."[293]

Abayama Katara had already used this tactic once when fleeing the police. During a court hearing for some members of the New York chapter, including Abayama, there were officers standing behind them. They began to jab the Panthers with their nightsticks, cursing and taunting them. The Panthers looked straight ahead, but into their ears the police said, "White tigers eat black panthers."[294]

When the small group of Panthers left the courtroom, they were attacked. As *The New York Times* reported, "About 150 white men, many of whom were off-duty and out of uniform policemen, attacked a small number of Black Panther party members and white sympathizers yesterday on the sixth floor of the Brooklyn Criminal Court." Many of the off-duty officers wore buttons that said, "Wallace for President." George Wallace, who was running for president of the

A bullet hole following a police raid on Party headquarters in Oakland.

United States at that time, was the former governor of Alabama. He was also a White supremacist.

The Panthers tried to run but were still beaten, many with blood running down their faces. One Panther, section leader Tom McCreary, suffered a fractured skull. The New York Panther Chairman, David Brothers, was kicked and stomped on more than twenty times while he lay on the ground.[295]

Abayama and others tried to keep running, fleeing into an elevator. But the elevator went up instead of down, and when the doors opened, the off-duty police were there waiting for them. The Panthers looked in multiple offices for help and a way to escape, but there was no one. They finally rushed back to the courtroom, where they asked the judge for protection. He eventually called a court guard to escort the Panthers downstairs.

But when they were outside, there were still off-duty police officers circling. The remaining Panthers split up and ran.[296] Once Abayama reached the subway, he pulled off his black beret and black shirt. Now that Abayama was no longer recognizable as a Black Panther, the off-duty police didn't pay him any attention and he rode the subway home, heart racing but safe for the time being.[297]

This was just a small slice of the violence the Panthers faced every day, especially in New York, where the Party had a large and influential branch, with many people agitating and committed to the struggle.

On April 2, 1969, in the early morning hours, a New York grand jury indicted twenty-one members of this branch. The decision was based on allegations from three people who were all paid informants. The charges were for plotting to bomb police stations, department stores, and the Brooklyn Botanic Garden.

At 5:00 a.m., the New York police raided the homes of five Black Panthers, arresting twelve. Some members were already in police custody. A few escaped and went into exile. Those remaining were indicted and became the "Panther 21."[298] The evidence was not substantial,

211

but bail was set at $100,000 for most of the defendants, an amount that they could not raise.

As Afeni Shakur, one of the Panther 21, wrote, "We are not being tried for any overt act nor for the attempt to commit any overt act— we are being tried for bringing within our minds the focusing of the ideas of centuries and trying to bring this knowledge into a work-able plan to liberate our people from oppression."[299] The idea was that, just like Huey, the Panther 21 were political prisoners, imprisoned not for the actions they took but for the beliefs they held.

But these arrests, based on very little evidence, led to almost all the leaders of the New York Panther office being imprisoned for two years, unable to do on-the-ground work for the Party.[300]

▲

The Panthers were now on the national and international stage. What Huey and Bobby started had grown from a small local group into an organization that had power and influence across the world. People believed that not only was revolution necessary, it was also possible. Because the movement was spreading so quickly, because it was disorderly, there wasn't an easy way to contain it. Unlike small-scale riots, which could be stopped, this directed force spread swiftly and effectively, affecting people throughout the United States and beyond.

Now that they were so well known, all of the Panthers were in danger. Even those affiliated with the Party would become targets. There would be more arrests. There would be more violence. And there would be more deaths. But even with this intense repression from the United States government, the Black Panther Party continued to grow.

For now, the Panthers' martyrs—Alprentice "Bunchy" Carter, John Huggins, and Lil' Bobby Hutton—loomed large.

PART FIVE: UNSTOPPABLE

If I know any thing at all, it's that a wall is just a wall and nothing more at all. It can be broken down. I believe in living. I believe in birth. I believe in the sweat of love and in the fire of truth.[301]

Assata Shakur

JOIN THE
CONSPIRACY

DAYS OF RAGE · OCTOBER 8·11 · CHICAGO

MARK MORRIS DESIGN FOR THE CONSPIRACY · 28 EAST JACKSON BOULEVARD · CHICAGO · ILLINOIS 60604

CHAPTER 17

CHICAGO EIGHT

CHICAGO EIGHT

On August 19, 1969, one of the Panthers was getting married. It was a beautiful, breezy Sunday in Oakland, California. Everyone appreciated the chance to be happy, to take a short break from the all-consuming business of revolution.

When the celebration was over, the Panthers piled into their cars. Bobby and his brother, John, were driving together. In the same car were David's brother June and Masai Hewitt. Suddenly, five cars surrounded them. Masai looked out the window. "Those cats look like—"

"Pigs!" June said, his hands tight on the steering wheel. The FBI officers drew their guns, jumped out of their cars, and began to shout, "Get out of the car! Get out of the car!" Bobby got out of the car slowly, with his hands open, palms facing them, to show that he didn't have any weapons. They grabbed Bobby, placed him under arrest, and drove off.[302]

Aaron Dixon was standing guard at the house in Berkeley. When the phone rang he grabbed it. "Aaron. The pigs just arrested the chairman," June said urgently. "They might be coming to the house. I want you to secure the house and don't let the pigs in. Understand?"

"Right on," Aaron answered, grabbing the closest weapon.

He peered through the windows. There were police cars circling slowly. All of a sudden, one stopped. Aaron ran down the steps, his heart beating fast. He looked through the peephole in the front door, trying not to make any noise. There was a sergeant outside. When he knocked Aaron held his breath and his gun. The sergeant knocked again, looking around, to see if anyone was home. Aaron stayed still for minutes that felt like hours. Eventually, the sergeant got back in his car.[303]

Bobby was taken to Chicago under state custody. There was a new federal conspiracy law that made it illegal to cross state lines for the purpose of inciting a riot. Bobby, along with seven other men, were the first to be charged with this crime.[304] All of the defendants had attended the 1968 Democratic Convention in Chicago, where there had been protests and rioting.

The protests at the convention were met with violence. The mayor of Chicago, Richard Daley, refused to grant permits so the protesters could demonstrate legally. He had barbed wire put around the convention site. Then he requested that all of the 12,000 police officers in Chicago be on twelve-hour shifts. He called in over 5,000 National Guardsmen and 6,000 U.S. army troops. These troops had flamethrowers, bazookas, bayonets, and machine guns on top of Jeeps.[305] It was not a surprise, then, that there was violence and rioting, but there was no evidence that Bobby Seale was a part of it. Bobby stopped in Chicago only briefly, to give a couple of speeches at the convention.[306] He hadn't even met some of the other defendants until the trial began.

These other defendants were Abbie Hoffman and Jerry Rubin, who cofounded the Youth International Party (Yippies); David Dellinger and Rennie Davis, who both worked with the National Mobilization Committee to End the War in Vietnam; Tom Hayden, who cofounded Students for a Democratic Society, and activists John Froines and Lee Weiner. Of what would be called the Chicago Eight, Bobby was the only Black man.[307]

Nineteen public intellectuals, concerned with the precedent set by this new rioting law, wrote a letter to *The New York Review of Books*. "The effect of this 'anti-riot' act is to subvert the first Amendment guarantee of free assembly by equating organized political protest with organized violence. Potentially, this law is the foundation for a police state in America." Those who signed the letter included the famous White writers Norman Mailer, Susan Sontag, and Noam Chomsky.[308]

Bobby wanted Charles Garry as his lawyer for the trial, but Charles was in the hospital. Bobby requested a trial delay so that Charles could recover and come represent him. Charles was the main lawyer for the Oakland Black Panther Party and had worked with Bobby before.

A Black Panther and Young Lords rally in support
of Bobby Seale's trial.

But the judge, Julius Hoffman, would not delay the trial. So Bobby decided to represent himself. Hoffman refused to allow this. Instead, the judge assigned William Kunstler, who was already representing some of the other defendants, to represent Bobby.

Bobby didn't agree to have Kunstler represent him, but not because he had an issue with Kunstler. It was the principle of the thing—the judge was trying to deny Bobby his constitutional right to defend himself.[309] When Bobby tried to speak, the judge ordered him to sit down and be quiet. But Bobby refused. "You have George Washington and Benjamin Franklin sitting in a picture behind you," Bobby said, "and they were slave owners. That's what they were. They owned slaves. You are acting in the same manner, denying me my constitutional rights."[310]

The trial of the Chicago Eight did not proceed in the regular fashion. Two of the defendants, Abbie Hoffman and Jerry Rubin, made sure of that. They continued to make comments, not observing normal courtroom decorum. As the days went on, the courtroom began to resemble something closer to a circus. Those observing the trial provided affirmation and calls of "Right on!" when the defendants spoke.

The defendants also didn't rise when the judge entered the room, as they were supposed to, because they refused to acknowledge him as having power and superiority. Abbie and Jerry even came in mockingly wearing judges' robes.[311] Abbie blew kisses to the jurors,[312] making jokes and proclaiming his disdain for the proceedings. Eventually, Judge Hoffman sentenced all of the defendants and their attorneys, including William Kunstler and Leonard Weinglass, for contempt of court.[313] But, as Abbie said, "You know you cannot win . . . The only way you can is to put us away for contempt. We have contempt for this Court, and for you . . . and for this whole rotten system. That's the only justice."[314]

At one point, as Judge Hoffman continued to deny Bobby his right to defend himself, Bobby called the judge "a blatant racist."[315] When Hoffman kicked one observer out of the courtroom, Bobby said, "You are a pig for kicking him out." Those observing called back, "Right on! Right on!" The court marshal tried to regain order. "This

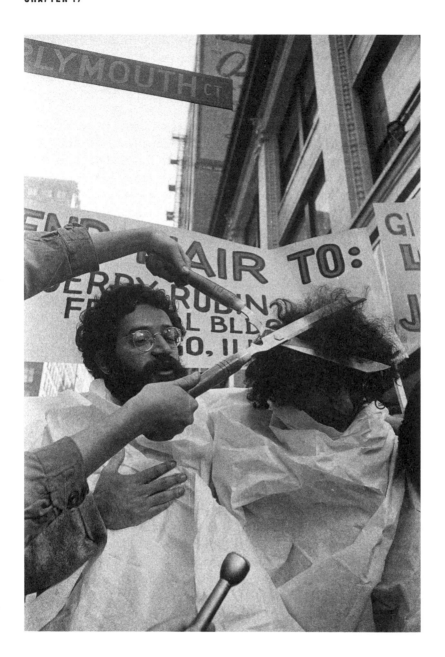

Abbie Hoffman of the Chicago Eight protests.

Honorable Court will now resume its session," he said. In response, those watching began to call out, "Oink oink. Oink oink."[316]

As the trial went on, Bobby continued to speak on his own behalf. Even as Hoffman was trying to hurry the jurors out of the room, Bobby kept speaking. "This racist administration government with its Superman notions and comic book politics," he said loudly. "We're hip to the fact that Superman never saved no black people. You got that?"[317]

On October 29, the judge asked Bobby, "Mr. Seale, are you going to disrupt this court anymore?"

"I'm not disrupting the court," Bobby said. "I am going to make my request and demand that I have a right to defend myself, because I know I have that right."

In response Judge Hoffman said, "Take the defendant and appropriately deal with him."[318]

The judge ordered that Bobby be bound to his chair and gagged. The court marshals took him out of the courtroom. They bound and gagged him as they were ordered and then carried Bobby back in, strapped to his chair. But Bobby would not be silenced. He struggled, banging his chair against the hard floor. He continued to make noise through his gag. "I object," he kept on saying. "I object."[319]

For days, Bobby was brought into the courtroom this way, shackled to a chair with a gag in his mouth. His voice was muffled and strained, but he still demanded his rights—he still fought for his freedom and his political beliefs. Defense attorney William Kunstler said, "This is no longer a court of order, Your Honor, this is a medieval torture chamber."[320]

"The next morning, when they tried to gag me, I thought I was going to die," wrote Bobby. "I mean, really die, because of the way they were doing things." When Bobby was not in the courtroom, he was kept in his cell, locked up.[321]

On November 3, Judge Hoffman said that Bobby could be in the courtroom without the gag and restraints if he remained quiet. But Bobby continued to speak on his own behalf. The judge ordered that he sit down. "This is a fascist operation," Bobby declared, and sat down. The court adjourned then for a break.

When they came back, Judge Hoffman read a list of all the ways in which Bobby was in contempt of court. He asked if Bobby had something to say in response. Bobby stood. "I'm not going to beg you for no time," he replied. Then he posed his own question. "How long have you been putting black people in jail and prisons and railroading people and denying them their constitutional rights?"[322] Judge Hoffman declared Bobby's trial a mistrial. He sentenced Bobby to four years in prison for contempt of court.[323]

As Bobby was taken out, the people in the courtroom chanted, "FREE BOBBY!"[324]

The repression, the silencing, the gagging of a leader of the Black Panther Party were all part of the efforts to stop the Party. But rather than flounder, the Panthers continued to grow. Even with the torture, the mistreatment, even staring death in the face, they went on.

As Fred Hampton said, "Bobby Seale is going through all types of physical and mental torture. But that's alright because we've said, even before this happened and we're going to say it after this and after I'm locked up and after everybody's locked up that you can jail a revolutionary, but you can't jail a revolution. You might run a liberator like Eldridge Cleaver out of the country but you can't run liberation out the country. You might murder a freedom fighter, like Bobby Hutton, but you can't murder freedom fighting."[325]

FREE
ERICA
HUGGINS

THE
CONNECTICUT
PANTHERS

4115

The Los Angeles office
following a SWAT raid
by LAPD, 1969.

CHAPTER 18

WHO CAN YOU TRUST?
LOS ANGELES RAID

WHO CAN YOU TRUST?

On December 3, 1969, Fred Hampton met with lawyer Jeff Haas to purchase the Panther office building in Chicago. The police were pressuring the Panthers' landlord to evict them. If they bought the building, the Panthers would have control over the space. They could make improvements and adjustments, but, most important, they could stay as long as they wanted. No one could force them to leave if they owned the building.

The Panthers raised the necessary $6,000 dollars, and Fred was ready to go ahead.

"Can we close tomorrow?" he asked Jeff.

"I have to draw up a deed and get the owner to meet us and sign it. I've got court in the morning and the coalition's housing proposal to finish after that. How about—"

"How's that housing plan coming?" Fred asked, before Jeff could finish.

The Panthers were working with the Young Patriots and the Young Lords through the Rainbow Coalition to draft a proposal for more low- and moderate-income housing in the area. The Panthers knew that a safe place to live was an important human need. As the fourth point of the Ten-Point Program said, "We want decent housing, fit for shelter [for] human beings."[326] By buying their own building, by trying to provide more safe places for people to live, the Panthers were working to make their community a better place.

"I have to file our proposal with the Department of Urban Renewal on Thursday morning. It really looks good." Jeff tried to steer the conversation back to the building. "How's the boiler, have you checked that out?"

Jeff had no doubt that the Panthers knew everything about the building, right down to every bullet hole from when the police had tried to raid the building, three consecutive times.

Fred Hampton at a Free Breakfast program.

"You can see, we get plenty of heat," Fred said, smiling in his T-shirt. Jeff had taken off his suit jacket as soon as he came into the sweltering office. "Except when the police bullets give us too much ventilation."

"We put some cement in our walls when we opened the People's Law Office last August. Maybe you should try that," Jeff said.

Fred became serious. "It's the windows they shoot at, not the walls. But I'll check it out."[327]

Fred led Jeff out soon after. As they passed Panthers in the halls, Fred stopped to talk to them. "Show up on time for the breakfast program," he said. "Sell your quota of Panther papers; be at political education class on Monday and Wednesday nights." The whole time Fred was talking, with a seemingly effortless rhythm and flow. Jeff was in awe of Fred's energy and the way it affected and inspired those around him.[328]

Fred turned to Jeff. "I'll see you Thursday. Power to the people."

"Power to the people," Jeff replied.

But Jeff wouldn't see Fred on Thursday. No one else would, either.

Fred worked late into the night with his staff. When it got too late, everyone stayed over at his house. Fred went to sleep beside his fiancée, Deborah Johnson (Akua Njeri), who was eight months pregnant. There were other Panthers sleeping in the living room and throughout the house. Nineteen-year-old Mark Clark, a Panther leader from Peoria, Illinois, was the only one on security duty. He remained awake, at attention, with his shotgun in his hand.

At 4:30 a.m. Mark thought he heard a noise at the door. The night was bitter cold. As the wind whipped, Mark padded up to the door. He couldn't hear anything or anyone. "Who is it?" he asked. Within seconds, shots were fired. Mark died instantly. His shotgun fell to the ground, firing a single bullet into the air.[329]

Fourteen men burst through the door. During a routine raid, officers usually brought tear gas and equipment to make loud warning sounds. In this case, the officers were armed with a submachine gun, shotguns, and pistols. They rounded up the Panthers, four of whom were wounded by the gunshots, in the living room.[330]

When Deborah heard the noises, she tried to wake Fred—but he barely responded. Only once did he slowly lift his head, when the gunshots got even closer. Deborah moved, covering Fred with her body to try to protect him. The bed was shaking with the gunshots. Someone cried out that there was a pregnant woman in the house. When the officers saw Deborah, they took her out of the bedroom, her blue and white nightgown stretched tight over her pregnant stomach. Fred never moved.

Two officers headed back into the bedroom. Deborah could no longer see into the room, but she could hear the officers inside. "He's barely alive. He'll barely make it." Then she heard two shots ring out. After a pause she heard, "He's good and dead now."[331]

Fred Hampton, the Deputy Chairman of the Illinois Black Panther Party, was dead at age twenty-one.

The Panthers that survived were charged with attempted murder, unlawful use of weapons, and aggravated battery.[332] The Cook County State Attorney, Edward V. Hanrahan, maintained that the Panthers fired first and that the officers were defending themselves.

In his statement to the press Hanrahan said, "The immediate, violent, criminal reaction of the occupants in shooting at announced police officers emphasizes the extreme viciousness of the Black Panther Party. So does their refusal to cease firing at the police officers when urged to do so several times." In stark contrast, the surviving Panthers said that the officers came in shooting without announcing themselves.[333]

How could this have happened? And why were the two versions of the story so radically different?

233

Fred's chief of security, William O' Neal, was an FBI informant. He had already been working for the FBI when he showed up at the Illinois Panther office on opening day. O'Neal seemed eager and helpful and became Fred's bodyguard, charged with keeping Fred safe.

O' Neal gave the FBI a detailed map of Fred's apartment so they would know where Fred would be sleeping. Once inside, they wasted no time.

The evening of the murder, Fred's bodyguard slipped Seconal, which induces sleep, into Fred's drink. Fred was knocked unconscious, unable to defend himself. Within fifteen minutes of the raid, Fred was killed, shot in the head twice while he slept. For the information that led to Fred's and Mark's murders, O' Neal received a $300 bonus.[334]

The FBI had successfully prevented what they were afraid of: the "rise of a black messiah."[335] But the officers made a crucial mistake. When their job was done, they left with the door open. Neighbors and reporters came into the apartment. Pictures were taken.

The next day, the police raided Bobby Rush's apartment on the South Side. But he wasn't there.[336] Very much alive, Bobby went to Fred's apartment. He spoke to those lined up to view the inside. "This was no shootout," he said. "Nobody in the apartment had a chance to fire a gun and we can prove it by the fact that there are no bullet holes outside in the hallways or outside, just big gaping holes in Fred's bedroom where they fired on him."[337]

Bobby Rush insisted that it was the government who killed Fred Hampton. When the independent autopsy on Fred's body came back, it was clear that Seconal was in his system when he died. Fred didn't take drugs or drink alcohol. Bobby Rush insisted that Fred must have been drugged by someone who had infiltrated the Party and was working for the FBI.[338]

On May 8, 1970, State Attorney Hanrahan dropped the charges against the surviving Panthers, admitting that there wasn't any proof they had, in fact, shot at the officers.[339] A week later, a federal grand

Civil Rights activist Ralph Abernathy tours the apartment where police shot
and killed Fred Hampton and Mark Clark.

jury issued a detailed 250-page report concerning the incident.
The grand jury found that the police had fired at least eighty-two
bullets in Hampton's home. The Panthers fired only one shot.[340] That
bullet most likely came from Mark Clark's gun when he hit the floor
as he died.

There was a huge outpouring of support for the Panthers after the
murders. The *Chicago Daily Defender,* the largest Black newspaper in the country, asked, "Are blacks to be murdered for what they
believe or what they say? Is the slaying of leaders of the Black Panthers
across the nation a part of a national conspiracy to destroy their
organization?"[341]

235

Bobby Rush speaks following the murder of Fred Hampton and Mark Clark.

There were calls for a public investigation. The Northern Area Conference of the NAACP issued a statement condemning the actions of the police and calling for an investigation by President Richard Nixon and the U.S Attorney General, John Mitchell. "Although we may differ with the Black Panthers in political philosophies," read the statement, "WE ARE ALL BLACK PEOPLE and when these kinds of actions are held by our police departments, we feel that Black people are being threatened with the loss of our very lives."[342]

State Attorney Hanrahan released pictures of Fred's apartment to the *Chicago Tribune,* claiming that there was photographic proof of a gun battle. After *The New York Times* conducted independent research, it became clear that the images in the photographs were misrepresented. Nail heads in the wall were labeled as bullet holes. The inside of a bedroom door was labeled as the outside of a bathroom door, changing the perspective of the bullet entry.[343] The truth was twisted and changed, the reality distorted like a fun house mirror to try to cover up what had really occurred that night. But the people were not fooled.

In the wake of Fred's murder, a coalition of more than a hundred Black community groups formed in Chicago. As Reverend C. T. Vivian, the leader of this coalition, noted, "In recent days, the forces of power in Chicago have stepped up their campaign to oppress and repress black people . . . We see these atrocities not as individual or isolated incidents but as a calculated pattern, a conspiracy by the forces of power in this city to crush the black drive toward liberation."[344]

The New York Times interviewed one protester at a rally shortly after Fred's death. "'They came in and killed Fred Hampton,' she said in a soft, very even tone, 'and if they can do it to him, they can do it to any of us.'"[345] It wasn't just the Panthers who were in danger. It was every Black person in America.

Black activist Robert Williams took this sentiment even further. "It is not just a campaign against the Panthers," he said. "It is not a campaign just against Blacks. It is a campaign against all of those who oppose what is taking place in America today. It is against the resisters, those who resist imperialism, those who resist fascism, those who are non-conformists . . . What is happening to the Panthers is happening to all of us."[346]

LOS ANGELES RAID

On December 8, just four days after the murder of Fred Hampton, the Los Angeles Police Department conducted a 5:00 a.m. raid of the Los Angeles Chapter of the Panthers. In both the L.A. raid and the raid of Fred's home, the officers claimed they were looking for illegal weapons.[347] They also raided Panther Geronimo Pratt's home and the Toure Community Center. The National Committee had recently placed Geronimo in charge of the Southern California Chapter of the Party.[348]

At Geronimo's home, the officers knocked down the door and began to shoot. They arrested everyone inside. This included Geronimo and his wife, Saundra; Bunchy Carter's widow, Evon Carter; and Evon's two children, Michelle, who was eight years old, and Osceola, who was only eight months old. At the community center, the officers also came in shooting and arrested all the Panthers inside.[349]

At the L.A. headquarters, the Panthers were prepared for an attack. A few weeks earlier, seventy-five officers had surrounded the building while the Panthers were meeting inside. There were sharpshooters on the roofs and police vans on the corners. In response, the Panthers called the media. When the reporters and the cameras, as well as the local residents, showed up, the officers left.[350]

After this event, the Panthers placed sandbags around the office, creating a type of fortress. They dug tunnels in the basement, filling the sandbags with the dirt. They also stacked tables and chairs against the door. Geronimo was the one that oversaw the fortification. "We stuffed sandbags in the panels behind our walls," he said, "below our ceilings, up under our roof. We put up *tons* of dirt. It was all defensive structure. No bullet was gonna penetrate three-foot walls."[351]

These raids of Panther offices were not new. In 1969, after Richard Nixon took office, there were countless raids of Panther offices throughout the country. Some locations, like the Chicago Panthers, were even targeted multiple times. These raids also took place in people's homes. When the Panther 21 were arrested, the police raided five private residences.

When Eldridge and Kathleen were still in the United States, the police raided their home. They experienced one of the earliest targeted raids and were unable to protect themselves, since they were unarmed at the time. That was when Huey issued the now-all-important Executive Mandate #3. Since then, all Black Panthers were ordered to arm themselves in self-defense, in case of unlawful entrance by the police. This meant that every time a raid occurred, both sides would have deadly weapons, escalating an already dangerous situation.

Unlike the other raids, however, the LAPD officers on December 8 were part of the very first SWAT team. These officers were dressed and prepared for war. They wore black jumpsuits and black boots. Their heads were covered. They wore gas masks and carried not only rifles but also belts full of ammunition strung around their shoulders. The SWAT team forced residents near the Panther office out of their homes so that the officers could use those buildings as cover.[352] They cordoned off the area to try to keep back onlookers.

The SWAT team borrowed vehicles from the National Guard and used these and armored cars to approach the Panther office. They burst through the front door, but the Panthers began shooting and drove them back. Three officers fell and were dragged away as the team retreated.[353] The officers fired 5,000 rounds of ammunition into the Black Panther office. They even went so far as to drop dynamite by helicopter on the roof. But they were unable to break through again.

Thick clouds of smoke and the scent of gunpowder filled the air. The Panthers fought back, throwing Molotov cocktails and adjusting their position to avoid the SWAT team's shots. Tommie Williams

239

accidentally moved her leg into a beam of light, and all too soon she was shot.[354] The walls became riddled with bullets, letting the early morning light in. Many of the Panthers were shot and wounded. But they were ready for this fight. It was what they had trained for and what they believed in: armed self-defense against an unjust attack by the police.

Gil Parker described the sound of the gunfire as music to his ears.[355] It was the perfect soundtrack to the story of his life as a Panther. It wasn't that these individuals were unafraid. It was that they all truly felt they had something worth fighting for. Wayne Pharr explained, "I felt free. I felt absolutely free . . . I was making my own rules. You couldn't get in. I couldn't get out. But in my space, I was the key. In that little space I had, I was the king."[356]

At one point a breeze blew in, clearing the air. The officers kept trying to change positions to gain the upper hand. But they were unsuccessful. They couldn't break into the building. As a result, they requested that their superiors let them use a grenade launcher, normally used only by members of the army. The Pentagon soon cleared the request and the fighting continued.[357]

After fighting for almost five hours, and running low on ammunition, the Panthers decided to surrender. Renee "Peaches" Moore came outside first. The men had talked it out for almost half an hour, trying to decide whether to go outside. Finally, Peaches said that she would go.[358]

Peaches's yellow dress was torn and stained with blood. In her hand she held a white flag, fluttering in the breeze. The rest of the Panthers filed out after her. They were almost all teenagers, with three in their early twenties. They had surrendered now, but they didn't intend to for long. As Peaches told the reporters, "We gave up because it's not the right time. We will fight again when the odds are more in our favor."[359]

During the Los Angeles raid, the Panthers experienced a feeling of true freedom, even while being violently attacked. When they surrendered, they didn't see it as giving up. Instead, they saw it as just biding their time for another opportunity to continue the struggle.

On Thursday, December 11, 4,000 people filled the area around Los Angeles City Hall to protest the raid. The majority of those in attendance were young Black people. In their hands they held signs that said, "Stop Mass Murder," "Stop Panther Killing," "End Political Repression," and "Free All Political Prisoners." Onstage were members of the NAACP, more mainstream Black supporters, and the Panthers themselves. As Elaine Brown said to those gathered, "These young warriors . . . established a lesson that

A protest following the SWAT raid of the LA office.

should never be forgotten—the power really does belong to the people."[360]

▲

By the end of 1969, the U.S. government had openly declared war on the Black Panther Party. The Panthers as a whole were experiencing oppression and state repression, but they continued to fight and remain resilient. In the face of violence and racism, the Panthers forged on, lifted up by their work and their commonly held goal: freedom.

It wasn't just about the work the Panthers were doing, though. It was about how the work imbued the members with power and purpose. The Party was a source of inspiration, a source of hope, and a source of meaning for its members. And for many, it was all-encompassing. As Panther Bobby McCall said, "I had totally dedicated myself to this organization. Regardless of what happened internally, I knew this was what I wanted to do, this was who I wanted to be, this was what I wanted my life to be about: uplifting the black community by any means necessary no matter what it took."[361]

David Hilliard and family.

CHAPTER 19

DAVID SPEAKS
WHO WE ARE

DAVID SPEAKS

In August 1969, Huey Newton's lifelong friend David Hilliard became the head of the Party. The youngest of twelve children, David was born in Rockville, Alabama, on May 15, 1942. He moved to Oakland when he was eleven years old, met Huey in elementary school, and they were friends ever since.[362]

David's first loyalty was to Huey. He believed in their friendship and he believed in Huey. "Huey became my friend when I was eleven. We've stayed by each other's side more or less ever since," wrote David. "But though I loved Huey, I was never fully comfortable with him; he was so extreme—talking at you, checking you out—that I was often on edge."[363] Still, David stuck with Huey. As Huey became more involved with the Black Panther Party, so did David.

When Huey went away to prison, David accepted the leadership of others, like Eldridge Cleaver and Bobby Seale. Then Eldridge went into exile in Algeria, where he formed the Intercommunal Section of the Party. When Bobby went away to stand trial as a part of the Chicago Eight, the Party needed a new leader.

David saw the Party like a big extended family, in line with what he experienced growing up in the rural South.[364] To this end, he became a major force in shifting focus away from the Party's armed tactics and toward the community programs and initiatives. These were the programs that gained the Party even more support from the broader community. They were also popular among many of the Panthers, who went into their communities, saw what needed to be done, and took steps to do it.

It was under David's leadership that the newly formed community programs flourished. And the FBI took notice. The more main-stream support and the more support from the broader Black community the Party received, the more the FBI saw them as an even greater threat. But even as the state began to repress the Party with greater force, the Party gained more allies and attention.

Some members, however, believed that these programs were at odds with what the Party was really about—armed self-defense and armed revolution that would overthrow the government and fight for Black liberation. Even though all of the members were Black Panthers, not everyone agreed on what this should mean. David did what he could to acknowledge and incorporate the different facets of the Party, but when he led the group further in the direction of the community programs, he began to alienate some members.

For example, Eldridge and the Intercommunal Section never wavered in their commitment to armed struggle and revolution. From Algeria, Eldridge became increasingly frustrated with the way the Party was headed in the United States. He could only hope that someone would take over from David and move the Party back in the right direction.

There were tensions, too, coming from outside the Party. On November 15, 1969, David spoke to over 100,000 protesters in Golden Gate Park in San Francisco. It was a mobilization rally against the Vietnam War. The crowd was diverse, with some waving their American flags. Everyone had a hope and a wish for peace.

David waited a long time to step up to the platform. The day was cold and raining, with gray skies. When David looked out over the audience, the applause was polite and brief. He took a breath and began with what he was supposed to say. But soon he left those words behind, letting his emotions guide him. He called the American flags symbols of fascism, which upset many. As his emotions rose, he began to shout over the crowd, who were growing more and more upset. Digging in, he denounced the president. That might have worked in a different setting, but before this crowd, his words fell flat. Still, David pushed on, going even further. "We will kill Richard Nixon . . . We will kill [anyone] that stands in the way of our freedom!"

He let his anger fly, even though he knew it was doing more harm than good. By this time he had said too much. The crowd was booing him and chanting "Peace! Peace! Peace!" David tried to continue, then he tried to join in the chants of peace, but he was eventually booed off the stage.[365]

The times were changing. The Party had helped to build this movement against the war in Vietnam, but now it was made up of many

247

more people, some of whom disagreed with the Panthers' methods and what the Panthers stood for. Many of these newer members might have heard only of the armed self-defense politics of the Party, and not of their community programs, or the Ten-Point Program, or any number of other aspects of the Black Panther Party.

As he left the podium, David felt "a sad, exhausted anger." He didn't want to have to fight any longer for public approval. He felt the weight of all that he had worked for, all the Panthers fought for, beginning to shift. Under David's leadership the Party had expanded their reach to include much more than just armed self-defense. But that was all many people in the public knew about the Panthers and this was the kind of rhetoric that David had fallen back on in his speech. "They don't want reconciliation," he thought as he walked away. "What I stand for scares these people."[366] David admitted that he wasn't sure he could handle all of the responsibility. His insecurity fed his anger, and, in this instance, it got the better of him.

Two weeks later, as David and Brenda Presley were driving toward the Bay Bridge, a group of cars came out of nowhere. Police officers jumped out, armed and running toward them. David knew this was coming. The Panthers' lawyer, Charles Garry, had warned him.

The officers told David he was under arrest. "What for?" he asked, knowing what they would say.

"You've gone too far," came the reply. "You've threatened the life of the president." They took David and Brenda into custody. In the car the FBI agent turned to Brenda. They tried again to appeal to her 'niceness.' "How'd you get mixed up in this?" the agent asked. "You're a nice girl."

"You seem like a nice guy," she replied, unfazed. "How'd you?"[367]

WHO WE ARE

The question of how to change in response to the times, of how to respond in the face of government repression, was not limited to the

Black Panther Party. Each group engaged in the revolutionary struggle at this moment had to make a decision.

The rhetoric of armed self-defense had gained the Party notoriety. But it had also resulted in incarceration and death. Most of the leaders in both the New York and Los Angeles Chapters were locked away. Lil' Bobby, John, Bunchy, Fred, and Mark were all dead. Executive Mandate #3, ordering all Panthers to keep weapons in their homes, escalated every interaction with a police officer.

From Algiers, Eldridge still argued for armed self-defense. Geronimo, the Panther 21, and others agreed with him. But there was a split beginning in the Party. Should their initial strategy, of armed self-defense, remain the central and most important one? Or should the Party move in other directions, like their community survival programs?

In reality, the notion of a violent, perpetually armed Panther was at odds with what most rank-and-file Party members did day in and day out. Many of the Panthers were involved in the work of the *Black Panther* newspaper or the community programs in their area. They weren't waging armed warfare in the street at all hours of the day. Unfortunately, this sensational image was all that so many people knew of the Panthers. It was also a decidedly masculine image, or as Panther Tracye Matthews called it, the Black Panther Party's "masculine public identity."[368]

Women were very often cut out of the picture. But by 1969, around 65% of the people in the Party were women.[369] Women founded many of the new branches and in many cases rose to leadership positions.[370] The women of the Party were just as essential to the work of revolution as their male counterparts. As Black actor Danny Glover said, "Those women in the Black Panther Party, you held it all together. The men—there was a lot of chaos going on. Things were wild. But it was the women who held it all together."[371] Or as Panther Frankye Malika Adams said, "Women ran [the Black Panther Party] pretty much."[372]

But all too often, the revolutionary standard was cast as male. As Black activist and educator Professor Angela Davis wrote, "Even

249

those of us who were women did not know how to develop ways of being revolutionaries that were not informed by masculine definitions of the revolutionary. The revolutionaries were male. The women who became revolutionaries had to make themselves in those images."[373]

Kathleen was often asked, "'What is the woman's role in the Black Panther Party?'" She disliked the question and usually gave a short, simple answer. "'It's the same as men.'" But when she sat with the question and picked it apart, she realized that the deeper implication was what troubled her so much. "The assumption held that being part of a revolutionary movement was in conflict with what the questioner had been socialized to believe was appropriate conduct for a woman. The convoluted concept never entered my head, although I am certain it was far more widely accepted than I ever realized."[374]

In July 1969, Eldridge published a call to end sexism in the Black Panther Party. "The incarceration and the suffering of Sister Ericka should be a stinging rebuke to all manifestations of male chauvinism within our ranks," he wrote. "That we must purge our ranks and our hearts, and our minds, and our understanding of any chauvinism, chauvinistic behavior of disrespectful behavior toward women. That we must too recognize that a woman can be just as revolutionary as a man and that she has equal stature, that, along with men, and that we cannot prejudice her in any manner, that we cannot relegate her to an inferior position. That we have to recognize our woman as our equals."[375]

This from the same person who, just a year earlier, published *Soul on Ice.* In the book, Eldridge admitted that he had committed violent sexual acts against White women, as a way of "getting revenge" against White men and "the white man's law." Not only this, but he had practiced on Black women first. "To refine my technique and *modus operandi,* I started out by practicing on black girls in the ghetto . . . and when I considered myself smooth enough, I crossed the tracks and sought out white prey." In the end Eldridge realized that he had "gone astray—astray not so much from the white man's law as from being human, civilized." In prison, in an attempt to save himself, Eldridge turned to writing.[376]

The ideas and practices of the creators of a movement shape that movement. In the Black Panther Party, everyone was not always on the same page when it came to gender equality. "I do not remember our ever constituting any value that said that a revolutionary must say offensive things . . . or that a revolutionary should make sure that women do not speak out about their own particular kind of oppression," wrote Huey. "As a matter of fact, it is just the opposite: we say that we recognize the woman's right to be free."[377] Huey made this statement in August 1970. What he said represented a forward-thinking position, one that expressed a desire for equality and unity. But it was also just a statement. While it was true that there had never been an explicit policy that discriminated against certain people, the day-to-day practice, the lived realities of Party members, was another matter.

JoNina Abron, who was at one time the editor of the *Black Panther,* vividly remembered the excitement of joining the Party. Then she was faced with the reality. "Throughout the 29 years of my life I have experienced the dual pain of being a Black woman in America," she said. "When I joined the Party five years ago, I was thrilled about becoming part of an organization that believes in the equality of men and women. However, I have since learned that my comrades and I have yet to overcome many of our backward ideas."[378]

Still, many of the members worked to change these ideas. As Bobby Seale wrote, "When Eldridge and Huey and the Party as a whole move to get rid of male chauvinism, we're moving on that principle of absolute equality between male and female: because male chauvinism is related to the very class nature of this society as it exists today."[379]

Historically, women and Black people have been disenfranchised and exploited so that others can come out on top. "The very nature of the capitalist system is to exploit and enslave people, all people," wrote Bobby. "A lot of black nationalist organizations have the idea of relegating women to the role of serving their men and they relate this to black manhood. But a real manhood is based on humanism and it's not based on *any* form of oppression."[380] Whether that was sexism, racism, classism, or any form of oppression.

Angela Davis

One approach to equality between women and men might be to try to change the behaviors of people to eliminate forces like racism. But the Black Panthers and others argued that trying to educate and change a person's behavior wasn't enough. This would be like putting a bandage on a festering wound. The Panthers believed that, instead, revolutionaries must also attack the root cause. For the Panthers, the root cause was imperialism, capitalism, and the Establishment.

Echoing a widespread belief, Fred Hampton famously said that "racism is a by-product of capitalism."[381] Fred and others in the Party believed that, in order to get rid of racism, the system that created and upheld it had to be eliminated. They argued that it would be impossible to eradicate racism without overthrowing capitalism. As Bobby Seale simply put it, "It is a class struggle."[382]

Why then, were certain images of the Party popularized while others were not? Why didn't most people know about the theory behind their practice? Or that women were over half of the Party's membership at its height? Why weren't the survival programs more well known? It was true that the first few members were men and that the initial focus was armed self-defense. But the reality was always more nuanced than that.

As Kathleen Cleaver pointed out, the popular ideas about the Party came down to who controlled the mainstream media. Who were the writers and the photographers? Who decided what was printed in the paper, played on the radio, and shown on television? What was their perspective and their aim? "Is it possible," she asked, "that the reality of what was actually going on day to day in the Black Panther Party was far less newsworthy and provided no justification for the campaign of destruction that the intelligence agencies and the police were waging against us? Could it be that the images and stories of the Black Panthers that you've seen and heard were geared to something other than conveying what was actually going on?"[383]

The popular images of the Party weren't purely based in reality. And they weren't the whole truth. They were small slices of a diverse and complicated organization. The members of the Party had a wide range of life experiences within and outside the Party. What was seen by the general public was just a tiny, curated portion. At times, these images were even distortions, like the mislabeling of bullet holes in Fred Hampton's apartment.

This was one of the reasons that the *Black Panther* newspaper was so important. It was a vehicle for the Panthers to represent themselves and speak for themselves, rather than relying on their portrayal in the mainstream media. It was also a way for the various chapters to be connected, since there was only one paper, printed through the National Headquarters in Oakland. It was a way for people, not just those in the Party but others too, to hear about what was going on throughout the country through the eyes of the Panthers.

As Huey wrote, "For years the Establishment media presented a sensational picture of us, emphasizing violence and weapons. Colossal events like Sacramento, the *Ramparts* confrontation with the police, the shoot-out of April 6, 1968, were distorted and their significance never understood or analyzed. Furthermore, our ten-point program was ignored and our plans for survival overlooked. The Black Panthers were identified with the gun."[384]

This image was an oversimplification, reducing the Panthers to just one aspect of their evolving program and history. All too often, the Panthers as a whole were represented by the superficial image that focused on the guns without the theory and the politics or on their other programs and strategies. As Panther Wayne Pharr said, "Everybody wanted this gun toting image of the big bad Black Shaft guy jumping through the window and you know, beating everybody up. I refute that. That's the image that was put up on us. I'm not Shaft. You know, as a Black man, that's all I am. I'm just a Black man."[385]

Above all, the women and men of the Black Panther Party wanted to be seen as human beings. They were fighting for human rights—theirs and those of other oppressed peoples. These were rights that had been denied Black people from the very start, when slavery in the United States began, over 400 years ago.

The Black Panther Party wasn't just about armed self-defense. It wasn't just about black berets and leather jackets. It was about revolutionary, anti-imperialist ideas. It was about demanding that Black people be seen as people. It was about standing up to police brutality. It was about feeding young children and clothing people of all ages, providing free medical care and a quality education. It was about the Panthers taking their place in the long Black freedom struggle.

Allies watch an Eldridge Cleaver speech on the UC Berkeley campus. Most large Panther rallies featured many non-Black as well as Black supporters.

CHAPTER 20

DIVERSE SUPPORT

DIVERSE SUPPORT

As 1969 led into 1970, the Party's growth continued. People were inspired by Huey's courage and Bobby's tenacity, by the community programs, by the examples of Fred, David, Ericka, and Elaine. They were excited about the international wing of the Party with Eldridge and Kathleen. They were not deterred by the efforts of the U.S. government to repress the Party. Even as the repression increased—and tensions arose between different viewpoints within the group—the Party continued to grow.

Even more new chapters sprouted up throughout the United States. So too did groups in other communities who drew inspiration from the Panthers, like the Puerto Rican Young Lords, the Latinx Los Siete de la Raza, the Chicanx Brown Berets, and the Asian American Red Guard. There were also countless allies and supporters within and outside of the Black community. People across the United States, around the world, were looking toward the Panthers as a model, as the true vanguard of the revolution.

But the Party was not monolithic. Each branch had a different flair and flavor, depending on the pressing needs and unique challenges of its area. The individuals who made up the branch also had an important effect on its character.

Kathleen put it this way, "The Panthers were almost like a network of black revolutionaries all calling themselves the Black Panthers, but when you say 'national organization' you imply a lot more cohesion and identity than in fact it had . . . If you go into every chapter nationwide that sprung up, the way the party was structured comes out of some 'preexisting set of local relationships.' "[386]

In the summer of 1969, the Black Panther Party hosted the United Front Against Fascism Conference. Out of the conference, the Party decided to form National Committees to Combat Fascism (NCCF). These groups would operate under the larger organization of the Black Panther Party. But, unlike in the Party chapters, the members did not have to be Black people. This was an important step in making even more space for allies, like the Students for a Democratic Society (SDS).

As SDS said, "The sharpest struggles in the world today are those of the oppressed nations against imperialism and for national liberation. Within this country the sharpest struggle is that of the black colony for its liberation; it is a struggle which by its very nature is anti-imperialist and increasingly anti-capitalist . . . Within the black liberation movement the vanguard force is the Black Panther Party . . . We must keep in mind that the Black Panther Party is not fighting black people's struggles only but is in fact the vanguard in our common struggles against capitalism and imperialism."[387] The

A SDS rally in support of Bobby Seale and the Chicago Eight.

NCCFs allowed people like those in SDS to show their support in an even more serious way, which helped the influence of the Party to grow and spread even further.

Bobby Seale often reiterated the idea that "Black racism is just as bad and dangerous as White racism."[388] The Black Panther Party was always open to incorporating different types of people into the struggle. In addition, the Party was always looking for allies within and outside of the Black community. Through the NCCFs more people could ally with the cause. By April 1970, there were National Committees to Combat Fascism operating in eighteen cities across the United States.[389]

On December 18, 1969, five students at Yale University in New Haven interrupted a large lecture class. They stood up and said the names of murdered members of the Black Panther Party. These students were expelled.[390] Months later, on April 21, 1970, Kenneth Mills, a Black assistant professor at the school, told the students that classes should no longer be their top priority. They were living in a racist country that was exploiting Black people, and it was time to recognize this and "close down" the university as a

A May Day rally at Yale University.

show of solidarity. In response his audience began to cheer, raising their fists. Their voices rose, strong and clear, into the air. "Strike! Strike! Strike!"

The next day, April 22, the students at Yale went on strike for the first time in the history of the university. The Black Panther Defense Committee, formed to free Panthers imprisoned in New Haven, planned for a nonviolent May Day protest on May 1, with growing support for their movement against oppression domestically and the war abroad.

Then, on April 30, President Nixon gave the go-ahead for the United States to invade Cambodia, a neighboring nation to Vietnam. For many in the nation, this was devastating news. Nixon had promised to decrease the draft, and many antiwar activists believed that the war in Vietnam would soon come to an end. But this action was an escalation, not a deescalation.

The president had some words to say about student activists too. On the front page of *The New York Times,* beside the coverage of the May Day protest, the president was quoted: "You see these bums, you know, blowing up the campuses. Listen, the boys that are on the college campuses today are the luckiest people in the world, going to the greatest universities in the world and here they are burning books and storming around."[391] Nixon painted a picture of young people who didn't know how good they had it. The implication was that rather than engaging in activism, rather than working for what they saw as positive change, these young people should be happy and grateful. They should sit down, not stand up. Rather than raising their voices, they should stay quiet and complacent, accepting the world just as it was.

Instead, 2,000 supporters of the Black Panther Party filed into Dwight Hall on the Yale campus. On May Day, Yale students came out in support of the Black Panther Party. They formed the National Student Strike Committee and discussed ways to take action not just locally, but across the United States. In the afternoon, Tom Hayden, of Students for a Democratic Society (SDS) and the Chicago Eight, called for a nationwide student strike. Students were asked to boycott classes until three demands were met. These were published in *The New York Times*:

> The United States must end its "systematic oppression" of all political dissidents, such as Bobby Seale and all other Black Panthers.

> The United States must cease "aggression" in Vietnam, Laos and Cambodia and unilaterally and immediately withdraw its force.

> Universities must end their "complicity" in war by ending war-related research and eliminating Reserve Officer Training Corps [ROTC] activities.[392]

Young people had had enough of war and violence. There was a call for a nationwide student strike against the war. Many of these students, when asked, agreed that the war in Vietnam was imperialist and that it was impossible for a member of the Black Panther Party to have a fair trial in the United States.[393] By May 4, student activists across the country had gone on strike.[394]

A protest against the Vietnam War and in support of Eldridge Cleaver, Chicago.

At Kent State University in Ohio, activists agitated in solidarity with the Panthers and with SDS against the war in Vietnam.[395] When the protests began to escalate, the mayor of the city called in the Ohio National Guard. In response, the Reserve Officers' Training Corps building was burned to the ground. On May 3, students staged a protest by sitting down in the middle of an intersection. The National Guard came toward them with bayonets, charging through those sitting and arresting many. That night sixty-nine students were arrested for protesting.

Then, on May 4, there was a rally. The National Guardsmen tried to disperse the crowd by firing tear gas. The canisters that didn't break open were thrown back by the protesters, along with other projectiles like bricks and rocks. The students were screaming and yelling and the situation rapidly escalated. Suddenly, the guardsmen opened fire into the crowd. Sixty-one shots were fired.

The shooting took just thirteen seconds. For each second, a young person was shot. But when the smoke cleared, it was clear that they weren't just wounded. Four of the students were killed.[396]

Across the country even more students began to strike. They protested the invasion of Cambodia, the continued war in Vietnam, the treatment of the Black Panthers, and the events at Kent State. The country had never seen a mass student protest like this. In the month of May, over 4 million students participated in protests. Five hundred and thirty-six college campuses were completely shut down by the over 1 million students who went on strike.[397] As a teacher in the Panthers' liberation schools said, "Youth makes revolution."[398] In this case the youth used their power to send a message. They wanted to live in a world without war, a world free of racism and violence. These students took a stand for freedom for all people. They rose up in support of personal and global liberation.

263

University of Washington students and faculty block
a highway in protest, May 5, 1970.

CHAPTER 21

HUEY'S RELEASE
AN EMERGING SPLIT

HUEY'S RELEASE

Finally, on August 5, 1970, came the moment that the Party and its supporters had been waiting for. For so long, they had braced themselves for the very real possibility that Huey would be sentenced to death. Instead, that day, he was released on bail.

Huey would walk the streets again, and now, most believed that he would lead the Party in the direction it should go. Change was in the air and the revolution seemed even closer.

But the transition wouldn't be easy. Huey had been away for years, and the Party was not what it had been before he went to prison. What began as a small local organization, with a membership of only a handful of people, was now a large, influential, "network of black revolutionaries" and their allies.

"What is [Huey's] political role going to be?" wondered David. "Huey has always said he's not the figure in Eldridge's poster. But Huey's now established as a movement leader, proven in both action and thought, a thinker and a doer who has changed history. Except that Huey doesn't picture himself a leader. He's not a speaker like Fred or Bobby. He's Huey."[399] David wasn't sure what Huey's next moves would be.

Eldridge, however, thought he had the answer. Huey would step in and reenergize the Party, taking it back to what he saw as its roots.

When he heard the news of Huey's release, Eldridge grew excited. He could feel the energy all the way in Algiers. Eldridge trusted that with Huey back in the lead, the Party would go in the direction that he believed it should: moving more toward armed self-defense and even guerrilla warfare if necessary. David had taken the Party in the direction of community programs, trying to attract allies and keep more mainstream supporters happy. But now David would step down and hand the Party back to Huey. Huey could return to the initial strategy and things would go back to the way they ought to be.

There were different ideas of what Huey could accomplish now that he was out of prison. For now, they would rally around their excitement at his release. But very soon, much would be expected of Huey. There would be conflicting opinions and ideas about where the Party should focus its energies. Huey would have to adjust to the realities of a new political world. And he would have to rise to the occasion.

Huey's bail was $50,000, but the Party came up with it. It was the least they could do for the man who had started the movement.

Now, for the first time in twenty-two months, Huey was in a car. Officers were transporting him from the California Men's Penal Colony in San Luis Obispo, California, to Oakland. It was a disorienting experience, especially after spending half a year in solitary confinement.

As the officer drove through the night and into the early morning, there were a few people on the street. Huey was struck by how bright and colorful their clothing was. "I could not get a clear impression of any one thing," he remembered, "everything tended to blur and become indistinct. The whole experience was devastating. Where I had been for thirty-three months everyone wore the same clothes, did the same things, and went to the same place every day."[400]

As Huey looked out from the backseat of the car, he was extremely aware of the simple things, like other cars stopping at stoplights and people walking freely in the street. All of it was an assault on his senses. He did his best to stay calm. He didn't want to show how unsettled he was, how nervous this all was making him.[401] Back home in Oakland, Huey was imprisoned once again, waiting on his bail hearing.[402]

On the day of his release, Huey tried to make his way to the elevator from the courthouse with his brothers Walter Jr. and Melvin, David Hilliard, Geronimo Pratt, and a few other Panthers. Reporters were crowding around, lunging toward them. Huey's freedom was close, but the elevator was too packed and it stalled on the fourth floor. The men got out and took the stairs the rest of the way.

The building's door opened on a beautiful sunny day, with blue skies for miles. Lake Merritt sparkled. All Huey could see was the light and the thousands of people gathered to receive him. Once the crowd saw him, they began to shout.

Huey had dreamed of this moment over and over again, hoping that it would happen, even when he knew he might never be released. Now, it was here. His freedom had finally come. "It was a bright, blue-sky day, just the kind of day I had wanted," he remembered. "Looking ahead, I could see thousands of beautiful people and a sea of hands, all of them waving. When I gave them the power sign, the hands shot up in reply and everyone started to cheer. God, it was good."[403]

Huey's sisters rushed up to him, hugging him close. The sun warmed his face, and the air had never been sweeter, even as the people surrounded him. He hardly had any room to breathe as the crush of people carried him, lifting him off his feet. Still, he gave in to the sense of floating, the euphoria, the rising tide of emotion that couldn't be contained.

Eventually, they got to their waiting car, but it was impossible to move with so many people around. Huey climbed on top of the car, unable to stop smiling.

On one side was David, Huey's lifelong friend and Chief of Staff. His long black trench coat swept the top of the hot car, his eyes hidden behind sunglasses. David reached his arms out to the crowd, full of pride, showing that, yes, his friend Huey was finally free.

Geronimo stood beside them, watching. His job was to keep Huey safe. Behind his black sunglasses his eyes surveyed the crowd; his dark hat and jacket absorbed the day's sunlight.[404]

As the people chanted and the sun beat down, Huey started to sweat. The reality of his release began to set in. Suddenly, he felt completely free. Nothing could hold him back now. Jubilant, he took his shirt off, smiling, waving, letting the excitement of the crowd and his newfound freedom wash over him like a healing, cleansing wave. His life was about to start again.

Huey opened his mouth to speak. He could tell that the people wanted it. He was ready to hold a rally on the spot, to give the speech to end all speeches. But now that he was higher up, he could see the police beginning to encircle the group. They had clubs and shields; their helmets were in place. The police were set up to stop a riot. This was not how Huey wanted his release to end. All that beauty and freedom, squashed.

Huey lied, telling the people that the rally would happen at Lil' Bobby Hutton Memorial Park. People began racing for their own cars, ready to hear Huey speak. Huey sent a Panther ahead to talk to the people when they got there, telling them that it wasn't safe for Huey to appear and the rally would have to happen some other time. It was all too likely that Huey would be shot out in the open, so soon after his release.[405]

Instead, Huey went to see his mother in the hospital. She didn't even know he had been released. He made sure to change out of his prison clothes before he saw her. Their reunion was full of joy. His reunion with his father was more emotional. Melvin began to cry. He admitted to his son that he hadn't thought he would live long enough to see Huey's release.[406]

For Huey, reintegration into society didn't come easily. "During the first few days out of jail, I wondered when reality would come again—in relation to myself, to the world around me, to all that was happening to me. I had literally forgotten how to live outside."[407] He had to readjust to the simple, everyday things that most people took for granted. There were too many sounds and too much light and too much movement all the time. People were talking and phones were ringing and the television was blaring and the radio was constantly announcing the latest news. Even the ring of the doorbell felt alien to Huey. "Ordinary life seemed hectic and chaotic, and quite overwhelming," he admitted. "I even had to figure out what to eat and what time I was going to bed. In prison, all this had been decided for me."[408] It was clear. Huey had to figure out how to live again as a free man.

Still, even just walking down the street now was a beautiful revelation. Huey was recognized, and the people greeted him with love, with joy and pride. He was their Huey. He was the Black Panther

Party's Minister of Defense, Huey P. Newton. "Walking through the streets was an indescribable experience, the closest I have ever felt to being truly free," he wrote, "with people walking by, recognizing me, and waving."[409] For Huey, being able to get out again into the community, to walk and talk and organize with the people, meant everything.

But, of course, it was only a certain kind of freedom. He was still a Panther. He was still a Black man in America. There wouldn't be true freedom until all the people were free.

"Although people received me warmly, I was at first a symbol. Our relationship had changed. There was now an element of hero worship that had not existed before I got busted."[410] Even though Huey hoped that this dynamic would shift eventually, it could never fully return to what it had been before. Kathleen and Eldridge had created something with the "Free Huey!" movement that couldn't be undone, even once Huey was released. People still saw him as an image, as the leader on the throne. He had become a myth. And now, what would happen?

Once Huey was released, he was pressured to appear on talk shows and to attend speaking engagements. He was even approached by Hollywood, with a letter saying that he had "star quality." But this was not Huey's goal. He had never sought fame. He didn't want to be the one held up as the star, speaking in front of huge crowds. As he wrote, "The task is to transform society; only people can do that— not heroes, not celebrities, not stars. A star's place is in Hollywood; the revolutionary's place is in the community with the people. A studio is a place where fiction is made, but the Black Panther Party is out to create nonfiction. We are making revolution."[411]

But the reality wasn't what people expected. They wanted someone that Huey was not. When they constructed the "Free Huey!" movement, the Panthers had created a godlike image. Now, they had just a man, one who was complicated and fallible. A hothead, sure, but also a person who in some ways was sensitive, shy, and withdrawn. Huey never wanted to be the one giving all the speeches. He was a thinker, an intellectual, who, while he was never afraid of a fight, liked to bury his head in theory and books.

The jubilation over Huey's release proved to be short-lived. Many of the Panthers had joined while he was incarcerated. They had only a notion of Huey, not an experience of the real person. They had rallied behind the movement without having met the man.

But David had known Huey before all of this. They were friends first. That's what was important to David. What David rallied around. What he prioritized.

After Huey's release, David and Huey would sit on the bed in the mornings, side by side, like they'd done ever since they were kids. They talked about the Party, how it had changed, and how things worked now.[412]

But it wasn't just the Party that had changed.

One weekend, Huey, David, Melvin, and his wife went out to Santa Cruz to spend time in a cabin near the redwood forest. The ground in the mornings was wet, smelling like soil and fallen needles. Huey and David would walk and talk, surrounded by the giant trees, older than their movement, older than all the people and conditions that surrounded them.

One afternoon they came inside. They started listening to Tchaikovsky's *Pathétique* Symphony.

"Huey, I didn't know you liked classical music," said David.

"Yeah. Don't you remember Melvin used to teach me piano?" said Huey.

David settled down into the majestic, soaring notes, into the moments of great sadness and great power. Sitting there alone with Huey, the notes of Tchaikovsky's final symphony dancing around them, David felt happy and at peace. He and Huey were picking up where they had left off. Rekindling their friendship, spending time together the way they used to. It felt good. It felt right.

"You know, David, I don't know you anymore."

David paused a moment. "What are you talking about?"

"I don't know you," Huey repeated. He stared into David's eyes, a kind of primal challenge.

"I'm David," David responded simply. Outside the trees stood still, silent, tall. Witnessing.

"Are you? Because you don't act like David. You act like Eldridge. When I sit here and listen to you, I might as well turn on Eldridge. Everything you do is Eldridge. I don't know who you are. You're an impersonator. You're not authentic. You're not David anymore."[413]

David was still, stunned by his friend's words. A moment ago, he had felt wrapped in their friendship, safe in the cabin in the woods. Now Huey was accusing David of behaving like Eldridge.

But David was unwilling to choose between Huey and Eldridge. He respected and revered them both. "Huey has frequently expressed his disapproval of Eldridge," wrote David, "but what he's saying now is more than a criticism of a style: it's an accusation of betrayal. But how can I betray Huey by identifying with someone who has done so much to get him free?"[414] David was trapped, facing an impossible decision.

The next morning David and Huey took another walk. The air still smelled fresh and inviting, wet with fog and dew. David was tired all the time. He couldn't sleep, and his stomach hurt from the moment he woke up until whatever small shred of sleep might come for him. He couldn't go on any longer. Especially now that he'd lost Huey's trust and respect.

David decided that he had to leave the Party. It was the only way. "I think you're right," David began. "I need time. I want to get out.

275

I'm tired. I did this out of friendship and now you're out so I can get out too."[415]

But Huey didn't agree. He asked David to stay, again and again. And David, like so many other people, could never go against Huey. Huey needed David—so David would stay.

AN EMERGING SPLIT

When Huey first came out of prison, he still supported not just armed self-defense, but armed revolution as well. Huey looked at the community programs as more of an emergency measure—and not the main substance of the revolution. He wrote, "During a flood the raft is a life-saving device, but it is only a means of getting to a higher and safer ground. So too with survival programs, which are emergency services. In themselves they do not change social conditions, but they are life-saving vehicles until conditions change."[416]

But soon Huey saw the political climate for what it was. He began to understand that the Party would lose much of its outside support if they went even further in the direction of armed revolution. The community programs drew a lot of widespread support. These programs were also the most essential and important part of the Party for many of its members. Huey saw how these could and should continue to be a focus, as they had been when David was in charge. Additionally, Huey was aware that the strategy of armed self-defense—and the result of his Executive Mandate #3—had led, in many cases, to more violence, imprisonment, and death. It was becoming increasingly clear that, ideologically, the Party was split. It would be impossible to please everyone, and it was becoming more and more challenging to figure out how to take the Party where it needed to go.

Huey was frustrated and overwhelmed in the months after his release. He had his doubts, not only about the Party, but also about his own role and the direction he should take. He had to admit to himself that the Party was not the same organization it had been when he went into prison. How would he adapt and how would he lead this new version of the Black Panther Party?

People in the Party began to take sides in a way they hadn't before. On one side were those that still argued for armed self-defense as the most important and essential tool in the liberation for Black people. Geronimo Pratt was one of those members.

Geronimo had fought in the Vietnam War and earned a Purple Heart after being wounded during service. He was ready to return to Vietnam if called on. But in 1967, he was asked to help put down the rebellions in Detroit. His mind began to change. "They took away our dignity as soldiers," he later said. "One month we're risking our lives for our country, and the next we're getting ready to fire on our own people. I knew if the order came I couldn't obey it."[417]

When Geronimo returned to Vietnam, he began having nightmares and quickly became critical of the war. "After a while," he said, "I began to see the war as another kind of racism . . . You got to make people subhuman before you kill 'em. I saw things I don't want to remember. I *did* things I don't want to remember. That second tour was a bad time."[418] Then, when Martin Luther King, Jr. was assassinated, Geronimo was fully convinced. There was a revolution approaching and he wanted to be on the right side of history.

In September 1968, Geronimo met Bunchy Carter. Geronimo joined the Party and became Bunchy's right-hand man. Since he had served in the military, Geronimo agreed to help train Panther members in L.A. Right from the beginning, he was seen as a warrior on the ground for the Panthers.[419] In January 1969, he became the Deputy Minister of Defense for the Southern California chapter of the Party. Geronimo became, for many people, a respected, powerful, and integral member of the Party.

In August 1970, Geronimo went underground to avoid multiple trials. But going underground was different from going into exile. The Panthers who left the country, like Eldridge, were no longer seen as direct and immediate challenges to the law in the United States. On the other hand, Geronimo was still in the country and seen as an outlaw. Living this way was difficult. Anyone that housed Geronimo was breaking the law.

It was also very expensive. Initially, the Party supported Geronimo going underground. He had served in the military and received thirteen medals before his honorable discharge. He used all of that training and experience in his work with the Party. "Due to what the U.S. knew he could do with the very knowledge they had given him," read the Party's statement, "and with his brilliant mind and devotion to his people, he suffered the severest attacks by the local and national police from that time on." The statement insisted that Geronimo had gone underground so that he could "continue his hard work for the people."[420]

After living underground for a few months, Geronimo asked for money so that he could stay on the run. But Huey refused and Geronimo felt abandoned. His friends said, "Newton stated that Geronimo demanded money. This is a half-truth. The leadership of the Panthers had refused to help him in his underground efforts while he and those with him were threatened with survival . . . The refusal to support Geronimo made it more difficult for him to elude the pigs."[421] On December 9, 1970, Geronimo was arrested in Dallas, along with Panthers Ellie Stafford, Roland Freeman, and Melvin "Cotton" Smith.[422] Geronimo kept calling Huey and the other members of the Central Committee, but he wasn't able to reach anyone.[423]

On January 19, 1971, the Panther 21 published an open letter to the radical group the Weather Underground, printed in the *East Village Other*. Originally, the Weather Underground was a part of the Students for a Democratic Society, but they broke away and began to engage in guerrilla warfare. They thought that their tactics, which included bombings and increased armed violence, would bring the people closer to revolution.

In their letter, the Panther 21 denounced the Black Panther Party. They called the Weather Underground "the true vanguard." The Panther 21 insisted that it was time for intense, extreme, widespread revolutionary violence. "The only thing that will deal with reactionary force and violence is revolutionary counter-force and counter-violence . . . The Amerikkkan machine and its economy must be destroyed—and it can only be done with intelligent political awareness and armed struggle—revolution . . . Let's talk about 'large scale material damage'—this economy must fall—There is a war on."[424]

From Algeria, Eldridge and others in the international wing of the Party—also called the Intercommunal Section—sided with the Panther 21. In January 1971, Eldridge and Field Marshal Donald Cox wrote an article for the *Black Panther*, calling for young Black people in the United States to commit violent acts against the U.S. government. As Cox wrote, "When a guerilla unit moves against this oppressive system by executing a pig or by attacking its institutions, by any means—sniping, stabbing, bombing, etc.—in defense against the 400 years of racist brutality, murder and exploitation, this can only be defined correctly as self-defense."[425]

This view was controversial and divisive. Very few people in the United States actually supported guerrilla warfare, and in a country like the United States, the state had great repressive power. The government would use this power to stop any kind of violent uprising. At this point, fewer and fewer people thought that the Panthers could win an armed struggle against the U.S. government.

As David said, "I speak to Eldridge every day and am mindful of the cadre who want to pick up the gun. But the concept of the Party as a liberation army overthrowing the American government is not realistic. When we begin our attack who's going to join us? Party comrades will jump off the moon if Huey tells them to. Our allies won't."[426] Many of the Panthers realized that a violent attempt to overthrow the U.S. government wouldn't succeed. Instead, people would die, the movement would be squashed, and the Party would lose its broad base of support.

In addition, many of the main supporters of this strategy were members of the Party who were no longer in the United States. The members in Algeria couldn't actually take the actions that they were recommending. Instead, they were inviting others to do so.

On January 23, 1971, just a few days after the Panther 21 published their open letter, Huey published his own letter in the *Black Panther.* He purged Geronimo, one of the most famous and respected Party members at the time. He also purged Geronimo's close friends and allies.[427] Huey said that Geronimo had issued an ultimatum. He wanted money and if the Party didn't give it to him, he would kill David Hilliard.[428] There were multiple versions of the same story. But no matter what really happened, the outcome was set. Geronimo Pratt was no longer a part of the Black Panther Party.

When Geronimo called Eldridge in Algeria, finally someone listened to him. "I tried to contact David," said Geronimo, "somebody, anybody to lend an ear. It was like I was already tried and convicted. When Papa [Eldridge Cleaver] contacted me, it was like a fresh breath of life. Eldridge told me that he knew what was going on, that the brothers were not expelled, that he would talk to Huey."[429]

On February 8, two of the Panther 21 did not appear for their scheduled court date. When Michael Cetawayo Tabor and Dhoruba Bin Wahad (Richard Moore) left, they gave up $150,000 in bail money that had been raised by people who supported the Panthers. The judge issued a warrant for the two men. The judge also revoked the $200,000 bail for Joan Bird and Afeni Shakur, who was four months pregnant. These two women were the only other Panthers who were out free on bail.[430]

Then Connie Matthews, Huey's secretary, disappeared. She took important records from the Party and contact information for Panther allies in Europe. It was later revealed that Connie had married Cetawayo in secret. It was possible that Connie had managed to get Algerian passports for Cetawayo and Dhoruba and they all had fled together to Algeria.[431]

The very next day, February 9, the Central Committee expelled most of the New York Panther 21. The following issue of the *Black Panther* had the headline "Enemies of the People." Pictured below were Cetawayo, Dhoruba, and Connie. The paper explained that nine members of the Panther 21, still in prison, had already been expelled for their open letter in January.

Up until now, the public hadn't known about this. The Party had been keeping the conflict under wraps as best as they could. But Cetawayo, Dhoruba, and Connie's disappearance forced the Party's hand. Those at the head of the Party decided to openly declare the split in the *Black Panther* newspaper.

The times had changed. The laws had changed. The Panthers' initial tactic of armed self-defense against the police was no longer as effective. This moment in history was one of great change and upheaval, of reaching beyond what seemed possible or even practical. At one point, the revolution had seemed within reach. But now, members of the Party were struggling to catch up to it.

Huey wrote," Revolution is not an action; it is a process. Times change, and the policies of the past are not necessarily effective in the present. Our military strategies were not frozen. As conditions changed, so did our tactics."[432] The Black Panther Party needed to evolve, to grow. They had to figure out how to hold on to their magic. They had to figure out a way to stay together, headed in one direction, toward a unified goal.

▲

At this point, the Party was large and the Party was popular. But its strength was being put to the test. Even though there was a Central Committee, the Party was beginning to split. Not only were there many chapters now, but each chapter had its own leadership. Those in power were appointed, not elected, which meant that the people in the Party didn't have a say over who was the head. There weren't real channels to address grievances. And even if they were voiced, it wasn't certain that those in power would listen.

The Party was still united around the struggle for Black liberation. Everyone agreed on the goal and the outcome. But how to get there was becoming less clear with each passing day.

The Black Panther Party was one of a kind. Unique, shining, and on the verge of breaking apart. If those in power were not careful, the pressures, the tensions, would shatter all that they believed in—all that they had built.

PART SIX: THE FALL

We know that you are trying to break us up because we are the truth and because you can't control us. We know that you always try to destroy what you can't control.[433]

Afeni Shakur

A Black Panther outside the Lincoln Memorial.

CHAPTER 22

THE SPLIT WIDENS
CHANGING TIMES

THE SPLIT WIDENS

On February 26, 1971, Huey gave a live radio interview. The purpose was to promote the Panthers' Intercommunal Day of Solidarity.[434] For him, the interview was a way to present a united front, to downplay and smooth over the Party's problems. Huey wanted to show everyone that the Party leadership throughout the world was on the same page. It was important to him that the Party at least appear strong and unbroken. But Eldridge destroyed that goal, on national television.[435]

At the interview's end, when asked if he wanted to add anything for his followers in the San Francisco Bay Area, Eldridge said that he disagreed with the expulsion of the Panther 21. He blamed David Hilliard, who had led for so long. Eldridge said that, under David's leadership, the party was "falling apart at the seams."[436] With that, the interview ended.

Huey was upset. Whatever he thought about his friend David, he kept it to himself. He didn't go on air, in public, making pronouncements. The longer Huey thought about it, the angrier he became. But most of all, he felt betrayed. Huey refused to give Eldridge another opportunity to embarrass him like that.

Huey didn't wait to calm down. Instead, he picked up the phone and called Eldridge back. Huey had to handle this. He didn't realize that Eldridge was recording the call.[437]

"Eldridge," Huey began.

"Hey, what's happening," Eldridge replied, his voice calm, cool, collected.

"Yeah, you dropped a bombshell this morning. It was very embarrassing for me. So, I'm warning you now or notifying you that the Intercommunal Section, you hear?"

"Yeah."

"The Intercommunal Section is expelled."

"That's not the best way to deal with that."

Huey's already high voice kept rising. His emotions barely stayed in check as he responded.

"Well, this is the way I want to deal with it."

"Well, then I think you're a madman too, brother." With every steady, measured word, Eldridge made Huey even more angry. Especially this last declaration—that Huey had lost his mind. But Huey delivered a glancing blow too.

"But I'm not a coward like you, brother," Huey said, "'Cause you ran off to get Little Bobby Hutton killed but I stayed here and faced the gas, you see? So, you're a coward and you're a punk, you understand?"

"I think you've lost your ability to reason, brother," Eldridge came back, seemingly unruffled, his voice clear and smooth as still water.

"Hey, brother, you know what I call you? That's what I feel about you now. You're a punk."

Huey hung up, slamming his phone down. He had never forgiven Eldridge for what happened to Lil' Bobby. There was a time when Huey felt that the Party needed Eldridge. But that time had come and gone.

"Brothers are bound together by the revolutionary love we have for each other," wrote Huey, "a love forged through loyalty and trust. It is an element of the Black Panther Party that can never be destroyed. Yet eventually Eldridge betrayed this love and commitment in ways I once never believed possible."[438] Huey was nothing if not decisive. Now he had expelled Eldridge, Kathleen, and the entire Intercommunal Section of the Party.

As it turned out, the FBI had targeted Huey and Eldridge specifically. They knew that their relationship was already tense, so they

287

jumped in and twisted the knife. As Kathleen said, "The FBI was picking at Huey and Eldridge and I don't know who else they were picking at to create this sense of distrust . . . What we thought the FBI wanted to do was kill us. Blow up our offices. Shoot us. I don't think we understood exactly how insidious their project was."[439]

The split in the Party only widened from that moment on. People began to line up on either side. Two days after the interview, Donald Cox called for expelling David and June Hilliard. "Conditions should be created so they can't even walk the streets," he said. "They must not be allowed to go to any office of the Black Panther Party. This machinery that they are now using was built on the blood of our comrades, like [Lil'] Bobby and Bunchy . . . And if Huey can't understand this and relate to this then he's got to go too."[440]

Many in the United States who supported Eldridge went underground. Members on both sides began to leave, disillusioned with the direction the Party was headed. There continued to be no real channels of communication to address the problems or the growing fractures in the Party. There was little room for dissension or a difference of opinion.

Panther Candi Robinson was called "crazy" by other members for disagreeing with the leadership, "not because they listened to my criticisms or tried to objectively anal[y]ze them but because they have built an attitude, that it is wrong to disagree with members of the Central Committee."[441] Those that didn't align with the Party's current vision were expelled. As Minister of Culture Emory Douglas put it, "If you don't want to hear it, if you don't like it, then you expel 'em."[442] And as the days went by, that vision became less and less about the people, as the violence within the Party itself increased.

On March 8, 1971, Panther Robert Webb was killed. He did not agree with Huey and Party leadership and there were allegations that the Central Headquarters orchestrated his murder. Those in charge denied this and no one was ever charged for Robert Webb's murder. Still, many believed that he was killed as a result of the fallout from the split between Huey and Eldridge.[443]

Then, on April 17th, the distribution manager of the *Black Panther* newspaper, Sam Napier, was murdered. He was aligned with national leadership, on the other side of the split from Robert Webb. After Napier was killed, the building he was in was set on fire and his body burned beyond recognition. This increasing brutality and violence surrounding the Party signaled an irrevocable split. The women and men that had joined had done so out of a love for the people and a desire for freedom. There was already intense government repression and numerous external threats, without the specter of internal violence. These events drove a large number of members to leave the Party.[444]

For the remaining members, the paranoia that the FBI had helped to create continued to settle over the Party like a thick cloud of poisonous smoke. The purges, the violence, and the expulsions continued.

Among those members who disagreed with the shift away from armed self-defense were some who committed violent acts, but without the blessing of the Party. What could the Party do when one of its members went rogue, and committed violent crimes that had nothing to do with the revolution? One response was to expel them.

Early on in the life of the Party, many chapters had grown quickly. There was no real way to decide who should be members, so they accepted everyone. At that time, the head of the New York chapter, Joudon Ford, called David Hilliard, trying to figure out how they could keep out people that wouldn't actually be good for the Party Some people might have been attracted by the opportunity to be violent, but without the training and focus on revolution and liberation. David didn't have the answer. "When I find out," he said to Joudon, "I'll let you know."[445]

Aaron Dixon had similar problems in Seattle. People had joined quickly and there wasn't a clear method to learn about their recruits, nor were there clear ideas of what they were supposed to be doing with all these ready, willing people. As Aaron said, "During those early days of the Seattle chapter, everything was happening so fast, and without a blueprint or methodology to guide us, we often had to learn how to operate on the fly, following our instincts. We had many

289

recruits, yet we lacked a clear understanding or model of exactly what we were supposed to be doing on a daily basis."[446] That's where the expulsions came in.

Eldridge had talked publicly about the need for purges, especially because of how rapidly people entered the Party in 1969 and 1970. "One thing that's important," he explained, "a lot of people don't understand why a lot of people were purged from the Party. During the time when Huey Newton was going to trial . . . because of the necessity of mobilizing as many people as possible . . . we started just pulling people in . . . In order to maximize the number of people we pulled in, we did not argue with people if they put on a black leather jacket or black berets, or said that they were Panthers. They just walked in and said they support Huey Newton and they wanted to join our organization. We didn't have time to conduct our political education classes . . . They proved to be very undisciplined . . . so we just came down hard."[447] Eldridge had no idea that, he too, would one day be expelled.

On May 12, 1971, the Panther 21 were acquitted of all 156 charges. But most of them had already been expelled from the Party. Many had been imprisoned for over two years, with bails set as high as $100,000. While they were imprisoned, they couldn't do the same kind of work they could on the outside. And once they were expelled, they couldn't do Party work at all. It was also unclear where all of the money that was raised for the Panther 21 had gone. Did it in fact go to the Panther 21? Or did some of it go elsewhere? Accusations began to fly.[448]

When the Panther 21 were freed, one of their lawyers, Gerald B. Lefcourt, said of the jury as a whole, "Together they have rejected once and for all a society which refuses to allow change. They said you must allow people to get together and think about changing life and the way they live. And it's a beautiful victory."[449] The battle was won. But the Panther 21 were still exiled from the Party, the place where they had fought for change and liberation, and where they had dared to hope for a better world for Black people.

CHANGING TIMES

George Jackson was an important member of the Black Panther Party. He was an author and a prison activist. He was also the head of the Black Panther Party Chapter at San Quentin Prison in Marin County, California. George organized among the other prison inmates, working to achieve revolutionary change. He was very influential, with great leadership capacity and international reach. His book *Soledad Brother* was a collection of prison letters that demonstrated his insight as a theorist of both Black revolution and Marxist thought. It also showed what a strong spokesperson for political prisoners, throughout the world, could look like.[450]

On August 7, 1970, George's younger brother Jonathan tried to break George out of the Marin County courthouse. Seventeen-year-old Jonathan took a judge hostage and was eventually killed. At that time, the Party praised Jonathan's efforts against the power structure. Eldridge said that Jonathan was a martyr for the revolution and that the actions he took to try to free his older brother were worthy of praise.[451]

Just over a year later, on August 21, 1971, George Jackson was shot and killed by guards at San Quentin. In the incident, three prison guards and two White inmates were also killed. Prison authorities said that George had killed the guards with a gun he managed to get into the prison and was trying to escape when he was shot.[452] Whether true or not—whether it was the full story or just part of the truth—still nothing could bring back George Jackson.

By the time George was killed, the Panthers were no longer advocating killing police officers in self-defense. They couldn't use the same rhetoric they had before. When Lil' Bobby Hutton, John Huggins, Bunchy Carter, Fred Hampton, and Mark Clark were murdered, the response had been to cast them as martyrs for the revolution. The *Black Panther* argued that these Panthers died for the revolution and that, when attacked, Panthers should retaliate against the police. The images in the paper were of guns and blood, calling for violence in self-defense.[453]

291

George Jackson

But George's death was painted in a very different light. The *Black Panther* had a large spread on George's funeral, which attracted thousands of mourners. They celebrated his life and his work. But the message was that his loss was tragic, not a reason to engage in violence.

This change was reflected in the *Black Panther* paper as a whole. Until 1969, around half of the articles in the paper called for "revolution now." In 1970, that number soared. The need for revolutionary change was portrayed as urgent and immediate. But in 1971, the number dropped significantly. In the years after, the proportion fell even further, below 1 percent.[454]

This was a very different public stance. And for many, it was a dividing line. For three years, the Party had thrived, growing at a rate that no one could have anticipated. Now, just as swiftly, it was on the decline.

The members of the Party no longer had a leadership that they could count on to provide a united goal and vision. They had worked hard, often under harsh and difficult conditions. They did so out of a belief, and also out of what the work itself provided. Being a part of the Panthers gave many members a sense of purpose and belonging. Through working toward the goal of liberation, by interacting with other like-minded people, the members of the Party had drawn inspiration. And they had obtained glimpses of true freedom. But now, that promise, that motivation, was no longer enough.

▲

Ironically, what so many Black Panthers had fought for—to have Huey back on the outside—was one of the factors that contributed to the Party's demise. When Huey was released, the Party had to be restructured. And when he wasn't able to solve the problems, and when he didn't do what members thought he should, the tensions within the Party were laid bare and increased. Huey was unable to hold the Panthers together.

But the Party didn't continue to fall apart just because of one person, a particular action, or a single event. The world around the

Panthers at this time was changing. Theirs wasn't the only revolutionary organization in decline, the only anti-imperialist movement beginning to collapse. Across the world, movements with similar political beliefs were all experiencing a sea change.

As the Vietnam War started to wind down in the early 1970s and the draft ended, the Panthers could no longer gain as much allied support as they had in the past. They had rallied against the draft and the concept that a person could be forced to go to war even if he was against it. Now those allies that had come to the Panthers specifically for the antiwar movement drifted away.

Also, the United States had begun to open diplomatic relationships with Cuba, China, and Algeria. These were countries where the Panthers had traveled, sought asylum, and found sympathetic allies. Now that they were more open to the United States, this support for the Panthers began to wane.

In 1968, Eldridge fled to Cuba and was given support and safe passage. Just a few years later, Cuba began to distance itself from the Panthers. They still allowed exiles, but were careful to not actively support Black revolution in a way that would provoke the United States.[455] In 1970, China sponsored a visit by members of the Black Panther Party, and in 1971 the Chinese gave Huey high state honors. But as the relationship between China and the United States improved, Chinese support for the Panthers disintegrated. Then, in 1972, the Algerian government took away the Panthers' diplomatic status and expelled them from Algiers.[456] Now the international wing of the Party was no more.

At home, the political climate had also changed. The U.S. government made official concessions to Black people and their allies. Through programs like affirmative action, Black people had begun to achieve greater access to federal and private sector jobs as well as elite college admissions and positions. It was harder for the Black Panthers to call for an armed revolution against the Establishment when it appeared that those in power were making strides in the right direction, without a violent overthrow of the government.

At the same time, the U.S. government had cracked down hard on the Panthers. The FBI played no small part in destroying the Panthers. After J. Edgar Hoover, the FBI director, declared that the Panthers were the "greatest threat to the internal security of this country," his agency wasted no time working to eradicate the Party.[457]

In 1971, *The New York Times* reported that, "a check of the Party's chapters across the country suggests that the operation is now only a shell of what it was a year ago."[458] That same year, the House Committee on Internal Security stated, "The Black Panther Party, as a national organization, is near disintegration . . . The committee hearings document the steady decline in [membership] during the last year. Furthermore, the feud between Eldridge Cleaver and Huey Newton threatens the start of a time of violence and terror within what remains of the Panther Party."[459]

But with all these challenges and pressures, internal and external, some would still attempt to preserve their beloved Party.

At this point, what could the Party try to do to resurrect itself?

BLACK COMMUNITY S
MARCH 2⁹
1972   SERVE THE PEOPL

HUEY P NE
SERVANT OF THE

Bobby Seale speaks, Oakland, 1972.

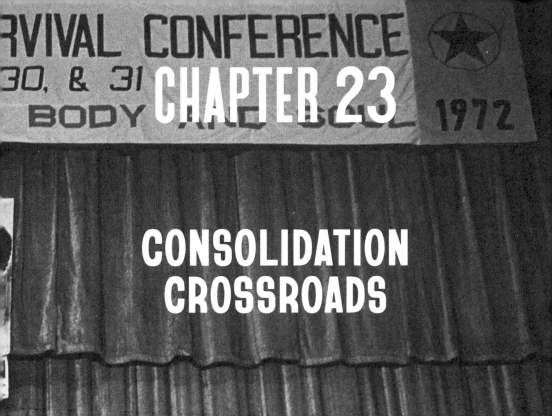

CHAPTER 23

CONSOLIDATION
CROSSROADS

CONSOLIDATION

As part of the plan to save and reenergize the Party, those in charge asked chapters throughout the country to close and come to Oakland. This consolidation was a calculated risk to strengthen the Party by putting everything in the birthplace of the movement.

But not everyone was down with the program. Many members decided to leave the Party rather than upend their lives and move to Oakland. "They began to resent things," Bobby Rush said. "People just wanted to move on, wanted to do something. So they said, 'Rather than go out to Oakland, we're just gonna disband. We're just gonna leave.' One by one they began to peter out."[460]

Those that went to Oakland got to work. They went out into the Black community encouraging people to register to vote.

Bobby Seale and Elaine Brown were both running for public office in 1973: Elaine for City Council and Bobby for Mayor of Oakland. As Elaine wrote, "Our campaign would, of course, have no impact on the dashed hopes of the past. It might not help realize the dreams of the next generation. Yet when Bobby Seale and I launched our campaign on the streets of West Oakland I could see on the faces of our constituents something I had never seen on my mother's face. I saw a resurgence of hope. Whatever the outcome of the campaign, that alone gave it worth."[461]

The Panthers' goal was not just to get people to vote for their candidates. It was also to create energy and excitement for exercising the right to vote, to get Black people registered and engaged in the political process.

This was no small action. Voter suppression was a real fact in Black communities. Many Black people fought and died to exercise their right to vote. "Blacks, in the South particularly, were murdered attempting to vote," wrote Elaine. "They were legally kept from voting by grandfather clauses and literacy tests. Blacks who actually made it to the ballot box found their votes decimated by the might of

white political machines. Thus, blacks had come to the realization that black votes, like black lives, were always extinguished by the majority rule of whites."[462]

The Panthers were fighting to show that Black votes, just like Black lives, mattered. That every vote, like every life, was important and should be counted.

This was a new strategy for the Panthers. Now they were explicitly working within the system, trying to gain power through political office. This was a far cry from a revolutionary overthrow of the government. Instead, it much more resembled the kind of agitation that took place as a part of the Civil Rights Movement. Was it possible for the Panthers to pivot this way and still hold onto their core identity?

An article in the *San Francisco Chronicle* commented on how support for the party had shifted over time. Now that the Party's policies had changed, the support came from a broad section of the African American community. "To many," wrote the author, "the most surprising thing of all was the presence at these meetings of a large number of middle-aged and elderly blacks, the hard-working family types, usually approachable to politicians via some Sunday morning speech from a Baptist or Methodist pulpit. It appeared the Panthers had pulled a coup."[463]

Elaine gained over 40 percent of the vote in her race for City Council, but it wasn't enough to win. Bobby, who wore a suit and a tie now, rode buses to spread the word about his bid for mayor. Even though he forced a runoff, Bobby didn't win either.

Afterwards, those who had come to Oakland didn't have anywhere else to go. Their local chapters were closed and now they no longer had a cause to rally around in Oakland either. The Panthers always knew that their candidates might not win, but they had operated with the hope that they would. Many of the remaining members who moved to Oakland left the Party. The Party numbers dwindled even further.

The remaining members of the Party went in different directions. Some moved toward the community survival programs. The Oakland Community School, run by Ericka Huggins, became one of the Party's most important remaining programs.

Other members, those who believed that the revolution could only come about through bloodshed, moved toward more radical armed violence. The Black Liberation Army (BLA) was in part an offshoot of the Black Panther Party, just as the Weather Underground was an offshoot of the Students for a Democratic Society.

Many members of the Black Panther Party respected the goals of the BLA, which were very closely aligned with those of the Panther Party. As BLA member Assata Shakur explained, "The Black Liberation Army is not an organization: it goes beyond that. It is a concept, a people's movement, an idea . . . The idea of a Black Liberation Army emerged from conditions in Black communities: conditions of poverty, indecent housing, massive unemployment, poor medical care and inferior education. The idea came about because Black people are not free or equal in this country . . . The concept of the BLA arose because of the political, social and economic oppression of Black people in this country. And where there is oppression, there will be resistance."[464]

But for many other Panthers, the methods of the BLA were not sustainable. As BLA member Sundiata Acoli wrote, the function of the BLA was to "defend Black people and to organize Black people militarily, so they can defend themselves through a people's army and war."[465] Some members of the BLA saw themselves as the direct descendants of the Panther Party. "[We are] a politico-military organization," wrote member Jalil Muntaqim from prison, "whose primary objective is to fight for the independence and self-determination of Afrikan people in the United States. The . . . BLA evolved out of the now defunct Black Panther Party."[466]

The BLA saw themselves as upping the ante against the Establishment by engaging in guerrilla warfare. A crucial difference between this and the early armed self-defense strategies of the Panthers, though, was that, politically, the BLA was never able to gain the allied support that the Panthers did. Many, if not most antiwar activists and moderate Black community members who had supported the Panthers, now saw the activities of the BLA as too extreme and often criminal.

Also, the members of groups like the BLA were isolated. Once they were captured or in exile, they didn't receive the same support from allies. They were unable to grow in the way the Panthers had. As Jalil wrote, "By 1974–75 the fighting capacity of the Black Liberation Army had been destroyed."[467]

CROSSROADS

"[I have] come to a crossroads in my life," wrote Tommie Williams, a member of the L.A. Party, "one path is the Party and the other path is my personal happiness . . . Some comrades have to struggle each month to pay rent, bills, food and to buy necessities for their children and some comrades don't have a source of income at all. Other comrades do not have to worry about their financial necessities . . . Our children are growing up—half the children don't know their parents or their parents don't know their children."[468] Tommie had fought and been arrested in the December 8, 1970 raid of the L.A. headquarters. She was a loyal and committed Party member. But for Tommie, like so many members, the current situation in the Party- was unsustainable.

Too many of the Black Panthers lived in poverty. They couldn't continue to fight for freedom, for liberation, when their own needs were barely being met. As Panther Amar Casey said, "I was able to see, you know, how we were basically living off the donations that you collected when you went out into the field . . . you got a percentage, sometimes 30 percent, sometimes 50 percent, it depends. And that's what you had to live on. And it worked a bit because you were supported, you got food and housing, but you were pretty dirt poor for the most part."[469]

Over the years, many Panthers' main income came from selling the *Black Panther* paper. As Party member Bobby McCall recounts, "The newspaper was our major source of income . . . The IRS was constantly harassing us about taxes. The Oakland Community School was constantly harassed about the grants we were getting. Huey was constantly being harassed about anything they could harass him about. Court costs were costing us an arm and a leg, and funds were just drying up. As soon as we could raise some money, they would figure out a way to take it away from us. . . . I had to go out and get a job which I did and gave all my money back to the party."[470]

Some of the Panthers even separated from their families to protect their loved ones and focus solely on the work of the revolution.

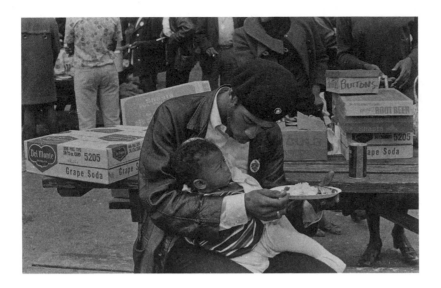

There were also young people who didn't yet have children of their own. They only had to sustain themselves. As Cleveland Panther Bill Davis noted about these younger members, "They were willing to work. They had the energy. They were willing to organize, go downtown and stand on the corner for eight hours a day selling papers."[471] But this situation could last for only so long. Eventually the members would start to have children, more responsibilities, and more people to support.

As Fred Hampton's wife, Deborah (Akua), said, "I was in the first group of women to become pregnant and have babies within the context of the Black Panther Party. There was nothing set up after the birth of Fred Hampton, Jr. that spoke to the issue of childcare, of how we would continue to function in the structure of the Party and continue to provide for our children."[472]

The members of the Party wanted to work toward a goal of group liberation, but at what cost to themselves and their families?

Members were feeling the strain. Many felt isolated and despondent, yearning for a different kind of life. Members wanted to leave to pursue different paths. Some wanted to go back to school, or spend more time with their children, or try to make more money so they could become financially independent.[473] As Panther Amar Casey said, "So many comrades have left and so many are on the verge of leaving because we suffer from loneliness, the lack of personal lives, extreme poverty and the lack of personal development."[474]

In 1974, Huey vanished after he was charged with the murder of a young woman named Kathleen Smith, eventually ending up in Cuba.

That year, Elaine Brown became the Chairwoman of the Black Panther Party. Elaine faced backlash as the head of the Party for many reasons, not the least of which was that she was a woman. In fact, women had always held important and essential positions in the Black Panthers. But with Elaine at the head, intraparty sexism was even more obvious.

Even before Elaine became the head of the Party, women were operating in many positions of power. "Before the time of Huey going to Cuba, women were in leadership," explained Ericka Huggins. "And that again was organic. Because of the male-predominate society we live in, when the police arrested and killed they tended to seek out men, thinking that men were the leaders. They didn't know that behind the scenes women ran almost every program, were involved in every level of the party . . . The greater numbers of men were taken away from leadership, [the more] women rose in the ranks of leadership. And it became apparent at one point that women should become a really viable part of the Central Committee. And some of that had to do with women asking for it and some of it had to do with the fact that women were the ones who were running everything anyway."[475]

Even though the Panther women fought against sexism, in the Party and in society at large, they couldn't upend it all alone. Especially when members of the Party were perpetrating it. As JoNina Abron said, "I know we are all products of this society, but we should expect more from each other because we are members of the Black Panther Party. Why can't we love and respect each other as human beings instead of males and female?"[476]

But within the party, even while members worked to root out sexism within their own ranks, the problem persisted. "We knew Brothers dragged their old habits into the party," wrote Elaine. "We all did. The party's role, however, was not limited to external revolution but incorporated the revolutionizing of its ranks . . . Black men were our Brothers in the struggle for black liberation. We had no intention, however, of allowing Panther men to assign us an inferior role in the revolution."[477]

While the Party line was one of inclusion, the practices did not always align. When Huey returned from Cuba and took control of the Party again, things began to get worse.

Elaine had always planned on handing the Party back to Huey. After he was acquitted, she did just that. But this time wasn't the same as when he reemerged in 1970. Now, years later, there was no fanfare. There were no arms outstretched. No blue water sparkling for miles. The thousands of people that once gathered just to see him were gone, all living their own lives. It was not a triumphant return.

Huey lived alone in his Lake Merritt penthouse, overlooking the water. From his window he could see not only the beauty of the lake, but also the Alameda County jail. The building stood there in his vision, a constant reminder of his years spent in prison, the long months in solitary confinement.

Now to see Huey, the remaining members of the Party had to go up an elevator to his private floor. In the dark, quiet cage they slowly ascended. They were met and searched by Huey's bodyguards. Once the members walked through the door, they were in Huey's world. And it had become a twisted place. They were subjected to all manner of things. To the new Huey, who had come to believe in his own mythology, who believed he was above the law. In the penthouse, Huey began to make his own rules.

"I loved being queen in his world," admitted Elaine, "for he had fashioned a new world for those who dared. Yet I had come to hate life with him. His madness had become as full-blown as his genius."[478]

The stories of abuse began to surface. It was clear that Huey was drinking and using drugs, which was against Party rules. But he

306

wasn't going to leave his position, and there was no effective way to remove him. That was not the way the Panthers were created.

Throughout the Party's history, everyone was appointed. There were never formal elections. The people who worked for the Party didn't have a say in the leadership. Huey was one of the founders, and now that he was back in charge, he wasn't going anywhere. Instead, the last members of the Party began to leave.

When Huey ordered that Regina Davis, who worked in the Oakland Community School, be beaten because of the way she spoke to a male member of the Party, Elaine called Huey. She explained to him that Regina was integral to the Oakland Community School and that treating her this way signaled something unacceptable to the women of the Party.[479] "The women were feeling the change," she wrote. "The beating of Regina would be taken as a clear signal that the words 'Panther' and 'comrade' had taken on gender connotations, denoting an inferiority in the female half of us. Something awful was not only driving a dangerous wedge between Sisters and Brothers, it was attacking the very foundation of the party."[480]

Elaine let Huey know all of this. He was quiet for a long time. She knew he was thinking. She could only hope that he would say the right thing. Finally, Huey spoke.

"You know, of course, that I know all that. But what do you want me to do about it? The Brothers came to me. I had to give them something."[481]

"You gave them Regina?"[482] Elaine asked. For her, there was no coming back from this. Even though some part of her still loved Huey, even though she had worked hard to hold the Party together in his absence, she had to leave.[483]

"It was absolutely devastating for me to leave the Black Panther Party," Elaine recalled many years later. "There was no other life. There was no other thing greater."[484]

CHAPTER 24

NO OTHER LIFE
CODA

NO OTHER LIFE

For years, the Black Panther Party had been at the center of many people's lives. Without the Party, the members had to find something else to believe in. But that wouldn't come easily. As Aaron Dixon wrote, "I would eventually have to come to grips with my past, my anger, and my detachment. The end of the Black Panther Party left a bitter taste in my mouth, as it had for many others. It would take at least a decade for the negative feelings to subside and the righteousness of what the party and its members stood for to resurface."[485]

In 1973, Bobby Seale resigned from the Black Panther Party. He who had believed in Huey first, before all others. But Bobby refused to be part of a Party that wasn't about the people.

When Bobby and Huey had first conceived of the Party, they made it about the community, about the liberation of Black people. As one Party member said, "The exploited . . . people's needs are land, bread, housing, education . . . clothing, justice and peace and the Black Panther Party shall not, for a day, alienate ourselves from the masses and forget their needs for survival."[486] The Party was the people. Without them, the Party ceased to have real meaning or purpose.

When the Party succeeded, it was because it encouraged the members to look outside of themselves, to work toward a commonly held goal of Black liberation. By doing this work, by arming themselves in self-defense, by going into their communities and making a difference, the Panthers operated in a long tradition of activists who found purpose not solely in working for themselves, but in working for others. Now, that era of the Panthers had ended.

Bobby could no longer walk down the path beside Huey. The young man Bobby first met, with his head buried in his books, who inspired people with his courage and bravery, who stood up to the police, who stood up to injustice—that young man was a memory. Bobby would continue to organize in his community, to speak and to agitate and keep up the spirit of the Party. But, to do that, he would leave Huey behind.

When Eldridge decided to be a member of the Black Panther Party, he gave himself over fully, to the organization and the purpose. He put his trust and his belief in Huey. Up until the end, Eldridge said what he thought. He was clear on the direction he thought the Party should go. But Huey had disappointed him. Huey hadn't stuck to the initial strategy, to the position of strength that had first attracted Eldridge. And now it was over for Eldridge too.

Kathleen would stay by Eldridge's side for many years after they were expelled from the Party. Even when Eldridge was separated from Kathleen and the children, when they had to live in separate countries, she loved and supported Eldridge. But in 1981, Kathleen left him. Too much had changed. They were not the people they once were. Kathleen went back and got her undergraduate degree and her law degree from Yale University. She continued to fight for the underdog, to speak out publicly, to agitate, and to fight, but never again as a member of the Black Panther Party.

On February 24, 1974, a memo was sent out saying that David resigned and was then expelled. There were rumors circulating that David was planning to take back the organization in a coup. When David heard about his expulsion in prison, he was shocked. He couldn't reach anyone, so he poured his feelings into a letter.

"Huey, I have tried always to give what you expected of me, striven to become what you are by following your example. You said in a conversation we had that I had proven my loyalty to you . . . You have full control of your organization and I bear no ill will against you. I am not your enemy and you know it. I want to be your friend Huey, not because I fear you, but because I love you."[487] After writing the letter, David fell into anger and despair. He couldn't believe that he hadn't seen this coming. Maybe his love, his loyalty, had blinded him.

The few Panthers that stayed had a hope for the future, for what the Party might still be able to accomplish. These members maintained a few important parts of the Party, like the *Black Panther* newspaper and the Oakland Community School.

The *Black Panther* newspaper was one of the most important contributions of the Black Panther Party. It gave the Panthers a space to control the production and the distribution of their own media. That way, they decided what was said about them and how. They decided the images and the tone and content of the articles. The paper was an essential step in self-definition. As Minister of Culture and primary visual artist for the paper, Emory Douglas explained that the goal of the *Black Panther* was to put Black people and their lives at the center. Whereas so often, blackness was relegated to the outskirts, to the honorable mentions and the edges, what Emory wanted to do with his images was to make everyday Black people the main characters and the protagonists. Also, it allowed the members of the Party to make money, through selling and distributing the paper.[488]

But even the *Black Panther* eventually ended. The last issue was printed in October 1980.

While Ericka stayed for many years, committed to the Party, to its ideals, and to her beloved community school, she too had to leave. She would never lose her commitment to the community, to making the world a better place for all people. But it was clear that she could no longer do so as part of what was more and more just a disintegrating group, orbiting around Huey. In 1981, the Oakland Community School closed.

One man was left standing alone in the wreckage. But one man does not a Party make. Especially when that Party was created to represent the interests of the people as a whole.

Those around Huey could see that now, not only had he given up on the Party, he had given up on himself. "As he became more and more addicted to multiple substances I don't think he wanted to live," said Ericka, "and I don't think he wanted the Party to live anymore. From there on he was less and less the Huey I knew and more and more listening to his demons."[489] On August 23, 1989, Huey would be killed by a drug dealer on the very streets he worked so hard to transform.

Earlier in his life, Huey had imagined a world where Black people could be free. And he thought about what it would look like and what it would take to get there. With his new friend, Bobby Seale, he started the Black Panther Party. Then Huey brought in Eldridge Cleaver, when he saw what Eldridge could do. The three began to make something, to create and to dream. At that time, what they had was limitless potential.

But it eventually all came to an end. In 1982, the last Black Panther office closed its doors.

For the women and men of the Party the dream, the promise of the Party was shattered. Friendships had fallen apart. Lives were lost. People experienced abuse and violence at the hands of those they thought they could trust. The betrayals and the pain ran deep. But the former members who were still living had to go on.

The Party changed everyone it touched. Being a Panther was, for all involved, a powerful and transformative experience. As the Reverend Julius Thomas wrote, "Regardless of their public image, the Black Panthers need to be understood. I have worked intensively with the Panthers for three years and have been amazed at how few people, Black or White, have made any effort to understand why there is a Panther Party. In the few years I have worked with the Black Panthers, I have become convinced that there is a cathartic and therapeutic element in this revolutionary force. I have seen their anguish, frustrations and undying love in their attempts to make not only the masses whole, but themselves as well. I have observed that for those who became a part of the Panthers, life is no longer meaningless. They find purpose, and that purpose is restoring human dignity and pride."[490]

For years, the members of the Black Panther Party would work and struggle together. They would fight to open the door to their liberation. Each member would experience the brightness of true freedom spilling from that open door. But eventually the door would close.

As the members made their way back to their lives, as they contemplated what had happened to them as members of the Party, they would not remember only the hard times. They would also remember what made the Party work, what gave it such power and such potential. There was a reason the members were drawn to the Party in the first place. That reason, that striving for something outside of themselves, would never go away. The Party would take its place in history and would not be forgotten. And there was still work to be done. Black people would continue to strive for liberation, to work within the long Black freedom struggle. But no longer as members of the Black Panther Party.

CODA

Each of us is positioned in our context, in our histories: personal, political, and global. While it might seem, at times, that we are alone, that our struggles are isolated, in fact, we are parts of a great swath of human experience.

The Black Panther Party exists in a long tradition of people who worked and continue to work to create a more just world. They dared to hope and they dared to dream.

The Black Panther Party grew out of the work of Civil Rights organizations like the National Association for the Advancement of Colored People, founded in 1909; the Congress of Racial Equality, founded in 1942; the Southern Christian Leadership Conference, founded in 1957; and the Student Nonviolent Coordinating Committee, 1960 to 1968.

The Party also grew out of the work of Black Power organizations like the Universal Negro Improvement Association, founded in 1914; the Nation of Islam, founded in 1930; and Malcolm X's short-lived but influential Organization of Afro-American Unity, 1964 to 1965.

Many different traditions have helped to make up this long Black freedom struggle, including the Civil Rights and Black Power movements and, now, the Black Lives Matter movement. At times these traditions have achieved a kind of unity and at others, they have been in conflict. But most important, as shown in the history of the Black Panther Party, the overriding goal of all of these traditions is freedom for Black people.

Martin Luther King, Jr. said, "The arc of the moral universe is long, but it bends toward justice."[491]

The Panthers believed that peace and justice wouldn't come without a fight. They believed that to become who you wanted to be, who you should be, you had to stand up and refuse to take no for an answer.

You might hope that the world is headed in a just direction, that the moral universe does in fact bend toward justice. But the Panthers firmly believed that, to make it so, you can't just sit back and wait. It is essential to act, to help it along.

You have to, in effect, bend the universe. And that takes great belief. That takes great courage. It takes a lot of hard work: mobilizing, organizing, planning, and agitating. It takes a concerted effort from many, many people.

At times, the struggle may seem impossible, the obstacles insurmountable. But as Huey wrote, "We will touch God's heart; we will touch the people's heart and together we will move the mountain."[492]

At their best, the Panthers lived for the people. They worked for something outside of themselves and, in so doing, touched greatness. They did so out of a sense of community, of collective understanding and shared experience. Of turning to the person next to you and saying, "I see you and in you I also see myself."

Those who worked, lived, and died for the Party were not perfect people. They were humans, with all the complications and contradictions that being human brings. The members knew that they were up against a great deal. But they didn't let that stop them. They were fighting for their lives. They were fighting for their commonly held goal of Black liberation.

Maybe they wouldn't see the finish line. Maybe their children and their children's children would be the ones to keep fighting, to keep agitating and keep believing. The Black Panthers fought and many Black Panthers died for this belief.

As Fred Hampton said, "If you dare to struggle, you dare to win."[493] And this is just what the Black Panthers did.

They saw the world as it was and refused to accept it. Instead, they fought, they organized, and they struggled to create a more just society. Not only for Black people in the U.S., but for oppressed people across the world.

Recently, while having a conversation with Ericka Huggins, a member of the Party from 1967–1981, she said something that really struck me. "Usually the story of the Black Panther Party begins and ends with the men." As a Black woman, writing this particular book, it was crucial to me to offer the stories and voices of both the women and the men of the Party.

This book proceeds in a mostly chronological order, but my hope is that *FREEDOM!* paints a more balanced picture of the experiences of the people of the Party, not just a single person or a few better known figures.

My co-authors and I have spent years researching and contributing to the scholarship on the Party to lay the foundation for this book. Still, this book is only a slice of the Party's history. In writing *FREEDOM!*, I decided to emphasize people's subjective experiences. I relied heavily on retrospective firsthand accounts and memoirs, fully understanding that these are subjective accounts which are, in many instances, recounted years after the fact.

My hope in writing this book is to energize a new generation of readers and activists. Over fifty years later, the history of the Party continues to inspire, as shown in contemporary examples like the Black Lives Matter Movement. The legacy of the Panthers, however, is a complicated one. I didn't shy away from the complexities and the contradictions. Instead, I tried to look at the history, to present it, and to get at the core of what the Panthers stood for and achieved.

I believe that the key to the Panther's legacy is living for the people. The Panthers endure because they stood for this. When individuals work for something truly important outside of themselves, they can achieve greatness.

The Panthers had love for the people and they worked hard for the poor and the oppressed. They desired Black liberation—in fact, human liberation—and believed in the necessity of change, evolution, and revolution.

Revolution is a process. It is not an end state or a destination. We are, as a people, and especially as writers and activists who are committed to positive change, always striving and working toward the world that we want to see. And we are not alone. We are part of a long river of history, of agents of change, who came before us and will go on long after us.

It is true. The revolution has not yet come. But that's because the revolution is all around us. We are the ones who are shaping our world. We are the ones who have the power to create the world that we want to live in and pass on to future generations.

First, thank you to the people who lived and worked in the Black Panther Party. It was my privilege and my honor to engage with your stories.

To my mother Catherine Macklin for your personal sacrifices, your intelligence, your understanding, and for always supporting my drive to be an artist. To my sister Coral Martin, the first person to read my writing, the first person to say that I was her favorite author, thank you for being my sister, and my best friend. To Corey Wade and my daughter Josephine Wade for their love, their support, and the space that we created, as a family, so that I could write this book. To my friends who supported me throughout this process, thank you. You know who you are and I love you.

Thank you to Ericka Huggins for encouraging me to stay true to myself, to have confidence in my voice, and to trust in what I have to say. Thank you to Nick Thomas for being the best Senior Editor around, for believing in my work, and championing this project. Not only are you superb at what you do, you are also a wonderful human being. To Irene Vázquez, Antonio Gonzalez Cerna, and the whole team at LQ, thank you for all that you do and all that you are. Thank you to Jon Key for your artistry, the beautiful cover art, and the striking interior design. I couldn't wish for a more lovely group of people to work with.

Thanks to Rho Bloom-Wang who read an early version of this manuscript. Having their critical eye on the text was invaluable. I would like to thank my co-author Joshua Bloom. Working with you has both enriched this process and created something that I never could have envisioned alone. Last, but definitely not least, thank you to my father, Waldo E. Martin Jr. You are a constant source of joy, inspiration, and stability in my life. Thank you all those years ago for letting me use your blue typewriter to write my very first story.

1962 • Huey Newton and Bobby Seale meet

1965 • February 21 — Malcolm X is assassinated
• August — Watts rebellion

1966 • September — Hunters Point uprising
• October — Huey and Bobby found the Black Panther Party for Self-Defense

1967 • February — Black Panthers escort Betty Shabazz at the airport
• April 1 — Denzil Dowell is murdered by police
• April 25 — first issue of the *Black Panther* newspaper is released
• May 2 — the Panthers protest at the California state capitol against Mulford's Bill
• May 15 — the Black Panther Party publishes the Ten-Point Program
• July 12 — Newark rebellion
• July 23 — Detroit rebellion
• October — Huey charged with the murder of John Frey; Free Huey! movement launched

1968 • February — Bunchy Carter founds the Los Angeles chapter of the Party
• April 4 — Martin Luther King, Jr. is assassinated
• April 6 — Lil' Bobby Hutton is murdered by the police
• April — Seattle and New York chapters formed
• November — Students at San Francisco State begin their strike in protest of the Eurocentric education and lack of diversity at the University
• November — Eldridge Cleaver flees the US

1969 • January 17 — John Huggins and Bunchy Carter are murdered
• January — the Panthers launch the Free Breakfast Program

327

- April 2 — New York City grand jury indicts the Panther 21
- June — Fred Hampton organizes the Rainbow Coalition
- June — First liberation school is organized
- July — the Panthers open the Afro-American Center in Algiers
- August — David Hilliard becomes the head of the Party
- September — Trial of the Chicago Eight begins
- November — Hemispheric Conference to End the War in Vietnam
- December 4 — Fred Hampton assassinated

1970
- May 1 — May Day protest at Yale and other colleges around the country
- August 5 — Huey released from prison

1971
- January 19 — the Panther 21 publish an open letter denouncing the Party
- January 23 — Huey begins purges of Party members
- May 12 — Panther 21 acquitted
- August 21 — George Jackson is murdered

1973
- Elaine Brown runs for city council and Bobby Seale runs for mayor in Oakland

1974
- Elaine Brown becomes Chairwoman of the Party
- Bobby Seale and Elaine Brown leave the Party

1980
- October — last issue of the *Black Panther* newspaper is published

1981
- Oakland Community School closes

1982
- Last Black Panther Party office closes

"All Power to the People" — a cultural and political cry frequently used by the Panthers and their allies.

"Free Huey!" — the movement to free Huey Newton which the Panthers rallied behind from his arrest in 1967 through release in 1970, organized especially by Kathleen and Eldridge Cleaver.

"Law and Order" platform — a political platform and slogan of being "tough on crime" which first became popularized during campaigns of George Wallace, Ronald Reagan, and Richard Nixon in the late 1960s.

Aaron Dixon — co-founder and Chairman of the Seattle Branch of the Party, the first chapter outside of California.

Afeni Shakur — a member of the New York chapter and the Panther 21; mother to Tupac Shakur.

Algiers — the capital and largest city of Algeria, which gave official diplomatic status to Eldridge Cleaver and other Panthers and allowed them to establish an international headquarters for the Party.

Alprentice "Bunchy" Carter — founder and leader of the Los Angeles Party branch, the first outside of Oakland.

Angela Davis — a political activist, philosopher, academic, scholar, and author, whose work has focused on feminism, class, and the US prison system among other things, and who was affiliated with the Panthers.

antiwar movement — the broad movement protesting against the U.S. involvement in the Vietnam War, of which the Panthers were a part and drew numerous allies from.

armed self-defense — the principal strategy of the Black Panther Party; inspired by Malcolm X.

Assata Shakur — a member of the Panthers who later joined the Black Liberation Army (BLA); while serving a life sentence for murder she escaped prison and was granted political asylum in Cuba; her autobiography *Assata* has become an essential text.

Betty Shabazz — Civil Rights advocate and educator; wife to Malcolm X.

Beverly Axelrod — a White civil rights lawyer who worked with a variety of activists and organizations in the 1960s and later, including the Black Panthers; she assisted Eldridge Cleaver while he was in prison and with the publication of *Soul on Ice*.

Black Liberation Army (BLA) — an offshoot of the Black Panther Party that formed in the early 1970s as the Party shifted to more non-violent tactics, which practiced armed violence in their stated goal of liberation and self-determination of Black people in the U.S.

Black nationalism — a movement originating in the 19th century—when some Black people emigrated from the U.S. to nations like Liberia and Haiti—which advocated for Black people to control their own economic, political, social, and cultural development.

Black Panther (symbol) — an image of Black Power that originated with the Lowndes County Freedom Organization in Alabama and would be used by others, most notably the Black Panther Party.

Black Panther, The — the newspaper and primary channel of communication for the Party which ran from 1967–1980 and at its height had international distribution and a circulation in the hundreds of thousands.

Black Power — a movement that began in the early 1960s and which advocated for Black pride, economic independence, and new social and cultural institutions for Black people; it did not necessarily seek to integrate with White society; the Black Panther Party were a primary organization within this movement.

Black Studies — an academic field devoted to the study of the history, culture, and politics of Black people; Party member George Murray helped lead the movement to create a department at San Francisco State University which ultimately led to the birth of ethnic studies programs across the country.

Bobby Rush — co-founder and later acting Chairman of the Illinois branch of the Party; later served as a representative in Congress for more than two decades.

Bobby Seale — co-founder and Chairman of the Black Panther Party.

bourgeoisie — as defined in Marxist philosophy, the social class that came to own the means of production during modern industrialization and who is focused on the value of property and preservation of capital; equivalent with the middle or upper middle class.

Brown Berets — a pro-Chicanx group that emerged during the Chicago Movement in the late 1960s, inspired by the Black Panthers and organizing around farmworkers' struggles, educational reform, and against police brutality and the Vietnam War.

capitalism — an economic and political system in which a country's trade and industry are controlled by private owners for profit, rather than by the state.

Chicago Eight — eight defendants—Abbie Hoffman, Jerry Rubin, David Dellinger, Rennie Davis, Tom Hayden, John Froines, Lee Weiner, and Bobby Seale—who were charged by the federal government under a new law for crossing state lines with intent to incite a riot at the 1968 Democratic National Convention.

Civil Rights Act — a civil rights and labor law enacted in 1964 which outlawed discrimination based on race, color, religion, sex, national origin, and later sexual orientation and gender identity; one of the primary achievements of the Civil Rights Movement.

Civil Rights Movement — the movement in the 1950s and 60s—preceded by similar campaigns in previous decades—by African Americans and allies to end legalized racial discrimination, disenfranchisement, and racial segregaion in the U.S.

class struggle — the tension and conflict that occurs between social classes.

COINTELPRO — a series of covert and illegal operations by the FBI aimed at surveilling, infiltrating, and disrupting domestic American political groups, including the Black Panthers and other Civil Rights and Black Power groups.

colonialism — the practice or policy of control by one people or power over another, often by establishing colonies through occupying settlers, and generally with the aim of economic dominance.

Communism — a form of socialism whose goal is a society with common ownership of the means of production and the absence of social classes, money, and state.

Community Alert Patrol (CAP) — an organization in the Watts community which monitored and documented police activity; an inspiration for Huey in founding the Party.

community survival programs — a series of Party programs, announced in 1968 and beginning in 1969, which achieved great success and garnered tremendous support in their communities; programs included Free Breakfast for Children; free health care clinics; Busing to Prisons; Free Food; Free Shoes and Clothing; a Free Ambulance Program; and others.

concession — something that is granted, especially in response to demands.

David Hilliard — childhood friend of Huey Newton and later Chief of Staff of the Party; during his time as leader he oversaw the Party's shift in focus to community survival programs.

Denzil Dowell — a young Black man from North Richmond, CA murdered by police in 1967; his mother, Ruby, and brother George worked with the Panthers to investigate.

Detroit rebellion — a rebellion by Black citizens of Detroit, MI lasting for five days; the most significant event of the "long hot summer" of 1967.

Elaine Brown — Los Angeles branch member and eventual Chairwoman of the Black Panther Party; her work in later years has focused on prison reform.

Eldridge Cleaver — Minister of Information for the Party, author of *Soul on Ice*, and head of the Intercommunal Section in Algiers; his split from Huey was a contributing factor to the decline of the Party.

Emory Douglas — Minister of Culture and primary visual artist for the *Black Panther* newspaper.

Ericka Huggins — Party member and leader in both the Los Angeles and New Haven branches of the Party; director of the Oakland Community School from 1973–1981.

Establishment — generally speaking, a term used to describe a dominant or elite group.

Executive Mandates — a series of statements by Party leadership which established key positions of the Party.

fascism — a form of far-right, authoritarian government; most notably implemented in Nazi Germany and Fascist Italy in the 20th century.

FBI — Federal Bureau of Investigation; the domestic intelligence and security system of the U.S. and its principal federal law enforcement agency.

Fred Hampton — Chairman of the Illinois branch and Deputy Chairman of the national Party; founder of the Rainbow Coalition; murdered by Chicago police in 1969.

George Jackson — author, prison activist, and head of the Party chapter at San Quentin Prison in Marin County, CA; he was killed by prison guards in 1971 and the reaction to his death from the Party illustrated the growing shift in tactics and approach.

George Murray — Minister of Education and teacher at San Francisco State University who helped lead a student strike calling for greater non-White representation in the student body and the creation of Black studies departments there and throughout the country.

Geronimo Pratt — Deputy Minister of Defense for the Los Angeles branch and right-hand man of Bunchy Carter; his expulsion from the Party by Huey Newton was another key moment in the eventual split of the Party.

Huey P. Newton — co-founder and Minister of Defense for the Black Panther Party.

imperialism — a policy or ideology of extending a country's power and influence through colonization, use of military force, or other means.

integration (racial) — the process of leveling barriers to association; creating equal opportunities regardless of race; and the development of a culture that draws on diverse traditions, rather than merely bringing a racial minority into the majority one; includes the process of desegregation, but desegregation is considered largely a legal matter, whereas integration largely a social one.

Intercommunal Section — the international wing of the Party, headquartered in Algiers and led by Eldridge Cleaver; a prime advocate for the continuation of armed struggle and revolution.

J. Edgar Hoover — director of the F.B.I. from 1935 until his death in 1972.

Jim Crow laws — state and local laws that enforced racial segregation in the South; generally these laws were ended by the Civil Rights Act in 1964 and Voting Rights Act in 1965.

John Huggins — Deputy Minister of Information for the Los Angeles branch; husband of Ericka Huggins.

José "Cha Cha" Jiménez — founder of the Young Lords Organization.

Kathleen Cleaver — Communications Secretary for the Party and a major organizer of the "Free Huey!" movement; her photo with the accompanying caption "Shoot Your Shot!" became one of the most enduring images of the Party; joined Eldridge in Algiers as part of the Intercommunal Section.

Kent State shootings — the killings of four and woundings of nine other unarmed Kent State students by National Guardsmen during May Day protests in 1970.

Kerner Commission — a Presidential Commission established by President Johnson to investigate the causes of the "long hot summer" of 1967.

liberation — the action of setting someone free from imprisonment, slavery, or oppression.

liberation schools — a series of schools founded and run by the Party across the country, most notably the Oakland Community School.

Lil' Bobby Hutton — Huey and Bobby's first recruit into the Party; killed in a shootout with police on April 6th, 1968, just two days after Martin Luther King, Jr.

Los Siete de la Raza — a group of young Latinx people in the Mission District of San Francisco who, inspired by the Panthers, worked to free seven men charged with the killing of a policeman.

Lowndes County Freedom Organization — A political party in Lowndes County, Alabama, devoted to registering Black votes, who first used the Black Panther symbol and inspired Huey and Bobby.

Lyndon B. Johnson — President of the United States from 1963–1969.

Malcolm X — a primary leader of the Black Power movement, initially within the Nation of Islam, who advocated for liberation "by any means necessary"; a tremendous influence on Huey, Bobby, and many others.

Martin Luther King, Jr. — the most prominent leader of the Civil Rights Movement and practitioner of non-violent civil disobedience.

martyr — a person who is killed because of their beliefs.

May Day protests, 1970 — a series of protests which began at Yale University, in support of the Panthers and against the Vietnam War, which soon spread to protests on campuses around the country.

messiah — a savior or liberator of a group of people.

Mulford Act — a 1967 California bill that prohibited the public carrying of loaded firearms; it was created by assemblyman Donald Mulford to eliminate the Panthers' initial main tactic of armed police patrols.

Nation of Islam — a religious and political Black nationalist organization, founded in 1930; Malcolm X was a prominent leader within it from 1952–1964.

National Association for the Advancement of Colored People (NAACP) — an organization founded in 1909 to address ongoing violence and discrimination against Black people; a prominent group during the Civil Rights Movement through the present.

National Committees to Combat Fascism (NCCF) — a series of groups founded by the Party following the United Front Against Fascism Conference in 1969, designed to create more space for allies to contribute.

Newark rebellion — a rebellion by Black citizens of Newark, NJ lasting for five days; along with Detroit one of the most significant actions in the "long hot summer" of 1967.

non-violent civil disobedience — the active, professed refusal of a citizen to obey certain laws or commands in order to effect change; the primary tactic of the Civil Rights Movement.

oppression — the unjust or cruel exercise of authority or power.

Pan-African Cultural Festival — the inaugural festival was organized by the president of Algeria, Houari Boumedienne, in order to promote African unity and support liberation struggles across the world; numerous Panthers were invited and attended.

Panther 21 — A group of twenty-one Panthers from the New York office charged with planning to bomb various locations, whose cause became a rallying point for the Panthers and their allies; all were acquitted.

Peace and Freedom Party — a major voice in the antiwar movement, made up primarily of White members, and an early ally of the Panthers.

Pig — a term and image for "policeman" popularized by Huey Newton and the Party, designed to call attention to police brutality and challenge stereotyping, preudice, and implicit bias.

police brutality — the excessive and unwarranted use of force by law enforcement.

prejudice — a bias or preconceived opinion, idea, or belief about something or someone.

racism — prejudice, stereotyping, or discrimination against a person or people on the basis of being part of a marginalized racial or ethnic group.

Rainbow Coalition — a union of diverse groups, including the Panthers, the Young Lords, the Young Patriots, and the Brown Berets, founded by Fred Hampton and devoted to ending poverty and class hierarchy in their communities.

***Ramparts* Magazine** — published by Edward Keating, an independent Catholic publication and an influential voice in Vietnam War opposition.

rebellion — open and armed defiance of or resistance to an established government.

Red Guard — a group of Asian-American from Chinatown in San Francisco who led a series of community-based programs and actions to assist poor and working class members of their communities.

reform — the action of changing an institution or practice in order to improve it.

repression — the action of subduing someone or something by force.

revolution — a forcible overthrow of a government or social order, in favor of a new system.

Revolutionary Action Movement (RAM) — a national radical and internationalist Black organization, of which Huey, Bobby, and Eldridge were members prior to the Panthers.

Richard Nixon — President of the United States from 1969–1974; he was elected under a "Law and Order" platform and under his administration repression of the Panthers greatly increased.

Robert Webb — a member of the Panthers killed in 1971 during the split between wings of the Party; afterwards many Panther members left the Party.

Ron Karenga — founder and leader of the US organization which clashed with the Panthers in Los Angeles; also the creator of the holiday Kwanzaa.

Sacramento protest — a protest by the Panthers at the California Capitol in 1967; one of the first and most influential actions taken by the Party.

Sam Napier — the distribution manager of the *Black Panther* newspaper killed in 1971 during the split between wings of the Party; afterwards many Panther members left the Party.

segregation (racial) — the systematic separation of people into racial or other ethnic groups in daily life, in realms such as housing, medical care, education, employment, and transportation; in the context of the U.S., refers primarily to the separate between White and Black people.

self-determination — the process by which people form their own state and choose their own government; more broadly, the ability or power for a person or people to make choices for themselves.

sexism — prejudice, stereotyping, or discrimination—typically against women—on the basis of sex.

socialism — an economic and political system where workers own the general means of production.

Soul Students Advisory Council (SSAC) — an offshoot of RAM, which Huey and Bobby were a part of prior to founding the Party.

stereotype — a widely held but fixed and oversimplified image or idea of a person or thing.

Stokely Carmichael (later known as Kwame Ture) — a prominent leader within the Civil Rights and Black Power movements; he

339

succeeded John Lewis as the leader of SNCC; briefly a member of the Black Panther Party.

Student Nonviolent Coordinating Committee (SNCC) — the principal group for students participating in the Civil Rights Movement; they later became a prominent ally of the Panthers and merged with them before dissolution.

Students for a Democratic Society (SDS) — a leftist White radical group and ally of the Panthers.

Tarika Lewis — one of the first women to join the Party and a contributor of artwork to the *Black Panther* newspaper.

Ten-Point Program — the party platform, written by Huey and Bobby, published in every issue of the Black Panther newspaper.

The "long hot summer" of 1967 — a series of 164 rebellions that erupted in Black communities across the U.S. in response to government oppression.

vanguard — a group of people leading the way in new developments or ideas; also, the foremost part of an advancing army or force.

Vietnam War — a conflict in Vietnam, Laos, and Cambodia from 1955–1975, fought between North Vietnam and its communist allies and South Vietnam and its anti-communist allies, including the U.S.

voter suppression — an election strategy designed to discourage or prevent specific groups of people from voting.

Voting Rights Act — a law enacted in 1965 that prohibited racial discrimination in voting; a major achievement of the Civil Rights movement.

Watts rebellion — a major uprising by Black citizens in the Watts neighborhood of Los Angeles, CA in 1965; a precursor to the "long hot summer" of 1967.

Young Lords — an organization, founded in Chicago and inspired by the Panthers, which advocated for rights and change for the Puerto Rican community; a member of the Rainbow Coalition.

Young Patriots Organization — a leftist group of mostly White Southerners living in Chicago who organized to support migrants from the Appalachia region living in poverty; a member of the Rainbow Coalition.

P. 2, 10, 42, 48–49, 60, 63, 64, 84, 109, 130–131, 150, 171, 172, 174, 176–177, 180–181, 252, 266, 296–297 — Stephen Shames/Polaris

P. 7 — Newton, Huey P. at press interview in the apartment of Jane Fonda (New York, New York), 1970, James E. Hinton photographs and papers, 1954–2006, Stuart A. Rose Manuscript, Archives, and Rare Book Library, Emory University.

P. 14–15 — Danny Lyon/Magnum Photos

P. 16, 55 — Ernest Cole/Magnum Photos

P.18 — Eve Arnold/Magnum Photos

P. 28, 76, 83 (bottom), 209 — Collection of the Smithsonian National Museum of African American History and Culture

P. 32, 284 — Courtesy of the Library of Congress

P. 34 (top) — Express/Getty Images

P. 34 (bottom), 197 — Los Angeles Times Photographic Archives, UCLA, Library Special Collections, Charles E. Young Research Library

P. 37, 110–111, 299 — Ron Riesterer/Photoshelter

P. 52–53, 65, 66, 80, 113, 115, 146, 151, 168, 210, 244–245, 256–257, 292, 303, 304 — © Regents of the University of California. Courtesy Special Collections, University Library, University of California Santa Cruz. Ruth-Marion Baruch and Pirkle Jones Photographs.

P. 56, 143 — Courtesy of the Marxists Internet Archive

P. 72–73 — AP Photo/Walt Zeboski

P. 83 (top) — SNCC Political Education Materials by Courtland Cox and Jennifer Lawson

P. 88–89 — New York Times Co./Getty Images

P. 92, 135, 308–309 — Bettmann/Getty Images

P. 96 — Keystone-France/Getty Images

P. 100 — Alan Copeland

P. 118, 132, 166 — Bob Fitch Photography Archive, Department of Special Collections, Stanford University Libraries

P. 122–123 — Leonard Freed/Magnum Photos

P. 127 — Bobby Hutton Murdered, flier, Social Protest Collection, 1943–1982 (bulk 1960–1975), BANC MSS 86/157 c, The Bancroft Library, University of California, Berkeley

P. 138 — MOHAI, Seattle Post-Intelligencer Collection, 1986.5.50982.1

P. 139 — Black Panthers on steps of Legislative Building, Olympia, 1969, State Governors' Negative Collection, 1949–1975, Washington State Archives, Digital Archives, http://www.digitalarchives.wa.gov, accessed 30 September 2021.

P. 141 — Jack Garofalo/Getty Images

P. 148 — Photograph by Terry Schmitt courtesy of San Francisco State University Archives, J. Paul Leonard Library.

P. 154–155, 160, 179 — Hiroji Kubota/Magnum Photos

P. 157 — ST-19030979-0006, Chicago Sun-Times collection, Chicago History Museum

P. 159 — ST-17101234-0002, Chicago Sun-Times collection, Chicago History Museum

P. 162 — ST-70004742-0019, Chicago Sun-Times collection, Chicago History Museum

P. 163 — ST-70004742-0011,Chicago Sun-Times collection, Chicago History Museum

P. 184, 188–189 — Bruno Barbey/Magnum Photos

P. 190 — Robert Wade

P. 194 — Eldridge Cleaver (in sunglasses) with Alprentice "Bunchy" Carter, Eldridge Cleaver photograph collection, BANC PIC 1991.078—PIC, box 1:1, The Bancroft Library, University of California, Berkeley.

P. 202–203 — Courtesy of the National Archives

P. 208 — Martin Petersilia, Courtesy of the National Museum of American History

P. 212–213 — ST-19030961-0003, Chicago Sun-Times collection, Chicago History Museum

P. 218 — Courtesy of the National Portrait Gallery, Smithsonian Institution

P. 222 — ST-19030997-0017, Chicago Sun-Times collection, Chicago History Museum

P. 224 — ST-19080078-0002, Chicago Sun-Times collection, Chicago History Museum

P. 228–229, 241 — Los Angeles Herald Examiner Photo Collection/Los Angeles Public Library

P. 231 — ST-19031010-0001, Chicago Sun-Times collection, Chicago History Museum

P. 235 — ST-19030972-0024, Chicago Sun-Times collection, Chicago History Museum

P. 236 — ST-19030958-0011, Chicago Sun-Times collection, Chicago History Museum

P. 259 — ST-70006726-0010, Chicago Sun-Times collection, Chicago History Museum

P. 260 — John Hill

P. 264–265 — MOHAI, Seattle Post-Intelligencer Collection, 1986.5.52212.1, Photo by Paul Thomas

P. 264 — Raymond Depardon/Magnum Photos

P. 271 — Associated Press

Part 1: In the Beginning

1. Aaron Dixon, *My People Are Rising: Memoir of a Black Panther Party Captain* (Chicago: Haymarket Books, 2012), p. 311.

FREEDOM! was written as a narrative intended for a general audience and not meant to be considered "objective history." For a scholarly, peer-reviewed history of the Party, see Joshua Bloom and Waldo E. Martin, Jr., *Black Against Empire: The History and the Politics of the Black Panther Party* (Oakland: University of California Press, 2016).

Chapter 1.

2. Bobby Seale, *Seize the Time: The Story of the Black Panther Party and Huey P. Newton* (1971; repr. Baltimore: Black Classic Press, 1990), pp. 93–98; and tour of the site of the incident with Joshua Bloom and Bobby Seale January 19, 1999.

3. Seale, *Seize the Time*, p. 97.

4. David Hilliard and Lewis Cole, *This Side of Glory: The Autobiography of David Hilliard and the Story of the Black Panthers* (New York: Little, Brown, 1993), p. 71; Huey Newton, *Revolutionary Suicide*, (1973; repr. New York: Penguin Group, 2009), p. 20.

5. Newton, *Revolutionary Suicide*, p. 30.

6. Ibid., p. 18.

7. Ibid., pp. 45–55, 60.

8. Bobby Seale, *Lonely Rage: The Autobiography of Bobby Seale* (New York: Times Books, 1978); Bobby Seale interview by Joshua Bloom, April 25, 1999; Joshua Bloom, "Bobby Seale," in *Civil Rights in the United States*, vol. 2, ed. Waldo E. Martin, Jr., and Patricia Sullivan (New York: Macmillan, 2000) p. 677.

9. Seale, *Lonely Rage*, pp. 19 and 26.

10. Ibid., part 3.

11. Ibid., p. 91 and part 4.

12. Seale, *Seize the Time*, p. 11.

13. Ibid.

14. Ibid., pp. 11–12.

Chapter 2.

15. https://www.naacp.org/about-us/

16. Seale, *Seize the Time*, p. 14.

17. Ibid.

18. Ibid.

19. Ibid.

20. Seale, *Seize the Time*, pp. 13–21; Robin D. G. Kelley, *Freedom Dreams: The Black Radical Imagination* (Boston: Beacon Press, 2002), pp. 74–77; Donna Jean Murch, *Living for the City* (Chapel Hill: University of North Carolina Press, 2010), pp. 75–95.

21. Newton, *Revolutionary Suicide*, pp. 64–65.

22. Seale, *Seize the Time*, p. 33.

23. Malcolm X and Alex Haley, *The Autobiography of Malcolm X* (New York: Ballantine Books, 1965); Walter Dean Myers, *Malcolm X: By Any Means Necessary* (New York: Scholastic, 1993).

24. Malcolm X and George Breitman, ed., *Malcolm X Speaks* (New York: Grove Press, 1965), p. 165.

25. Ibid., p. 22.

26. Ibid., pp. 31–32.

27. Malcolm X and Haley, *Autobiography of Malcolm X,* p. 439.

28. Ibid., pp. 4 and 437.

29. Seale, *Lonely Rage*, pp. 133–36; Seale, *Seize the Time,* p. 3.

Chapter 3.

30. Seale, *Seize the Time,* p. 27.

31. Ibid., pp. 27–28.

32. Ibid., p. 28.

33. Deborah Gray White, Mia Bay, Waldo E. Martin Jr., *Freedom on My Mind: A History of African Americans with Documents,* (Boston: Bedford/St. Martin's, 2017), p. 548.

34. The People of the State of California v. Bobby Seale, case 38842; Seale, *Seize the Time*, pp. 27–28.

35. Seale, *Seize the Time,* pp. 28–29, 33. Megan Miladinov, "Former Black Panther Leader," *Athens News,* February 12, 2004.

36. Seale, *Seize the Time,* p. 29.

37. Ibid., p. 35.

38. Parker quoted in Tracy Tullis, "A Vietnam at Home: Policing the Ghettos in the Counterinsurgency Era" (PhD diss., New York University, 1999), p. 208.

39. Ibid.

40. Gerald Horne, *Fire This Time: The Watts Uprising and the 1960s* (New York: Da Capo, 1997), pp. 54–55.

41. Ibid., pp. 58, 66.

42. Ibid., pp. 36–38. In the end 34 people were killed, almost all Black. In addition, more than 1,032 were wounded and 3,952 were arrested; Jack McCurdy and Art Berman, "New Rioting: Stores Looted, Cars Destroyed, Many Fires Started; 75 Reported Injured in 2nd Violent Night," *Los Angeles Times*, August 12, 1965, p. 1.

43. Thomas C. Fleming, "Wild Rioting by Oakland Youths," *Sun Reporter*, October 22, 1966, in Daniel Edward Crowe, "The Origins of the Black Revolution: The Transformation of San Francisco Bay Area Black Communities, 1945–1969" (PhD diss., University of Kentucky, 1998), p. 196; Amory Bradford, *Oakland's Not for Burning* (New York: D. McKay, 1968), p. 194.

44. Ibid.

45. Terence Cannon, "A Night with the Watts Community Alert Patrol," *Movement*, August, 1966, p. 1; article in Huey Newton's possession, Huey P. Newton Collection, series 7, flat box 9, folder 13, Stanford University; Horne, *Fire This Time*, p. 54.

46. Newton, *Revolutionary Suicide*, pp. 115, 129–130; Seale, *Seize the Time*, pp. 73, 89.

47. Diane C. Fujino, *Samurai Among Panthers: Richard Aoki on Race, Resistance, and a Paradoxical Life* (Minneapolis: University of Minnesota Press, 2012), pp. 11–20, 28, 66, 79, 105, 134. For evidence that Richard Aoki was working with the FBI see Seth Rosenfeld *Subversives: The FBI's War on Student Radicals and Reagan's Rise to Power* (New York: Picador, 2013).

48. Seale, *Seize the Time*, pp. 72–73.

49. Newton, *Revolutionary Suicide*, p. 126.

50. Ibid.

51. Ibid.

52. Seale, *Seize the Time*, p. 77.

Part 2: Take a Stand

53. Newton, *Revolutionary Suicide*, p. 213.

Chapter 4.

54. Seale, *Seize the Time*, p. 132.

55. Lauren Araiza and Joshua Bloom, "Eldridge Cleaver," in Mark Carnes, ed., *American National Biography* (New York: Oxford University Press, 2001).

56. Eldridge Cleaver, *Soul on Ice* (New York: Random House, 1968, repr., 1992), p. 22.

57. Newton, *Revolutionary Suicide*, pp. 136–37.

58. Seale, *Seize the Time*, p. 133.

59. Newton, *Revolutionary Suicide*, pp. 136–37.

60. Gene Marine, *The Black Panthers: Eldridge Cleaver, Huey Newton, Bobby Seale—A Compelling Study of the Angry Young Revolutionaries Who Have Shaken a Black Fist at White America* (New York: Signet 1969), pp. 52–53; Wyatt Buchanan, "Edward Keating, Ramparts Founder," *San Francisco Chronicle*, April 10, 2003.

61. The escort of Betty Shabazz and the incidents directly preceding and following are drawn from five firsthand accounts: Eldridge Cleaver, "The Courage to Kill: Meeting the Panthers," June 1968, in *Eldridge Cleaver: Post-Prison Writings and Speeches*, ed. Robert Scheer (New York: Random House, 1969); Marine, *The Black Panthers*, pp. 52–56, Earl Anthony, *Spitting in the Wind: The True Story Behind the Violent Legacy of Black Panther Party* (Santa Monica, CA: Roundtable Publishing, 1990), pp. 22–23; Seale, *Seize the Time*, pp. 113–32; "Frightening 'Army' Hits the Airport," *San Francisco Chronicle*, February 22, 1967, p. 1.

62. Newton, *Revolutionary Suicide*, p. 139.

63. Nessel quoted in "Frightening 'Army' Hits the Airport," p. 1.

64. Seale, *Seize the Time*, p. 134.

65. Cleaver, "The Courage to Kill," p. 36.

66. Spencer, *The Revolution Has Come*, p. 47.

67. Ashley D. Farmer, *Remaking Black Power: How Black Women Transformed an Era* (Chapel Hill: University of North Carolina Press, 2017), p. 62.

68. Spencer, *The Revolution Has Come*, p. 48.

Chapter 5.

69. *Black Panther*, April 25, 1967, pp. 1–2.

70. "Sudden Death: Suspect in Robbery Shot Down," *Oakland Tribune*, April 1, 1967, p. 1.

71. Marine, *The Black Panthers*, pp. 57–59; Anthony, *Spitting in the Wind*, p. 28; *Black Panther*, April 25, 1967, pp. 1–2.

72. *Black Panther*, April 25, 1967, p. 2; "Youth Sought in Slaying Investigation," *Oakland Tribune*, December 11, 1966, p. 1B.

73. Newton, *Revolutionary Suicide*, p. 146.

74. Marine, *The Black Panthers*, p. 57; Newton, *Revolutionary Suicide*, p. 146.

75. Newton, *Revolutionary Suicide*, p. 146.

76. George Dowell, interview published in the *Black Panther*, May 15, 1967, p. 2; Marine, *The Black Panthers*, p. 58.

77. Newton, *Revolutionary Suicide*, pp. 147–51.

78. Marine, *The Black Panthers*, p. 60.

79. Newton, *Revolutionary Suicide*, pp. 147–51.

80. Ibid., pp. 147.

81. Ibid.

82. Marine, *The Black Panthers*, p. 61; Seale, *Seize the Time*, pp. 143–47; Jerry Belcher, "It's All Legal: Oakland's Black Panthers Wear Guns, Talk Revolution," *San Francisco Chronicle*, April 30, 1967, p. 1; *Black Panther*, April 25, 1967, p. 2.

83. Gilbert Moore, *A Special Rage* (New York: Harper and Row, 1971), p. 58; *Black Panther*, April 25, 1967; Anthony *Spitting in the Wind*, p. 31; Marine, *The Black Panthers*, p. 62; Newton, *Revolutionary Suicide*, p. 151.

84. Belcher, "It's All Legal," p. 1; *Black Panther*, April 25, 1967, p. 1; Anthony, *Spitting in the Wind*, p. 29.

Chapter 6.

85. Oakland police officer Richard Jensen interviewed for *Eyes on the Prize II: America at the Racial Crossroads 1965–1985,* episode 3, "Power!" 1967–1968), produced and directed by Henry Hampton, aired 1987 (Washington, DC: PBS, 2010), DVD.

86. For more details about AB 1591, see California Legislature, *Final Calendar of Legislative Business,* 1967, pt. 2,506.

87. Statutes of California, 1967 Regular Session, ch. 960.

88. Newton, *Revolutionary Suicide*, p. 154.

89. Ibid.

90. Ibid., p. 155.

91. Huey was on probation for stabbing Odell Lee at a party with a steak knife. Huey argued that he could read the cues and knew that Odell was getting ready to attack him, so Huey attacked first. An all-White jury disagreed. Huey spent six months in jail, most of them in solitary confinement for not following the guards' orders, before he was released. Newton, *Revolutionary Suicide,* pp. 88–91, 156.

92. Seale, *Seize the Time*, pp. 153–63; Marine *The Black Panthers*, pp. 63–64; *Eyes on the Prize II*; Newton, *Revolutionary Suicide,* p. 157.

93. Marine, *The Black Panthers*, pp. 63–64.

94. Seale, *Seize the Time*, pp. 153–63; "Black Panthers Disrupt the Assembly," *San Francisco Chronicle*, May 3, 1967, p. 1.

95. "Black Panthers Disrupt the Assembly," p. 1; Footage from Sacramento in *Eyes on the Prize II*, pt. 3.

96. Executive Mandate No. 1, quoted in Philip S. Foner, ed., *The Black Panthers Speak* (Philadelphia: Lippincott, 1970; repr. New York: Da Capo, 1995), p. 40.

97. "Black Panthers Disrupt Assembly," p. 1.

98. TV footage from *Eyes on the Prize II;* concerning the concealed weapons charges see Marine, *The Black Panthers,* p. 65; about Forte's arrest see Seale, *Seize the Time*, p. 165.

99. Seale, *Seize the Time*, p. 171.

100. For this point see Bobby Seale's February 1968 speech printed in the *Black Panther*. "Now I'm gonna show you how smart Brother Huey is when he planned Sacramento. He said, now, the papers gon call us thugs and hoodlums. A lot of people ain't gon know what's happening. But the brothers on the block, who the man's been calling thugs and hoodlums for four hundred years, gon say, 'Them some out of sight thugs and hoodlums up there!'"

101. Interview with Emory Douglas in *Eyes on the Prize II*.

102. Interview with George Dowell in *Black Panther*, May 15, 1967, pp. 2, 4.

Chapter 7.

103. Seale, *Seize the Time*, p. 185.

104. Ibid.

105. Ibid., p. 182.

106. The language of the Ten-Point Program changed over time, but it was always included in the Party paper.

107. *Black Panther,* May 15, 1967, p. 3.

108. Newton, *Revolutionary Suicide,* p. 119; https://designobserver.com/feature/the-women -behind-the-black-panther-party-logo/39755.

109. Seale quoted in Jim Hyde, "Protest Police Brutality: Black Panthers Defend Negro," *Daily Californian*, May 11, 1967, p. 3.

110. Barbara Arthur quoted in Jim Hyde, "Protest Police Brutality: Black Panthers Defend Negro," *Daily Californian*, May 11, 1967, p. 3; "Panther Rally Postponed," *Daily Californian*, May 5, 1967, p. 1; "Black Panthers at UC—Friendly Unarmed Visit," *San Franciscco Chronicle*, May 11, 1967, p. 2.

111. Newton, *Revolutionary Suicide*, p. 125.

112. Bobby Seale, "The Coming Long Hot Summer," *Black Panther*, June 20, 1967, pp. 4, 7. When Bobby uses the phrase "long hot summer" he is referencing the way Malcolm X talked about the Harlem rebellion.

113. Newton, *Revolutionary Suicide*, p. 163.

114. Malcolm X and Haley, *The Autobiography of Malcolm X,* p. 360.

115. This account draws on five sources: U.S. Riot Commission, *Report of the National Advisory Commission on Civil Disorders* (New York: Bantam, 1968); Robert L. Allen, *Black Awakening in Capitalist America: An Analytic History* (Garden City, NY: Anchor Books, 1969); Komozi Woodward, *A Nation within a Nation* (Chapel Hill: University of North Carolina Press, 1999); Tom Hayden, *Rebellion in Newark* (New York: Vintage, 1967); and Kevin Mumford, *Newark: A History of Race, Rights and Riots in America* (New York: New York University Press, 2007).

116. LeRoi Jones quoted in Allen, *Black Awakening in Capitalist America,* p. 135.

117. *Black Panther,* July 20, 1967, pp. 12–13.

Chapter 8.

118. Many of the details concerning the Detroit rebellion are taken from Sidney Fine, *Violence in the Model City: The Cavanagh Administration, Race Relations, and the Detroit Riot of 1967* (Ann Arbor: University of Michigan Press, 1989), unless specifically noted.

119. Ibid., p. 160.

120. Sol Stern, "America's Black Guerillas," *Ramparts,* September 2, 1967, p. 26; Fine, *Violence in the Model City,* pp. 191–201.

121. Campbell-Schuman survey in Fine, *Violence in the Model City,* p. 177.

122. Ibid., pp. 170, 180, 181, 194, 206, 207, 224–25; US. Riot Commission, *Report of the National Advisory Committee on Civil Disorders,* p. 101.

123. Fine, *Violence in the Model City,* p. 249, 294; U.S. Riot Commission, *Report of the National Advisory Commission on Civil Disorders,* p. 107.

Part 3: The Panthers Rise

124. Robert Shellow et al., "The Harvest of American Racism," an unpublished report quoted in Andrew Kopind, "White on Black: The Riot Commission and the Rhetoric of Reform," in *The Politics of Riot Commissions,* ed. Anthony M. Platt (New York: Collier, 1971), p. 387.

125. Ibid.

126. www.poetryfoundation.org/poems/44694/if-we-must-die Claude McKay wrote this poem in 1919 as a response against the White mobs who were attacking Black Americans. Here is the full text of the poem:

If we must die, let it not be like hogs
Hunted and penned in an inglorious spot,
While round us bark the mad and hungry dogs,
Making their mock at our accursed lot.
If we must die, O let us nobly die,
So that our precious blood may not be shed
In vain; then even the monsters we defy
Shall be constrained to honor us though dead!
O kinsmen! we must meet the common foe!
Though far outnumbered let us show us brave,
And for their thousand blows deal one
    death-blow!
What though before us lies the open grave?
Like men we'll face the murderous, cowardly
    pack,
Pressed to the wall, dying, but fighting back!

Chapter 9.

127. Seale, *Seize the Time,* p. 187.

128. Newton, *Revolutionary Suicide,* p. 184.

129. Ibid.

130. Marine, *The Black Panther,* pp. 100–101.

131. Ibid., ch. 9.

132. Newton, *Revolutionary Suicide,* p. 185–87.

133. Ibid., p. 188.

134. Ibid., p. 184.

135. Eldridge Cleaver, "Huey Must Be Set Free!" *Black Panther,* November 23, 1967, p. 1.

136. Marine, *The Black Panthers,* pp. 128–29.

137. Kathleen Cleaver and George Katsiaficas, *Liberation, Imagination, and the Black Panther Party* (New York: Routledge, 2001), p. 126.

138. Kathleen Cleaver, "On Eldridge Cleaver," *Ramparts,* June 1969, p. 4.

139. Ibid.

140. Interview with Kathleen Cleaver in the *Washington Post,* February 1970, cited in Foner, ed., *The Black Panthers Speak,* p. 145.

141. Cleaver and Katsiaficas, *Liberation, Imagination, and the Black Panther Party,* pp. 124–25.

142. Marine, *The Black Panthers,* p. 129.

143. Huey Newton, "Executive Mandate No. 3," *Black Panther,* March 16, 1968, p. 1.

144. The photo of Kathleen Cleaver taken for Executive Mandate No. 3, *Black Panther,* September 28, 1968, p. 20.

145. Cleaver and Katsiaficas, *Liberation, Imagination, and the Black Panther Party,* p. 125.

146. Mike Parker, KPFA Radio, February 15, 1968, recording BB1632, 18:30, Pacifica Radio Archives, North Hollywood, CA.

147. "B.P.P. and P.F.P.," editorial, *Black Panther*, March 16, 1968, p. 3.

148. Newton, *Revolutionary Suicide,* p. 162.

149. *Black Panther,* July 3, 1967, various articles, pp. 1, 6, 7; "Carmichael 'Drafted' by Panthers," *San Francisco Chronicle,* June 30, 1967, p. 48.

Chapter 10.

150. Martin Luther King, Jr., "My Trip to the Land of Gandhi," *Stanford University* (July 1, 1959), https://kinginstitute.stanford.edu /king-papers/documents/my-trip-land -gandhi.

151. "Martin Luther King's Last Speech: 'I've Been to the Mountaintop,'" YouTube, uploaded by NewsPoliticsInfo (April 4, 2010), https://www.youtube.com/watch?v =Oehry1JC9Rk.

152. White, Bay, and Martin, *Freedom on My Mind,* p. 555.

153. King Papers Project, Martin Luther King Jr., Research and Education Institute, Stanford University; for the Memphis rebellion, see Caldwell, "Guard Called Out," p. 1.

154. *The Black Power Mixtape,*. directed by Goran Hugo Olsson (IFC Films), 20:35–20:40.

155. Hilliard and Cole, *This Side of Glory,* p. 186.

156. Stanley Nelson, *The Black Panthers: Vanguard of the Revolution, 2015, 46:29–46:50.*

157. Eldridge Cleaver, "Affidavit #2: Shoot-Out in Oakland," in *Post-Prison Writings*, p. 80; "Oakland Police Attack Panthers," *New Left Notes,* April 15, 1968, p. 1; "Panthers Ambushed, One Murdered," *Black Panther,* May 4, 1968, p. 4; Daryl E. Lembke, "Oakland Tense in the Wake of Police, Panthers Battle," *Los Angeles Times,* April 8, 1968, p. 3; "Black Panther Chief Demands Indictment," *Los Angeles Times,* April 13, 1968, p. A16; Hilliard and Cole, *This Side of Glory,* pp. 182–93.

158. Seale, *Seize the Time,* p. 235.

159. Lawrence E. Davies, "Black Panthers Denounce Policemen," *New York Times,* April 13, 1968, p. 12; "Brando at Oakland Funeral for Slain Black Panther, 17," *Los Angeles Times,* April 13, 1968 , p. B1.

160. Hilliard and Cole, *This Side of Glory,* p. 194.

161. Ibid.

162. Newton, *Revolutionary Suicide,* p. 127.

163. Hilliard and Cole, *This Side of Glory,* p. 164.

164. Bobby Seale, press conference at Oakland Hall of Justice, recording BB 5543, Pacifica Radio Archives, North Hollywood, CA.

165. Billy John Carr quoted in Sol Stern, "The Call of the Black Panthers," New York Times Magazine, August 6, 1967. This story took up two full pages in the magazine. It had large photos and the article itself took up three extra pages.

166. Malcolm X and Haley, *The Autobiography of Malcolm X,* p. 439.

Chapter 11.

167. Michele Russell, "Conversations with Ericka Huggins. Oakland, California, 4/20/77," 10, box 1, Huey P. Newton Papers, cited in Robyn Ceanne Spencer, "Repression Breeds Resistance: The Rise and Fall of the Black Panther Party in Oakland, CA 1966–1982" (PhD diss., Columbia University, 2001), p. 105.

168. Donald Freed, *Agony in New Haven: The Trial of Bobby Seale, Ericka Huggins, and the Black Panther Party* (New York: Simon and Schuster, 1973), pp. 62–64.

169. Elaine Brown, *A Taste of Power: A Black Woman's Story,* (New York: Pantheon Books), p. 87.

170. Ibid., pp. 87–89; chs. 2–5.

171. Ibid., pp. 123–25; Judson L. Jeffries, ed., *Comrades: A Local History of the Black Panther Party* (Bloomington: Indiana University Press, 2007), pp. 262–63.

172. Brown, *A Taste of Power*, p. 118.

173. Cleaver and Katsiaficas, *Liberation, Imagination, and the Black Panther Party,* p. 227.

174. Brown, *A Taste of Power,* pp. 110–20, quotes on pp. 120 and 121. With the statement "In revolution one wins or dies," Bunchy was quoting Che Guevara.

175. Dixon, *My People Are Rising*, p. 78.

176. Ibid., pp. 79–81.

177. Ibid., pp. 80–83.

178. Ibid.

179. Ibid., p. 111.

180. In Harlem, the chapter of the Black Panther Party had its own distinct flavor and character. The members there drew on the strong historical roots of Black nationalism and had cultural nationalist tendencies. Many

of the members took on African names, spoke in Swahili, and wore dashikis. Murray Kempton, *The Briar Patch: The Trial of the Panther 21* (1973; repr. New York: Da Capo Press, 1997), p. 54.

181. Ibid., p. 43.

182. Lumumba Shakur in Kuwasi Balagoon, Joan Bird, Cetewayo, Robert Collier, Dhoruba, Richard Harris, Ali Bey Hassan, Jamal, Abayama Katara, Kwando Kinshasa, Baba Odinga, Shaba Ogun Om, Curtis Powell, Afeni Shakur, Lumumba Shakur, and Clark Squire, *Look for Me in the Whirlwind: The Collective Autobiography of the New York 21* (New York: Random House, 1971), p. 295; Kempton, *The Briar Patch*, pp. 45–46.

183. Jasmine Guy, *Afeni Shakur Evolution of a Revolutionary* (New York: Atria Books, 2004), pp. 60–61.

184. Afeni Shakur is known not only as an important leader in the New York 21 but also as rapper Tupac Shakur's mother. Afeni married Lumumba, took his name, Shakur, and also gave that name to Tupac. But Lumumba was not Tupac's father. Tupac Shakur would go on to become one of the most famous and well-loved rap artists of all time. Afeni Shakur in Balagoon et al., *Look for Me in the Whirlwind*, pp. 287–88.

185. Earl Caldwell, "Black Panthers: 'Young Revolutionaries at War,'" *New York Times,* September 6, 1968, p. 49.

186. Abayama Katara in Balagoon et al., *Look for Me in the Whirlwind*, p. 273.

187. Newton, *Revolutionary Suicide*, pp.173–75.

188. Ibid., p.175.

189. Ibid.

190. Balagoon et al., *Look for Me in the Whirlwind*, pp. 277–78, 295–96. Also McCandlish Phillips, "4 Pupils Arrested at Brandeis High: Brown Appearance Barred before Trouble Erupts," *New York Times,* June 6, 1968, p. 58; David K. Shipler, "Classes Go On Despite District Woes," *New York Times,* June 11, 1968, p. 49; Sidney E. Zion, "5 Black Panthers Held in Brooklyn," *New York Times,* September 13, 1968, p. 93; David Bird, "Judge Forbids Slogan Buttons at Panther Hearing in Brooklyn," *New York Times,* September 19, 1968, p. 32; Steven Roberts, "Race: The Third Party in the School Crisis," *New York Times,* September 22, 1968, p. 182; Leonard Buder, "Shanker Rejects Offer to Protect Ocean Hill Staff," *New York Times,* September 25, 1968, p. 1; Peter Kihiss, "Open Schools, Galamison Tells Rally,"

September 26, 1968, p. 56; "20,000 in N.Y. March for Black Control," *Black Panther,* October 26, 1968, p. 15.

191. Balagoon et al., *Look for Me in the Whirlwind*, p. 277–78, 295–96; Also McCandlish Phillips, "4 Pupils Arrested at Brandeis High: Brown Appearance Barred before Trouble Erupts," *New York Times,* June 6, 1968, p. 58; David K. Shipler, "Classes Go On Despite District Woes," *New York Times,* June 11, 1968, p. 49; Sidney E. Zion, "5 Black Panthers Held in Brooklyn," *New York Times,* September 13, 1968, p. 93; David Bird, "Judge Forbids Slogan Buttons at Oanther Hearing in Brooklyn," *New York Times,* September 19, 1968, p. 32; Steven robets, "Race: The Third Party in the School Crisis," *New York Times,* Septemeber 22, 1968, p. 182; Leonard Buder, "Shanker Rejects Offer to Protect Ocean Hill Staff," *New York Times,* September 25, 1968, p. 1; Peter Kihiss, "Open Schools, Galamison Tells Rally," September 26, 1968, p. 56, "20,000 in N.Y. March for Black Control," *Black Panther,* October 26, 1968, p. 15.

192. George Murray, "For a Revolutionary Culture," *Black Panther,* September 7, 1968, p. 12.

193. "Black Students Union," *Black Panther,* October 12, 1968, p. 9.

194. "Black Student Union News Service," *Black Panther,* December 21, 1968, p. 11; "10 Point Program and Platform of the Black Student Unions" and "'Important' Black Student Unions," *Black Panther,* February 2, 1969, p. 22; San Francisco State Black Student Union demands are reprinted in *Black Panther,* January 25, 1969, p. 10.

195. Dikran Karagueuzian, *Blow It Up! The Black Student Revolt at San Francisco State College and the Emergence of Dr. Hayakawa* (Boston: Gambit, 1971), pp. 33–36.

196. Ibid.

197. Jason Michael Ferreira, "All Power to the People: A Comparative History of Third World Radicalism in San Francisco, 1968–1974," (PhD diss., University of California, Berkeley, 2003), p. 116.

198. George Murray quoted in Karagueuzian, *Blow It Up!,* pp. 38–39.

199. George Mason Murray, "Panthers' Fight to the Death against Racism," *Rolling Stone,* April 5, 1969, p. 14.

200. Ron Dellums quoted in William H. Orrick Jr., *Shut It Down! A College in Crisis, San Francisco State College, October 1968– April 1969: A Staff Report to the National Commission on the Causes and Prevention of*

Violence (Washington, D.C.: Government Printing Office, June 1969), p. 73.

201. Statement quoted in Ferreira, "All Power to the People," p. 154, also see pp. 154–60.

202. Kathleen Cleaver in Henry Hampton and Steve Fayer, *Voices of Freedom: An Oral History of the Civil Rights Movement from the 1950's through the 1980's* (New York: Bantam Books, 1990), p. 514.

203. Mumia Abu-Jamal, *We Want Freedom* (Cambridge, MA: South End Press, 2004), p. 197.

204. Ibid., p. 247.

205. Ibid., p. 44.

206. Ibid., p. 247.

Part 4: The Glory

207. Hilliard and Cole, *This Side of Glory,* p 227.

Chapter 12.

208. Bobby Rush in Hilliard and Cole, *This Side of Glory*, pp. 214–15; *The Murder of Fred Hampton*, directed by Howard Alk (Chicago: Film Group, 1971), DVD; Jesse Jackson, "On Fred Hampton," *Chicago Daily Defender,* December 13, 1969, p. 1; Jeffrey Haas, *The Assassination of Fred Hampton* Chicago: Lawrence Hill Books, 2019), p. 16.

209. Haas, *The Assassination of Fred Hampton,* pp. 18–19.

210. Ibid., pp. 16 and 18.

211. Ibid., p. 27.

212. Dave Potter, "Martial Law in Maywood Provokes More Boycotts," *Chicago Daily Defender,* September 27, 1967, p. 3; some anecdotes come from Akua Njeri, *My Life with the Black Panther Party* (St. Petersburg, FL: Burning Spear Publications, 1991), p. 29.

213. Jon Rice, "Black Radicalism on Chicago's West Side: A History of the Illinois Black Panther Party" (PhD diss., Northern Illinois University, 1998), pp. 71–72; Bobby Rush in Hilliard and Cole, *This Side of Glory,* pp. 214–15.

214. Dixon, *My People Are Rising,* p. 142.

215. Ibid.

216. Johanna Fernández, *The Young Lords* (Chapel Hill: University of North Carolina Press, 2020), p. 42; Hilliard and Cole, *This Side of Glory,* pp. 229–30; "The Patriot Party Speaks to the Movement," *Black Panther,* February 17, 1970, p. 12; "Pigs Bust Nine Young Patriots," *Black Panther,* June 7, 1969;

Carlton Yearwood quoted in Michael T. Kaufman, "Black Panthers Join Coalition with Puerto Rican and Appalachian Groups," *New York Times,* November 9, 1969, p. 83.

217. Farmer, *Remaking Black Power,* p. 77.

218. Fernández, *The Young Lords,* p. 44.

219. David Hilliard, "Statement from Chief of Staff: Attack on Chicago Office," *Black Panther,* October 11, 1969, p. 3.

220. *Murder of Fred Hampton,* 6:08.

221. On April 9, 1969, Bobby Seale was arraigned as a part of the Chicago 8. Bobby, along with seven other men, was charged with conspiracy to incite a riot at the 1968 Democratic National in Chicago.

222. Clark Kissenger, *Guardian* Midwest Bureau, "Chicago Panthers Busted," reprinted in *Black Panther,* May 4, 1969, p. 6.

223. *Murder of Fred Hampton.,* 29:46–29:50

224. Fernández, *The Young Lords,* p. 22.

225. Iris Morales, "¡Palante, Siempre Palante!: The Young Lords, "in Andres Torres and José E. Velásquez, eds., *The Puerto Rican Movement: Voices from the Diaspora* (Philadelphia: Temple university Press, 1998), p.212; Jimenez quoted in "Interview with Cha Cha Jimenez, Chairman—Young Lords Organization," *Black Panther,* June 7, 1969, p. 17.

226. Ibid.

227. "S.F. Pigs Attempt to Arrest Entire Brown Community," *Black Panther,* May 19, 1969, p.14.

228. Jason Michael Ferreira, "All Power to the People: A Comparative History of the Third World Radicalism in San Francisco, 1968–1974" (PhD diss., University of California, Berkeley, 2003); *Black Panther* articles various 1969.

229. Ibid.

230. "Red Guard," *Black Panther,* March 23, 1969, p. 9

231. http://www.fightbacknews.org /2003winter/brownberets.htm.

232. Spencer, *The Revolution Has Come,* p. 71.

Chapter 13.

233. "Breakfast for Black Children," *Black Panther,* September 7, 1968, p. 7; "Volunteers Needed to Help Prepare and Serve Breakfast for School Children," *Black Panther,* October 19, 1968, p. 2.

234. Robyn C. Spencer, *The Revolution Has Come: Black Power, Gender, and the Black Panther Party in Oakland,* (Durham: Duke University Press), p. 85.

235. Tim Findley, "School Kids: The Panther Breakfast Club," *San Francisco Chronicle,* January 31, 1969; "Breakfast for School Children," *Black Panther,* December 21, 1968.

236. JoNina Abron, "'Serving the People': The Survival Programs of the Black Panther Party," in *The Black Panther Party [Reconsidered],* ed. Charles E. Jones (Baltimore Black Classic Press, 1998), p. 182; Judson L. Jeffries, "Revising Panther History in Baltimore," in *Comrades,* p. 23, for similar opinions.

237. "Capitalist Attacks Breakfast for Children," *Black Panther,* April 20, 1969, p. 15; "Vallejo Chapter Starts Breakfast for Children," *Black Panther,* March 31, 1969, p. 9; "Indiana Breakfast," and "Boston Breakfast," *Black Panther,* July 19, 1969, p. 16.

238. *Black Panther,* October 4, 1969, p. 7.

239. *Black Panther,* May 2, 1969, p. 14.

240. Flores Forbes, *Will You Die with Me? My Life and the Black Panther Party,* (New York: Washington Square Press) p. 50.

241. Dixon, *My People Are Rising,* p. 191.

242. Benjamin Friedman, "Fighting Back: The North Carolina Chapter of the Black Panther Party," (master's thesis, George Washington University, 1994), pp. 80–81.

243. Alondra Nelson, "Black Power, Biomedicine, and the Politics of Knowledge," PhD diss., New York University, 2003) pp. 103–206 Abron, "Serving the People," p. 184; Andrew Witt, *The Black Panthers in the Midwest: The Community Programs and Services of the Black Panther Party in Milwaukee, 1966–1977* (New York: Routledge, 2007), p. 63.

244. Statistic from the National Institutes of Health, Bethesda, Maryland.

245. Clarence, Peterson cited in Omari L. Dyson, Kevin L. Brooks, and Judson L. Jeffries, 'Brotherly Love Can Kill You,': The Philadelphia Branch of the Black Panther Party," in Jeffries *Comrades,* p. 243.

246. White, Bay, and Martin, *Freedom on My Mind,* p. 581.

247. *Black Panther,* May 15, 1967, p. 3.

248. https://www.erickahuggins.com/

249. Newton, *Revolutionary Suicide,* p. 18.

250. Ibid.

251. Murch, *Living for the City,* p. 179.

252. Ibid., p. 176.

253. Ibid., p. 181.

Chapter 14.

254. "Opening Salvos from a Black/White Gun," *Black Panther,* October 5, 1968.

255. Eldridge Cleaver interview in Paris by Henry Louis Gates Jr., winter 1975, p. 61, transcript with Joshua Bloom.

256. Kathleen Cleaver, "Back to Africa: The Evolution of the International Section of the Black Panther Party (1969–1972)," in *The Black Panther Party [Reconsidered],* p. 220.

257. Ibid., p. 218.

258. Eric Pace, "African Nations Open 12-Day Cultural Festival with Parade through Algiers," *New York Times,* July 22, 1969, p. 9; "Algerian Leader Opens Arts Festival," *New York Times,* July 22, 1969, p. A8.

259. Photo, *Black Panther,* August 9, 1969, p. 14; Cleaver, "Back to Africa," p. 213.

260. Cleaver, "Back to Africa," p. 220.

261. Ibid., pp. 228–30; Eldridge Cleaver, interview by Gates, p. 67.

262. https://www.nytimes.com/1970/11/01/archives/our-other-man-in-algiers-our-other-man-in-algiers.html; Sanche de Gramont, "Our Other Man in Algiers," *New York Times Magazine,* November 1, 1970.

263. Ibid.

264. Ibid.

265. Jean Tainturier, "A la Conférence de Montréal," *Le Monde,* December 3, 1968, p. 3.

266. Ibid.; Seale quote from Raymond Lewis, "Montreal: Bobby Seale—Panthers Take Control," *Black Panther,* December 21, 1968, p. 5.

267. Lewis, "Montreal," p. 5; Bobby Seale, "Complete Text of Bobby Seale's Address," *Black Panther,* December 21, 1968, p. 6.

268. Lewis, "Montreal," p. 5; Interview with David Hilliard by Joshua Bloom, June 29, 2005.

269. The following articles from the *Black Panther:* "Bobby Seale in Sweden," March 31, 1969, p. 14; "Chairman Seale and Masai Return to U.S.," March 31, 1969, p. 14; "Free Huey Demonstration in Scandinavia: Black Panther Spokesman Connie Matthews Speaks at Free Huey Rally in Sweden," June 21, 1969, p. 18; Connie Matthews, "Scandinavian Solidarity with the BPP," September, 13, 1969, p. 9; "Connie Matthews at San Jose State on the Vietnam Moratorium," transcript, October 25,

1969, p. 11; Klaus Pedersen, "Interview with Scandinavian Rep. of Black Panther Party: Connie Matthews," reprinted from *Land of Folk*, October 18, 1969, p. 9.

Chapter 15.

270. Hilliard and Cole, *This Side of Glory*, p.164.

271. Scot Brown, *Fighting for US: Maulana Karenga, the US Organization and Black Cultural Nationalism* (New York: New York University Press, 2003). Please see for a more full treatment of the US organization.

272. Seale, *Seize the Time*, p. 272.

273. Brown, *Fighting for US*.

274. Seale, *Seize the Time*, p. 271.

275. Brown, *A Taste of Power*, p. 164.

276. Ibid., p. 167.

277. Ibid., p. 168.

278. Ibid., p. 180.

279. Dixon, *My People Are Rising*, p. 144.

280. Ibid., p. 146.

Chapter 16.

281. Melvin Small, *Johnson, Nixon and the Doves* (New Brunswick, NJ: Rutgers University Press, 1988), p. 158.

282. Memo, J. Edgar Hoover to Field Offices, "Counter Intelligence Program, Black Nationalist Hate Groups, Racial Intelligence (Black Panther Party)," November 25, 1968. All of the FBI memos are available in the FBI Reading Room, FBI Headquarters, Washington, D.C.

283. Bobby Seale quoted in William Drummond, "2 Black Panther Students Slain in UCLA Hall," *Los Angeles Times*, January 18, 1969.

284. Memo, G. C. Moore to W. C. Sullivan, September 27, 1968.

285. Kenneth O'Reilly, "*Racial Matters*": *The FBI's Secret File on Black America, 1960–1972* (New York: Free Press, 1991), ch. 1.

286. Select Committee to Study Governmental Operations with Respect to Intelligence Activities [Church Committee], *Supplementary Detailed Staff Reports on Intelligence Activities and the Rights of Americans*, Final Report, S. Doc. No. 94–755 (April 1976), bk. 3, pp. 79–184 (hereafter Church Committee Report).

287. Memo, J. Edgar Hoover, FBI Director, to Field Offices, August 25, 1967.

288. Memo, J. Edgar Hoover to Field Offices, March 4, 1968; see also Memo, G. C. Moore to W. C. Sullivan, February 29, 1968.

289. Spencer, *The Revolution Has Come*, p. 89.

290. Ibid., p. 95.

291. Ibid.

292. Memo, G. C. Moore to W. C. Sullivan, September 27, 1968.

293. Dixon, *My People Are Rising*, p. 178.

294. David Burnham, "Off-Duty Police Here Join in Beating Black Panther," *New York Times*, September 5, 1968, p. 1; "Brutality, New York Style," editorial, *New York Times*, September 5, 1968, p. 46; "News Flash . . . New York Pigs Use New Tactic to Vamp on 12 Panthers," *Black Panther*, September 7, 1968, p. 10; Balagoon et al., *Look for Me in the Whirlwind*, pp. 275–77.

295. Balagoon et al., *Look for Me in the Whirlwind*, pp. 275–77.

296. Abayama Katara in Balagoon et al., *Look for Me in the Whirlwind*, pp. 275–77.

297. Ibid.

298. The Panther 21 were Afeni Shakur, Lumumba Shakur, Jamal (Edie Joseph), Joan Bird, Cetawayo (Michael Tabor), Kuwasi Balagoon (Donald Weems), Robert Collier, Richard Harris, Ali Bey Hassan (John J. Casson), Sekou Odinga (Nathanial Burns), Dhoruba (Richard Moore), Kwando Kinshasa (William King), Baba Odinga (Walter Johnson), Shaba Ogun Om (Lee Roper), Curtis Poweel, Clark Squire, Larry Mack, Mshina (Thomas Berry), Lonnie Epps, Mkuba (Lee Berry), and Abayama Katara (Alex McKiever).

299. Afeni Shakur quoted in Foner, ed., *The Black Panther Speaks*, p. 161.

300. Kempton, *The Briar Patch* Balagoon et al., *Look for Me in the Whirlwind*.

Part 5: Unstoppable

301. Assata Shakur, *Assata: An Autobiography* (Chicago[:Lawrence Hill Books, 1987; repr. 2001), p. 1.

Chapter 17.

302. Bobby Seale was arrested for the murder of Alex Rackley, a crime of which he was acquitted. First, he stood trial as a part of the Chicago Eight. Seale, *Seize the Time*, pp. 289–91; Dixon, *My People Are Rising*, p. 175.

303. Dixon, *My People Are Rising*, p. 176.

304. A. G. Langguth, *Our Vietnam War, 1954–1975* (New York: Simon and Schuster, 2000), p. 552.

305. Todd Gitlin, *The Sixties: Years of Hope, Days of Rage* (New York: Bantam Books, 1987), pp. 321–23; *New York Times,* August, 29, 1968. There were sixty Black soldiers out of Fort Hood, Texas. They were asked to put a stop to the protests at the Chicago convention. But they refused. Forty-three of those Black soldiers were taken to the stockades: "60 Negro GIs Balk at Possible Riot Control," *Los Angeles Times,* August 25, 1968, p. F9.

306. "Chairman Bobby Seale and Chief of Staff David Hilliard in Chicago," *Black Panther,* September, 7, 1968, p. 3.

307. Mark L. Levine, George C. McNamee, and Daniel L. Greenberg, *Trial of the Chicago 7* (New York: Simon and Schuster, 2020); Langguth, *Our Vietnam War,* pp. 552–53.

308. https://www.nybooks.com/articles /1969/06/19/the-committee-to-defend-the -conspiracy/

309. Seale, *Seize the Time,* pp. 326–29.

310. Levine, McNamee, and Greenberg, *Trial of the Chicago 7,* p. 73.

311. Ibid., p. 280.

312. Ibid., p. 4.

313. Ibid., pp. 343–47.

314. Ibid., pp. 279.

315. Seale, *Seize the Time,* p. 328.

316. Levine, McNamee, and Greenberg, *The Trial of the Chicago 7,* p. 65.

317. Langguth, *Our Vietnam War,* p. 553.

318. Seale, *Seize the Time,* p. 337.

319. Ibid., p. 338.

320. Levine, McNamee, and Greenberg, *Trial of the Chicago 7,* p. 75.

321. Seale, *Seize the Time,* p. 342.

322. Ibid., pp. 348–49.

323. Ibid.

324. *The "Trial" of Bobby Seale*, edited transcript of the trial (New York: Priam Books, 1970), p. 90; J. Anthony Lukas, "Seale Put in Chains at Chicago 8 Trial," *New York Times,* October 30, 1969, p. 1; J. Anthony Lukas, "Seale Found in Contempt, Sentenced to Four Years," *New York Times,* November 6, 1969, p. 1; https://www.loc.gov/exhibitions /drawing-justice-courtroom-illustrations /about-this-exhibition/political-activists-on -trial/bobby-seale-bound-and-gagged/

325. *Murder of Fred Hampton,* 7:37–8:09.

Chapter 18.

326. *Black Panther,* May 15, 1967, p. 3.

327. Haas, *The Assassination of Fred Hampton,* p. 69.

328. Ibid., p. 70.

329. Dixon, *My People Are Rising,* pp.184–85,.

330. Fred P. Graham, "U.S. Jury Assails Police in Chicago on Panther Raid," *New York Times,* May 16, 1970, p. 1; Hampton v. Hanrahan, 600 F.2d 600 (7ᵗʰ Cir. 1970) pp. 66–81; Roy Wilkins and Ramsey Clark, *Search and Destroy: A Report by the Commission of Inquiry into the Black Panthers and the Police* (New York: Metropolitan Applied Records Center, 1973), pp. 35–36.

331. Haas, *The Assassination of Fred Hampton,* p. 5; *Murder of Fred Hampton* 1:09:49–1:11:37.

332. Graham, "U.S. Jury Assails Police," p. 1; Hampton v. Hanrahan, pp. 66–81; Wilkins and Clark, *Search and Destroy,* pp. 35–36.

333. *Murder of Fred Hampton,* 53:55; John Kifner, "State's Attorney in Chicago Makes Photographs of Black Panther Apartment Available," *New York Times,* December 12, 1979, p. 46.

334. Memo, Chicago Field Office to FBI Headquarters, December 8, 1969, quoted in Church Committee Report, bk. 3, p. 223. Regarding the bonus see John Kifner, "F.B.I. Files Say Informer Got Data for Panther Raid," *New York Times,* May 7, 1976, p. 14.

335. Memo, J. Edgar Hoover to Field Offices, March 4, 1968; Memo, G. C. Moore to W. C. Sullivan, February 29, 1968.

336. Faith C. Christmas, "Bobby Rush Surrenders before 5,000," *Chicago Daily Defender,* December 8, 1969, p. 2.

337. Faith C. Christmas, "'It Was Murder' Rush," *Chicago Daily Defender,* December 6, 1969, p. 1; John Kifner, "Inquiry into Slaying of 2 Panthers Urged in Chicago," *New York Times,* December 6, 1969.

338. John Kifner, "3 Panthers Snub Hampton Inquest," *New York Times,* January 7, 1970, p. 30.

339. Seth King, "7 Panthers Freed in Chicago Clash," *New York Times,* May 9, 1970, p. 1.

340. Graham, "U.S. Jury Assails Police," *New York Times,* May 16, 1970, p. 1.

341. "Was It Murder?" *Chicago Daily Defender,* December 8, 1969, p. 13.

342. Carter Gilmore, NAACP statement on December 11, 1969, reprinted as "N.A.A.C.P. against Pig Repression of Black Panthers," *Black Panther,* January 3, 1970, p. 3.

343. Kifner, "State's Attorney in Chicago," p. 46.

344. John Kifner, "Negroes in Chicago Impose a Curfew on Whites," *New York Times,* December 16, 1969, p. 21.

345. John Kifner, "The 'War' Between Panthers and the Police," *New York Times,* December 12, 1969, p. E3.

346. "Robert Williams Speaks at NCCF Panther Benefit; Detroit, Michigan," transcript of the speech, *Black Panther,* January 3, 1970, p. 20.

347. Dixon, *My People Are Rising,* p. 185.

348. Geronimo Pratt in Jack Olsen, *Last Man Standing: The Tragedy and Triumph of Geronimo Pratt* (New York: Doubleday, 2001), p. 53.

349. Ibid., pp. 63–64.

350. "L. A. Oppression," *Black Panther,* November 22, 1969, p. 2; Brown, *A Taste of Power,* pp. 201–2.

351. Olsen, *Last Man Standing,* p. 59.

352. Dixon, *My People Are Rising,* p. 185.

353. Nelson, *Vanguard of the Revolution,* 1:22:59–1:23:50.

354. Ibid., 1:27:10–1:27:18.

355. Ibid., 1:23:16–1:23:22.

356. Ibid., 1:25:58–1:26:23.

357. "Pigs Attack Southern California Chapter of Black Panther Party," *Black Panther,* December 13, 1969, p. 10; "Statement by Witnesses of Attack at Black Panther Headquarters," *Black Panther,* December 13, 1969, p. 10; Olsen, *Last Man Standing,* pp. 63–64; Kenneth Reich, "National Pattern Followed in Raid on Panthers Here," *Los Angeles Times,* December 9, 1969, p. 1; Phillip Fradkin, "Bombs, Gunfire Shatter Quiet of Central Ave," *Los Angeles Times,* December 9, 1969, p. 3.

358. Nelson, *Vanguard of the Revolution,* 1:27:49–1:28:05.

359. Renee "Peaches" Moore, in Dial Torgerson, "Police Seize Panther Fortress in 4-Hour Gunfight, Arrest 13," *Los Angeles Times,* December 9, 1969, p. 1.

360. Art Berman, "Thousands Protest Panther Raid in City Hall," *Los Angeles Times,* December 12, 1969, p. 1.

361. Spencer, *The Revolution Has Come,* p. 116.

Chapter 19.

362. Hilliard and Cole, *This Side of Glory,* pp. 24–26, p. 70.

363. Ibid., p. 4.

364. Ibid., p. 114.

365. Ibid., pp. 260–65; Wallace Turner, "More Than 100,000 on Coast Demonstrate in Moderate Vein," *New York Times,* November 16, 1969, p. 1; Darly Lembke and Philip Jager, "Thousands Parade Quietly in S.F. to Show War Frustrations," *Los Angeles Times,* November 16, 1969, p. 1.

366. Hilliard and Cole, *This Side of Glory,* pp. 261, 264–65.

367. Ibid., pp. 266–67.

368. Tracye Matthews, " 'No One Ever Asks, What a Man's Role in the Revolution Is'; Gender and the Politics of the Black Panther Party, 1966–1971," in *The Black Panther Party [Reconsidered],* p. 270.

369. Cleaver and Katsiaficas, *Liberation, Imagination, and the Black Panther Party,* pp. 125–26.

370. Farmer, *Remaking Black Power,* p. 67.

371. Cleaver and Katsiaficas, *Liberation, Imagination, and the Black Panther Party,* p. 127.

372. Frankye Malika Adams quoted in Abu-Jamal, *We Want Freedom,* p. 164.

373. Angela Davis interviewed by Tracye Matthews, in Matthews, " 'No One Ever Asks, What a Man's Role in the Revolution Is.' "

374. Cleaver and Katsiaficas, *Liberation, Imagination, and the Black Panther Party,* p. 124.

375. Eldridge Cleaver quoted in Foner, ed., *The Black Panther Speaks,* pp. 98–99. Both Ericka Huggins and Bobby Seale were indicted for the murder of Alex Rackley and both were cleared of all charges.

376. Cleaver, *Soul on Ice,* pp. 33–34.

377. Huey Newton, "Women's Liberation and Gay Liberation Movements," quoted in Farmer, *Remaking Black Power,* p. 79.

378. Spencer, *The Revolution Has Come*, p. 188.

379. Seale, *Seize the Time*, p. 394.

380. Ibid., p. 403.

381. *Murder of Fred Hampton*, 9:44–9:46.

382. Bobby Seale quoted in Earl Caldwell, "'Fascism' Decried at Black Panther Conference," *New York Times*, July 21, 1969, p. 48; "Chairman Seale Sums up Conference," transcript of speech, *Black Panther*, July 26, 1969, p. 4.

383. Cleaver and Katsiaficas, *Liberation, Imagination, and the Black Panther Party*, p. 126.

384. Newton, *Revolutionary Suicide*, p. 357.

385. Nelson, *Vanguard of the Revolution*, 1:48:28–1:48:53.

Chapter 20.

386. Kathleen Cleaver quoted in Spencer, *The Revolution Has Come*, p. 71.

387. Students for a Democratic Society resolution at the Austin National Council, "The Black Panther Party: Toward the Liberation of the Colony," *New Left Notes*, April 4, 1969, pp. 1, 3.

388. Bobby Seale quoted in Caldwell, "'Fascism' Decried," p. 48; "Chairman Seale Sums Up Conference," transcript of speech, *Black Panther*, July 26, 1969, p. 4.

389. Spencer, "Repression Breeds Resistance," p. 182.

390. "Yale Suspends 5 on Charges of Disrupting a Lecture," *New York Times*, December 19, 1969, p. 36.

391. Richard Nixon quoted in Juan de Onis, "Nixon Puts 'Bums' label on Some College Radicals," *New York Times*, May 2, 1970, p. 1.

392. Homer Bigart, "New Haven Rally Ends a Day Early; Attendance Down," *New York Times*, May 3, 1970, p. 1.

393. 1970 Rockefeller Foundation survey in Daniel Yankelovich, *The Changing Values on Campus: Political and Personal Attitudes of Today's College Students* (New York: Washington, 1972), pp. 62, 64, 70.

394. Michael T. Kaufman, "Campus Unrest over War Spreads with Strike Calls," *New York Times*, May 4, 1970, p. 1; Linda Charlton, "Antiwar Strike Plans in the Colleges Pick Up Student and Faculty Support," *New York Times*, May 5, 1970, p. 18; Richard E. Peterson and John A. Biloursky, *May 1970: The Campus Aftermath of Cambodia and Kent State* (Berkeley: Carnegie Commission on Higher Education, 1971), pp. 15–19; Nancy Zaroulis and Gerlad Sullivan, *Who Spoke Up? American Protest against the War in Vietnam* (New York: Doubleday, 1984), p. 319.

395. Joe Eszterhas and Michael Roberts, *Thirteen Seconds: Confrontation at Kent State* (New York: Dodd, Mead, 1970), pp. 57, 68.

396. Irwin Unger, *The Movement: A History of the American New Left, 1959–1972* (New York: Dodd, Mead 1970), pp. 183–86; Langguth, *Our Vietnam War*, pp. 569–70.

397. Peterson and Bilorusky, *May 1970: The Campus Aftermath*, pp. 15–19; Charles DeBenedetti and Charles Chatfield, *An American Ordeal: The Antiwar Movement of the Vietnam Era* (New York: Syracuse University Press, 1990), pp. 279–80; Gitlin, *The Sixties*, pp. 409–10; Jeffrey P. Kimball, *Nixon's Vietnam War* (Lawrence: University Press of Kansas, 1998), pp. 215–16.

398. Murch, *Living for the City*, p. 181.

Chapter 21.

399. Hilliard and Cole, *This Side of Glory*, p. 297.

400. Newton, *Revolutionary Suicide*, pp. 299–300.

401. Ibid.

402. Ibid., pp. 288–96.

403. Ibid., p. 312.

404. "Huey Freed," *Newsweek*, August 17, 1970; photos from *Black Panther*, August 15, 1970, p. 14.

405. Newton, *Revolutionary Suicide*, pp. 312–14.

406. Ibid., p. 314.

407. Ibid.

408. Ibid., p. 315.

409. Ibid.

410. Ibid.

411. Ibid., p. 316.

412. Hilliard and Cole, *This Side of Glory*, p. 300.

413. Ibid., p. 303.

414. Ibid.

415. Ibid., p. 304.

416. Newton, *Revolutionary Suicide*, p. 322.

417. Geronimo Pratt quoted in Olsen, *Last Man Standing*, pp. 32, 33.

418. Ibid., p. 4.

419. Ibid., pp. 38–39.

420. "Press Statement to the Press on Elmer Pratt, Deputy Minister of Defense Southern California Chapter Black Panther Party," *Black Panther,* October 3, 1970, p. 5; Also Craig Williams, Southern California Chapter, "Reflections of Geronimo . . . The Essence of a Panther," *Black Panther,* August 29, 1970, p. 14.

421. Committee to Defend Abandoned Panthers, "Free Geronimo—The Urban Guerilla," *Right On!* April, 3, 1971, p. 6.

422. "Metropolitan," *Los Angeles Times,* December 10, 1970, p. A2; "Metropolitan," *Los Angeles Times,* January 20, 1971, p. A2; Robert Finklea, "FBI Arrest Four Men Wanted in California," *Dallas Morning News,* December 9, 1970, p. 1.

423. "Metropolitan," *Los Angeles Times,* January 20, 1971, p. A2; In *Freedom, Humanity, Peace,* Geronimo says that he was being shut out by Huey and the Central Committee. *Freedom, Humanity, Peace* is a pamphlet that has transcripts of prison interviews. It was published by the Revolutionary Peoples Communication Network around 1971 and can be found in the Bancroft Library at the University of California, Berkeley.

424. Panther 21, "Open Letter to Weatherman Underground from Panther 21," *East Village Other,* January 19, 1971, p. 3.

425. Don Cox, "Organizing Self-Defense Groups," *Black Panther,* January 16, 1971, p. 8.

426. Hilliard and Cole, *This Side of Glory,* p. 284.

427. These friends and allies included George Lloyd, Saundra Lee, Will Stafford, and Wilfred "Crutch" Holiday.

428. Huey P. Newton, "On the Purge of Geronimo from the Black Panther Party," *Black Panther,* January 23, 1971, p. 7.

429. Pratt in *Freedom, Humanity, Peace,* p. 13. Also Ron Eintoss, "Former Black Panther Aide Held for Murder," *Los Angeles Times,* February 17, 1971, p. D5. Julius Butler's testimony led to Geronimo's conviction. When it became clear that Butler was a paid FBI informant, Geronimo was released, after having spent years in prison.

430. Rod Such, "Newton Expels 12 Panthers," *Guardian,* February 20, 1971, p. 4; Newton statement quoted in United Press International, "Panthers Oust Eleven," *Chicago Daily Defender,* February 11, 1971, p. 10; Edith Evans Asbury, "Newton Denounces 2 Missing Panthers," *New York Times,* February 10, 1971, p. 1.

431. Ibid. Newton statement quoted in UPI, "Panthers Oust Eleven," p. 10; Asbury, "Newton Denounces 2 Missing Panthers," p. 1. The FBI sent letters in Connie Matthews's name through COINTELPRO. There is speculation that Connie was working with the FBI, but that hasn't been proven.

432. Newton, *Revolutionary Suicide,* p. 356.

Part 6: The Fall

433. Afeni Shakur quoted in Foner, ed., *The Black Panther Speaks,* p. 161.

Chapter 22.

434. Spencer, *The Revolution Has Come,* p. 108.

435. "Black Panther Dispute," *Sun Reporter,* March 13, 1971, p. 2; Thomas A. Johnson, "Panthers Fear Growing Intraparty Strife," *New York Times,* April 10, 1971, p. 12.

436. Nelson, *Vanguard of the Revolution,* 1:35:37–1:35:51.

437. Hilliard and Cole, *This Side of Glory,* p. 323. David Hilliard provides many quotations from the discussion, potentially transcribed from a recording. David did play a cassette tape for Joshua Bloom. As the authors, we don't have a copy of the cassette tape or a full transcript, but what Joshua heard he believed to be genuine and the partial transcript in David's book is consistent with what Joshua heard. David said that Eldridge secretly recorded the call and then released it to a local Bay Area radio station and that's how David eventually got a copy. According to David, Eldridge played it cool, provoking Huey's anger. The dialogue used in this section of the text was taken from Stanley Nelson's documentary *Vanguard of the Revolution,* beginning 1:36:20.

438. Newton, *Revolutionary Suicide,* p. 144.

439. Nelson, *Vanguard of the Revolution,* 1:33:53–1:34:22.

440. "Black Panther Dispute," p. 2; Johnson, "Panthers Fear Growing Intraparty Strife," p. 24. On March 6, 1971, there was a *Black Panther* article titled "Free Kathleen Cleaver." The reported statements appear to have been made before this. There is some disagreement on the dates.

441. Spencer, *The Revolution Has Come,* p. 92.

442. Ibid.

443. "Black Panther Dispute," *Sun Reporter,* March 13, 1971, p. 2; Curtis J. Austin, *Up Against the Wall: Violence in the Making and Unmaking of the Black Panther Party* (Fayetteville: Universoty of Arkansas Press, 2006), p. 314; Michael Knight, "Death Here Tied to Panther Feud," *New York Times,* March 10, 1971, p. 29; United Press International, "Say N.Y. Panthers Balk in Death Probe," *Chicago Daily Defender,* March 13, 1971, p.2; Thomas A. Johnson, "Panthers Fear Growing Intraparty Strife," *New York Times, April 10, 1971, p.24.*

444. Spencer, *The Revolution Must Come,* pp. 111–113; Michael Knight, "A Black Panther Found Slain Here," *New York Times,* April 18, 1971, p. 1; "Murdered . . . Sam Napier, Black Panther Party, Intercommunal News Service, Circulation Manager Murdered by Fascists, Revolutionary Service Scheduled for April 24," flier, April 17, 1971," copy with Joshua Bloom; Robert D. McFadden, "4 Panthers Admit Guilt in Slaying," *New York Times,* May 22, 1973, p.1.

445. Spencer, *The Revolution Must Come.,* p. 56.

446. Dixon, *My People Are Rising,* p. 111.

447. "Eldridge Cleaver Discusses Revolution—An Interview from Exile," *Black Panther,* October 11, 1969, pp. 10–12.

448. Stanley Nelson, *Vanguard of the Revolution,* 1:33:03- 1:33:30.

449. Lefcourt interview cited in Nelson, *Vanguard of the Revolution,* 1:02:19–1:02:35.

450. Eric Mann, *Comrade George* (New York: Harper and Row, 1972).

451. San Quentin Branch, Black Panther Party, "TO Eldridge Cleaver and His Conspirators, FROM the San Quentin Branch of the Black Panther Party," *Black Panther,* March 20, 1971, p. 1; the quote from Eldridge about Jonathan Jackson appears in Eldridge Cleaver, "On the Case of Angela Davis," *Black Panther,* January 23, 1971, p. 5.

452. Wallace Turner, "Two Desparate Hours: How George Jackson Died," *New York Times,* September 3, 1971, p. 1.

453. *Black Panther,* January 25, 1969, images appearing on pp. 3, 24, 11, 16, 18, 9, 8, and 6; Randy, "Fred Hampton Murdered by Fascist Pigs," *Black Panther,* December 13, 1969, p. 2; *Black Panther,* December 13, 1969, pp. 1, 9–12, 16, 18–20.

454. Charles W. Hopkins, "The Deradicalization of the Black Panther Party: 1967–1973" (PhD diss., University of North Carolina at Chapel Hill, 1978), ch. 4.

455. Ruth Reitan, "Cuba, the Black Panther Party, and the U.S. Black Movement in the 1960s: Issues of Security," in Cleaver and Kastiaficas, *Liberation, Imagination, and the Black Panther Party*; Ruth Reitan, *The Rise and Decline of an Alliance: Cuba and African American Leaders in the 1960s* (East Lansing: Michigan State University Press, 1999).

456. Cleaver, "Back to Africa," p. 227, n. 253; for the U.S. and Algerian diplomatic status, see U.S. Department of State, Office of the Historian, Historical Documents: Foreign Relations of the United States; Gramont, "Our Other Man in Algiers."

457. Small, Johnson, Nixon and the Doves, p. 158.

458. Earl Caldwell, "The Panthers: Dead or Regrouping," *New York Times,* March 1, 1971, p. 1.

459. Committee on Internal Security of the House of Representatives, *GunBarrel Politics: The Black Panther Party, 1966–1971,* 92d Cong., 1st sess. (Washington, DC: Government Printing Office, 1971), p. 143.

Chapter 23.

460. Bobby Rush quoted in Hilliard and Cole, *This Side of Glory,* p. 327.

461. Brown, *A Taste of Power,* p. 322.

462. Ibid., p. 323.

463. Murch, *Living for the City,* p. 227.

464. Shakur, *Assata,* p. 169.

465. Sundiata Acoli in Akinyele Omowale Umoja, "Repression Breeds Resistance: The Black Liberation Army and the Radical Legacy of the Black Panther Party," in Cleaver and Katsiaficas, *Liberation, Imagination, and the Black Panther Party,* p. 12.

466. Jalil Muntaqim, *On the Black Liberation Army,* pamphlet (1979; repr. Oakland, CA: Abraham Gullien Press, 2002), p. 3.

467. Ibid., p. 12.

Chapter 24. Chairwoman

468. "Letter to Huey from Tommie Williams" cited in Spencer, *The Revolution Has Come,* pp. 196–97.

469. Spencer, *The Revolution Has Come,* p. 191.

470. Ibid., pp. 193–94.

471. Jeffries, *Comrades,* p. 107.

472. Akua Njeri [Deborah Johnson], "Difficulties of Being a Single Mother in the Black Panther Party," in *My Life with the*

Black Panther Party (Oakland: Burning Spear Publications, 1991), p. 45.

473. Ibid., p. 194.

474. "Letter to Huey from Amar Casey" cited in ibid., p. 198.

475. Spencer, *The Revolution Has Come*, p. 173.

476. Ibid., p. 189.

477. Brown, *A Taste of Power*, pp. 191–92.

478. Ibid., p. 7.

479. Ibid., p. 444.

480. Ibid., p. 445.

481. Ibid.

482. Ibid.

483. Ibid., pp. 445–50.

484. Nelson, *Vanguard of the Revolution*, 1:47:42–1:48:08.

485. Dixon, *My People Are Rising*, p. 310.

486. *Black Panther*, April 6, 1969, p. 14.

487. Spencer, *The Revolution Has Come*, pp. 166–67; Hilliard and Cole, *This Side of Glory*, p. 376.

488. Nelson, *Vanguard of the Revolution*, 39:33–39:49

489. Nelson, *Vanguard of the Revolution*, 1:45:52–1:46:13.

490. Jeffries, *Comrades*, page before the "Contents" section, not numbered.

491. While that quote is often attributed to King, he was inspired by the words of the nineteenth-century Unitarian minister and abolitionist Theodore Parker.

492. Newton, *Revolutionary Suicide*, p. 360.

493. This quote is derived from Black abolitionist Frederick Douglass, who said, "Without struggle there is no progress. Power concedes nothing without a struggle. It never did and it never will." *Murder of Fred Hampton*, 1:27:01–1:27:03.

Jetta Grace Martin is a debut author from the San Francisco Bay Area. She earned her A.B. with honors in Social Studies and African American Studies from Harvard University, where she won the Cornel West Prize and the Kathryn Ann Huggins Prize. Jetta is also an award-winning dancer, performer, and choreographer whose work has been presented nationally and internationally. Her research and writing focuses on the intersection of race, identity, and embodiment.

Joshua Bloom is Director of the Social Movements Lab and faculty in Sociology at University of Pittsburgh, where he studies the dynamics of insurgent practice and social transformation. He is the co-author of *Black Against Empire: The History and Politics of the Black Panther Party*, which won the American Book Award. Before earning a PhD, Bloom spent many years as an anti-racist organizer.

Waldo E. Martin Jr. is the Alexander F. and May T. Morrison Professor of American History and Citizenship at the University of California, Berkeley, and the co-author of *Black Against Empire: The History and Politics of the Black Panther Party*. The intersecting histories of the Modern Black Freedom Struggle, modern Black cultural politics, and modern U.S. social movements shape his current research and writing interests. His forthcoming book (for adults) is *"A Change is Gonna Come": Black Cultural Politics and the Making of Modern America*.

371

The cover art, a digital collage of historical images of the Blank Panther Party, was designed by Morcos Key. The text was set by Westchester Publishing in Danbury, CT, in Bradford, a serif font family designed by Laurenz Brunner and aimed to preserve the physical presence and distinctive character of hot metal type. The display was set in Bayard, a sans-serif designed by Tré Seals' Vocal Type Co. inspired by the signs from the 1963 March on Washington. The name is an homage to Bayard Rustin, an African American leader in social movements for civil rights, socialism, nonviolence, and gay rights. The book was printed on FSC™-certified 98gsm Yunshidai Ivory woodfree paper and printed in China.

Production was supervised by Leslie Cohen and Freesia Blizard
Book jacket, case, and interiors designed by Morcos Key
Editor: Nick Thomas
Editorial Assistant: Irene Vázquez

LEVINE QUERIDO